Crash Course in QBasic™

Greg Perry

JOHN G. RICE & ASSOCIATES
P. O. Box 4845
Annapolis, Maryland 21403

PROGRAMMING
SERIES

Crash Course in QBasic

Copyright© 1993 by Que® Corporation

Library of Congress Catalog No.: 92-63323

ISBN: 1-56529-165-4

96 95 94 93   8 7 6 5 4 3 2 1

Interpretation of the printing code: the rightmost double-digit number is the year of the book's printing; the rightmost single-digit number, the number of the book's printing. For example, a printing code of 93-1 shows that the first printing of the book occurred in 1993.

Trademarks

Dedication

Thanks to my friend and co-teacher, Pamela Chew, for encouraging me to learn a second language. *Grazie, Pam.*

Credits

Publisher
Lloyd J. Short

Associate Publisher
Rick Ranucci

Publishing Manager
Joseph B. Wikert

Production Editor
Jodi Jensen

Editors
Lori Cates
Kezia Endsley
Bryan Gambrel
Susan Pink

Technical Editors
Jay Munro
David Leithauser

Editorial Assistants
Elizabeth D. Brown
Stacey Beheler

Production Manager
Corinne Walls

Proofreading/Indexing Coordinator
Joelynn Gifford

Production Analyst
Mary Beth Wakefield

Book Designer
Scott Cook

Cover Designer
Jay Corpus

Graphic Image Specialists
Dennis Sheehan
Jerry Ellis
Susan VandeWalle
Jeff Shrum

Production
Claudia Bell
Brad Chinn
Jay Lesandrini
Cindy L. Phipps
Caroline Roop

Indexer
Suzanne G. Snyder

Composed in *ITC Garamond* and *MCPdigital*
by Prentice Hall Computer Publishing

About the Author

Greg Perry

Greg Perry has been a programmer and trainer for the past 14 years. He received his first degree in Computer Science and then completed a Master's Degree in Corporate Finance. He is currently a professor of computer science at Tulsa Junior College, as well as a computer consultant and lecturer. Mr. Perry is the author of more than a dozen computer books, including *QBasic By Example, C By Example, C++ By Example, Turbo Pascal By Example* (all by Que Corporation), and *Moving from C to C++* (by Sams Publishing). Additionally, he has written articles for several publications, including *PC World, Data Training,* and *Inside First Publisher.* He has traveled in several countries, attending computer conferences and trade shows, and is fluent in nine computer languages.

Acknowledgments

I want to thank Jodi Jensen, Joe Wikert, and Jay Munro, the top-notch three at Que who somehow turned my manuscript into a book.

I'd also like to thank Microsoft for continuing to support the QBasic language. Beginners, as well as advanced programmers, often have a special place in their hearts for BASIC and its derivatives. It was Microsoft's BASIC that started my entire computer career, and I'll always be grateful.

Finally, I'd like to thank my beautiful bride, Jayne, and my parents, Glen and Bettye Perry, who have supported everything I do. I'm proud that all three of them are in my life.

Contents at a Glance

Introduction 1

Chapter 1   Introduction to QBasic 5

Chapter 2   Using the QBasic Environment 11

Chapter 3   Working with Data 31

Chapter 4   Operators and String Variables 51

Chapter 5   Advanced Input and Output 71

Chapter 6   Making Decisions with Data 99

Chapter 7   Controlling Program Flow 123

Chapter 8   Data Structures 143

Chapter 9   Built-In Functions 167

Chapter 10   Modular Programming: Subroutines 187

Chapter 11   Disk Files 195

Chapter 12   Sound and Graphics 223

Index 237

Table of Contents

Introduction 1

Who Should Use This Book 1
Syntax at a Glance 2
Conventions Used 3
Get Ready, Get Set, ... Go! 3

1 Introduction to QBasic 5

What QBasic Can Do for You 5
The Background of QBasic 6
Programs and Data 7
Program Design 8
From Start to Finish 9
Summary 10

2 Using the QBasic Environment 11

Starting QBasic 11
Starting QBasic with Command-Line Options 12
The QBasic Screen 13
Selecting from QBasic's Menus 14
    Choosing an Option 15
    Menu Shortcut Keys 16
    Using Dialog Boxes 17
Getting Help 19
    The Help Survival Guide 19
    Help About Help 20
    The Help Menu 21
    Context-Sensitive Help 21
Loading a Program 21
Stopping a QBasic Program 22
Using the Program Editor 22
    Typing a Program 23

Your First Program 26
Spacing in Programs 27
If There Are Errors... 27
Saving the Program 27
Erasing the Program Editing Window 28
Printing a Program 28
Quitting QBasic 28
Summary 28

3 Working with Data 31

QBasic Data 31
Numeric Variables 31
Naming Variables 32
Variable Types 33
Assigning Values to Variables 35
QBasic Constants 36
Viewing Output 37
The *PRINT* Statement 38
More About *PRINT* 39
Printing String Constants 39
Printing More Than One Value on a Line 40
Using Semicolons with *PRINT* 41
Using Commas with *PRINT* 41
Printing with *TAB( )* 43
Printing to Paper 45
Clearing the Screen 46
Using the *END* Command 47
Program Remarks 48
Using Helpful Remarks 50
Summary 50

4 Operators and String Variables 51

The Math Operators 51
The Four Primary Operators 51
Integer Division and Exponentiation 52
Assigning Formulas to Variables 54
The Order of Operators 54
Using Parentheses 56

Printing Calculations 58
String Variables 60
   Creating String Variables 60
   Naming String Variables 61
   Storing Data in String Variables 62
   Printing String Variables 63
String Concatenation 67
Make Your Data Types Match 68
Summary 70

5 Advanced Input and Output 71

The *INPUT* Statement 71
   INPUT Fills Variables with Values 72
   Improving the Use of *INPUT* 74
   Prompting with *INPUT* 76
   Inputting Strings 77
   Match the *INPUT* Variables 78
   Eliminating the Question Mark 78
The *LINE INPUT* Statement 79
INPUT and *LINE INPUT*
   Cursor Control 80
Producing Better Output 81
   The *PRINT USING* Statement 82
   Printing Strings with *PRINT USING* 83
   Printing Numbers with *PRINT USING* 86
   Printing with *SPC( )* 90
   Using *BEEP* 92
   Printing Special Characters 92
   Printing with *COLOR* 94
   The *LOCATE* Statement 96
Summary 97

6 Making Decisions with Data 99

The *GOTO* Statement 99
Comparison Operators 101
The *IF* Statement 102
   Compound Logical Operators 104
   Complete Order of Operators 106

READ and *DATA* Statements 107
The *RESTORE* Statement 111
The Block *IF-THEN-ELSE* 112
Multiple Statements on a Line 112
   The *ELSE* Statement 114
   The Block 115
   The *ELSEIF* Statement 117
The *SELECT CASE* Statement 119
Summary 122

7 Controlling Program Flow 123

The *FOR* and *NEXT* Statements 123
   Nested *FOR-NEXT* Loops 127
   The *EXIT FOR* Statement 130
Other Loop Statements 132
   The *WHILE* and *WEND* Statements 133
   The *DO* Loop 134
      The *DO WHILE-LOOP* Statements 134
      The *DO-LOOP WHILE* Statements 136
      The *DO UNTIL-LOOP* Statements 137
      The *DO-LOOP UNTIL* Statements 139
      The *EXIT DO* Statement 140
Summary 142

8 Data Structures 143

What Is an Array? 143
Good Array Candidates 144
Using *DIM* to Set Up Arrays 146
The *OPTION BASE* Statement 152
Searching and Sorting Arrays 154
   Searching for Values 154
   Sorting Arrays 155
The *ERASE* Statement 159
An Array as a Table 159
   Dimensioning Multidimensional Arrays 160
Multidimensional Arrays 161
   Tables and *FOR-NEXT* Loops 163
Summary 166

9 Built-In Functions 167

Overview of Functions 167
Math Functions 168
    Integer Functions 168
    Other Common Math Functions 172
    The *LEN( )* Function 173
String Functions 174
    ASCII String Functions 174
    String Conversion Functions 176
    String Character Functions 179
    Justifying String Statements 182
    The *INKEY$* Input Function 184
Summary 185

10 Modular Programming: Subroutines 187

Subroutines 187
Subroutine Procedures 191
Outlining the Problem 192
Summary 194

11 Disk Files 195

Why Use a Disk? 195
Data Files and Filenames 196
Computer File Example 196
    Records and Fields 197
    Filenames 199
Types of Disk File Access 200
    Sequential-Disk Processing 200
    The *OPEN* Statement 201
The *CLOSE* Statement 202
Creating Sequential Files 203
Appending to Sequential Files 208
Random-Access Disk Processing 209
Random File Records 209
The Random-Access *OPEN* Statement 210
The *TYPE* Statement 211
Declaring Record Variables from Your *TYPE* 213
Accessing Fields in a Record 214

Reading and Writing to Random-Access Files 215
  Creating Random-Access File Data 215
Reading Random-Access Files 217
Changing a Random-Access File 219
Summary 221

12 Sound and Graphics 223

Your Screen 223
Drawing Pixels on the Screen 226
Drawing Lines and Boxes 228
Drawing Circles 230
Adding Color 231
QBasic and Color 231
Making Music and Special Sounds 233
The *SOUND* Statement 233
Summary 235

Index 237

Introduction

Put on your crash helmets and get ready to learn QBasic fast!
Crash Course in QBasic is one of several books in Que's new
line of "Crash Course" titles. The philosophy of these books is
a simple one: It is possible to learn a new programming language without a lot of "fluff" getting in your way. This book is
a tutorial of the QBasic language and is packed with command
descriptions and format syntax. While being as concise as possible, *Crash Course in QBasic* still offers numerous examples
of code; it also explains the more difficult concepts in enough
detail to enable you to understand the underlying concepts.
By reading *Crash Course in QBasic*, you should begin to reap
the rewards of QBasic programming in a very short time.

Who Should Use This Book

If you have programmed before but are new to QBasic, this
book sets you on the road to becoming a QBasic programmer
immediately. In today's fast-paced world, people do not have
time to spend months learning new skills. Adding a programming language to your bag of tricks can be useful both on the
job and at home. QBasic offers the advantage of being widely
available to everyone with DOS 5.0 or later. With this book
and DOS 5.0, you have everything you need to begin writing
QBasic programs.

If you are new to programming, but feel you can master programming concepts without too much trouble, this book is
intended for you as well. The concepts of entering, editing,
and running QBasic programs are fully explained before you
see your first example.

Syntax at a Glance

Crash Course in QBasic features a "How-To" approach that briefly explains why a command is important, and then provides one or two short code examples to illustrate the important features of each command. Throughout each chapter, you will see shaded boxes labeled "Syntax at a Glance." These boxes are chock full of important information and make *Crash Course in QBasic* an extremely valuable resource—one that you will return to throughout your QBasic programming career. A sample Syntax at a Glance box follows:

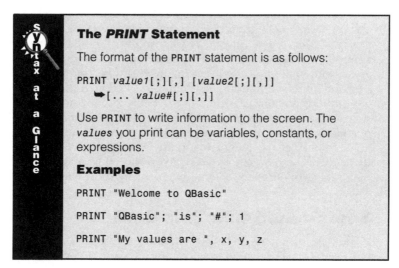

The *PRINT* Statement

The format of the PRINT statement is as follows:

```
PRINT value1[;][,] [value2[;][,]]
  ➡[... value#[;][,]]
```

Use PRINT to write information to the screen. The *values* you print can be variables, constants, or expressions.

Examples

```
PRINT "Welcome to QBasic"

PRINT "QBasic"; "is"; "#"; 1

PRINT "My values are ", x, y, z
```

Besides Syntax at a Glance boxes, you will find three other visual aids in this book that can help you on your QBasic journey.

TIP   Tip boxes offer you ideas for possible shortcuts and hints to make programming in QBasic easier and more efficient.

Note boxes provide you with additional information. Often, this information will help speed your learning or remind you of important information that bears repeating.

CAUTION

Caution boxes warn you of problem areas, including procedures that could possibly harm your computer or cause your program not to run.

Conventions Used

To get the most out of this book, you should know how it is designed. The following list introduces you to the general conventions used in this book.

- New terms and emphasized words appear in *italics*. Pay special attention to italicized text.

- Statements, commands, functions, and so on appear in a special `monospace` typeface.

- Anything you are asked to type appears in **bold**. Responses to program prompts appear in **`monospace bold`**.

- In code lines, placeholders—words that represent text you will insert—appear in `monospace italic`. For example, `filename` or `variable`.

- In syntax lines, brackets ([ ]) indicate optional items. Do not type the brackets when you include these parameters in your programs.

- Some lines of QBasic code are too long to fit within the margins of this book. A special line-wrap icon (➥) is used to indicate when two or more lines in the book should be typed as one line in your program.

Get Ready, Get Set, ... Go!

Without any further delay, turn the page and begin your quick journey towards mastering the QBasic language.

Introduction to QBasic

One of the biggest advantages of QBasic is its availability to almost anyone who owns a PC. Microsoft, the company who wrote QBasic, has included some form of the BASIC program on every copy of DOS it has sold. With DOS 5.0, Microsoft introduced QBasic. If you have DOS version 5.0 or later, you can write QBasic programs.

In this chapter, you are introduced to QBasic, and you learn a little about the programming process.

What QBasic Can Do for You

Have you ever wished that your computer could do exactly what you wanted it to do? Maybe you have looked for a program for your computer that will keep track of the records for your small (or large) business, but nothing is available that prints reports the way you like them. Or, maybe you have thought of a new use for a computer and want to implement that idea. QBasic gives you the power to incorporate your ideas and to make your computer work for you.

Even if you have never programmed a computer before, you will see that programming in QBasic is rewarding. Becoming an expert programmer in QBasic or any other computer language takes some time and dedication on your part. Nevertheless, you can start writing simple programs with very little effort. After you learn the fundamentals of QBasic programming, you can build on what you've learned and hone your programming skills. As you write more powerful programs, you will begin to imagine other uses for your computer, and you can use your programming skills to create programs that others can use as well.

The Background of QBasic

QBasic is based on earlier versions of the BASIC programming language. BASIC is an acronym for Beginner's All-purpose Symbolic Instruction Code—a name nearly as long as the QBasic language itself! As the acronym implies, QBasic is the perfect place for beginning programmers to start writing programs. Unlike its predecessors, however, QBasic includes lots of programming power that previously had been found only in the more complex programming languages. Because of its excellent built-in numeric and string-handling functions, QBasic is also a great language for those who have been programming for a while but are looking for more flexibility.

BASIC was created at Dartmouth College in 1964. The students there often struggled to learn FORTRAN, a language much more strict in its approach than BASIC. Some Dartmouth professors decided to create a new language that had a simpler structure and was easier for beginning programmers to learn, and BASIC was the result. Throughout the years, various companies have added to the BASIC language, often changing the name slightly (BASIC, BASICA, GW-BASIC, QuickBASIC, PowerBASIC, and several others), improving BASIC each step of the way, while still trying to maintain BASIC's ease of use.

Microsoft Corporation was one of the biggest promoters of BASIC during the years that microcomputers were maturing. Microsoft began writing versions of BASIC in the late 1970s and has been the flagship developer of BASIC programming tools ever since. With the introduction of QBasic, Microsoft abandoned the tradition of using a line editor and gave the program a new look. Despite the makeover, QBasic retains all the flair that is perfect for beginners, while utilizing the more advanced features of the language.

If you have programmed before in other versions of BASIC, such as BASICA or GW-BASIC, you will feel at home with QBasic because it runs programs written in most of the BASIC predecessors. Nevertheless, do not limit yourself to the old environment of BASIC. QBasic's improved editor, integrated environment, and program maintenance facilities make programming in QBasic easy.

If you have never programmed before, put on your thinking caps and hop aboard. Programming in QBasic is rewarding, fun, and easier than you might think.

Programs and Data

Simply stated, computers are machines. They are not smart—quite the opposite. Computers cannot do anything unless you give them detailed instructions. Those detailed instructions are called *programs*. Programs tell the computer what to do. If you have used a word processor, you were running a program of instructions that told your computer how to manipulate text in a particular way. If you have ever followed a recipe, you are familiar with the concept of programming. A recipe is just a program (a list of cooking instructions) that tells the cook how to make a certain dish. A good recipe gives these instructions in the proper order, completely describes how to cook the dish, and makes no assumptions that the cook knows anything about the dish.

If you want your computer to help you with your budget, keep track of names and addresses, or compute gas mileage for your travels, you must provide a program that tells the computer how to do those things. There are two ways to supply that program for your computer. You can either buy a program written by someone else or write the program yourself.

For many applications, writing the program yourself has one big advantage: the program does *exactly* what you want it to do. If you buy a commercially available program, you must adapt your needs to the intentions of the program designers. This is where QBasic comes into the picture. With QBasic (and a little study), you can make your computer perform any task.

Because computers are machines that do not think, you must supply QBasic with detailed instructions. If an instruction is not included in your program, don't expect the computer to know what to do.

Program instructions manipulate some type of data. The data can be payroll figures that QBasic turns into a paycheck or a list of test scores that QBasic averages. You probably have heard the term *data processing*. Data processing occurs when a program turns raw facts and figures (the *data)* into meaningful output. That meaningful output often is called *information*. Figure 1.1 illustrates the relationship between data, the program that processes the data, and the resulting output.

After you write a QBasic program, you must *run*, or *execute* it. Otherwise, your computer doesn't know to follow the instructions in the program. Just as a cook must follow a recipe's instructions to prepare a particular dish, your computer must execute the program's instructions before it can accomplish what you want.

Figure 1.1. *Your QBasic programs process input data into meaningful output.*

DOS (short for disk operating system) acts as an intermediary between QBasic and your computer's hardware. When a QBasic program issues a command that sends data to a device such as the screen, DOS takes over the job and writes the data. You don't have to know much about DOS to be a good QBasic programmer. The more thorough your understanding of DOS, however, the better you will understand what is going on "behind the scenes."

Program Design

Before you can begin typing your program into QBasic, you must plan what it is to do. When you want to build a home, the builders don't simply get out their hammers and nails and begin pounding. First, you must communicate your requirements to the builder, have plans drawn, order materials, gather a construction crew, and *then* the hammering begins. Some preparatory work also must go into every program you write.

The hardest part of writing a program is breaking it into logical steps that the computer can follow. Learning the language is a requirement; however, the language is not the only thing to consider. Learning the formal program-writing procedure makes your programming job easier. To write a program you should

1. Define the problem to be solved.

2. Determine what data will be required by the program.

3. Determine what output the program will produce.

4. Break the problem into logical steps to achieve the problem's solution.

5. Write the program (this is where QBasic comes into play).

6. Test the program to make sure it performs as expected.

As you can see, the actual typing of the program occurs as one of the last steps in creating a program. You must *plan* how to tell a computer to perform certain tasks.

Your computer can perform instructions only step-by-step. You must assume that your computer has no previous knowledge of the problem and that you must supply the computer with that knowledge. That is what good recipes do. A recipe for baking a cake that simply said, "Bake the cake," wouldn't be very good because it assumes too much on the part of the cook. Even if the recipe is written step-by-step, you must take care to ensure that the steps are in sequence (by planning in advance). Putting the ingredients in the oven *before* stirring wouldn't be prudent.

Designing a program in advance makes the entire program structure more accurate and keeps changes to a minimum. A builder knows that a room is much harder to add after the house is built than before. When you do not plan properly and think out every step of your program, creating the final working program takes longer. It is much harder to make changes after you have already written the entire program, than to make the changes during the design stage.

From Start to Finish

Once you have designed the program, you are ready to write it. Figure 1.2 illustrates the process of writing a QBasic program. After starting QBasic, you use the built-in *editor* (a word processor-like tool that lets you enter and change QBasic programs) to write the program. You then run the program using menus from within QBasic. If the program has errors (and it usually will the first few times you run it, so be patient), you must edit the program to fix the errors before running the program again.

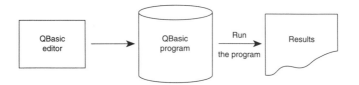

Figure 1.2. *Using QBasic to create and run programs.*

You can save your QBasic program to your hard disk or a floppy disk at any time while you are writing it. Once your program is stored on disk, it is safely tucked away and will remain there even after you turn off the power. If you do not save your program to a disk file, it will no longer be in memory the next time you turn on your computer. Save your programs often when you use the QBasic editor. If a power failure occurs, whatever you have saved to disk will still be intact.

Summary

This chapter introduced you to programming and to QBasic. It briefly explained what QBasic can do for you and described the history of the language. If you are new to programming, you should find QBasic easy to use. If you have previously programmed in BASIC, you will find that QBasic's programming environment offers a much more powerful platform from which to program than other versions of BASIC.

Here are some of the things you learned in this chapter:

- QBasic helps you make the computer do exactly what you want it to do.

- A program is a set of detailed instructions that takes input data and processes that data into meaningful output.

- QBasic is based on previous versions of the BASIC programming language and is a good computer language for beginners to learn.

- A program requires some advance thought. Don't go straight to the keyboard and start typing your program. Instead, think through the task that you want the program to accomplish.

- You use QBasic's built-in program editor to enter and make changes to QBasic programs.

- After you write a QBasic program, it may not always run the first few times. Usually, you will have to go back to the editor and correct problems until the program is accurate.

Using the QBasic Environment

QBasic offers a full array of helpful tools, such as a full-screen editor, pull-down menus, context-sensitive on-line help, and mouse support. This chapter introduces you to the QBasic environment and explains how to start QBasic, how to load and run programs, how to use the program editor, and how to end QBasic.

Using the QBasic editor, this chapter helps you to create programs from scratch. After you enter a program, you can make changes to it, save it to disk, print it on the printer, and erase it so you have a fresh workspace.

After you finish this chapter, you will have the tools you need to begin using the QBasic language.

Starting QBasic

To begin using QBasic, power-up your computer as you always do. QBasic resides in the DOS directory on your disk, which usually is called DOS. To load QBasic on most computers, you just type **QBASIC** in either uppercase or lowercase letters. After you type **QBASIC**, you see the QBasic opening screen, shown in Figure 2.1.

If an error message appears, the path to the DOS directory may not be properly set. You may first have to change to the DOS directory by typing **CD\DOS**. You should then be in the DOS directory, and you can type **QBASIC** to load QBasic into memory.

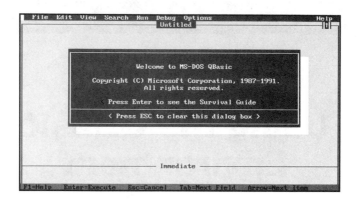

Figure 2.1. *The QBasic opening screen.*

If you use Microsoft Windows, one of the easiest ways to start QBasic is to select the File Manager, open the DOS subdirectory, and double-click QBASIC.EXE.

Starting QBasic with Command-Line Options

There are several options you can add to the QBasic startup command. These *command-line options* change the QBasic environment so that it works differently from the default environment.

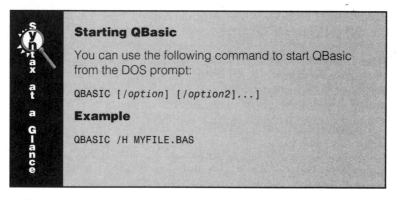

Starting QBasic

You can use the following command to start QBasic from the DOS prompt:

QBASIC [/*option*] [/*option2*]...]

Example

QBASIC /H MYFILE.BAS

Table 2.1 shows a list of these options. As you become familiar with QBasic, these will make more sense.

Table 2.1. QBasic startup command-line options.

Option	Description
/B	Forces QBasic to display in monochrome on computers with a monochrome monitor and a color graphics adapter. Good for laptop users.
/EDITOR (or /ED)	Uses the MS-DOS text editor called Editor. Otherwise, the QBasic text editor is used.
/G	Eliminates the snow, or flickering, from some CGA screens.
/H	Sets the number of lines for the QBasic screen to the maximum your video adapter allows (such as 50 for VGA screens).
/MBF	Used for numeric conversions. Without this option, QBasic stores numbers with more precision, as defined by the Institute of Electrical and Electronics Engineers (IEEE), and is better suited for math coprocessors. This option only maintains compatibility with some previous versions of BASIC.
/NOHI *filename*	For monitors that do not allow high intensity characters. Automatically loads the specified ASCII QBasic program (represented here by the placeholder *filename*) into the editor when QBasic starts.
/RUN *filename*	Loads the designated ASCII QBasic program (represented here by *filename)* into QBasic when QBasic starts, and then runs that program.
/?	Displays all the command-line options in this table.

You can type the options in any order, using either uppercase or lowercase letters.

The QBasic Screen

Figure 2.2 describes the various parts of the QBasic screen. It is from this screen that you create, modify, and execute QBasic

programs. If you have started the QBasic program, press Esc to
clear the copyright message, and you will see this screen. If you
have a mouse, move it around on your desk so that you can see
the mouse cursor move. QBasic works well with a mouse; if you
don't have one, you can still do anything you need to with the
keyboard.

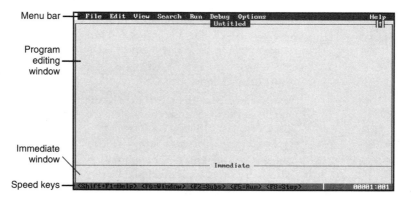

Figure 2.2. *The parts of the QBasic screen.*

The most important part of the screen is the *program editing window*—where you work with QBasic programs. This window acts
like the document-editing area in a word processor: you can move
the cursor with the arrow keys or mouse and make additions and
changes to the text.

The *menu bar* at the top of the screen makes using QBasic easy.
With older versions of BASIC, you had to memorize many commands, such as LOAD, SAVE, LIST, and RUN. In QBasic, you simply
select from the menu bar the command you want to execute.

Selecting from QBasic's Menus

The developers of QBasic understood that programmers did not
want to memorize an assortment of commands in order to use a
program. Instead, QBasic's developers decided to display a list of
available commands and let the programmer select the appropriate one.

The QBasic menu bar displays eight words across the screen: File,
Edit, View, Search, Run, Debug, Options, and Help. These eight
items are headings for the *pull-down menus* from which you can
choose commands. These menu bar items are called pull-down

menus because when you select one, it drops or can be pulled
down from the menu bar. Figure 2.3 shows what happens when
you select the File pull-down menu.

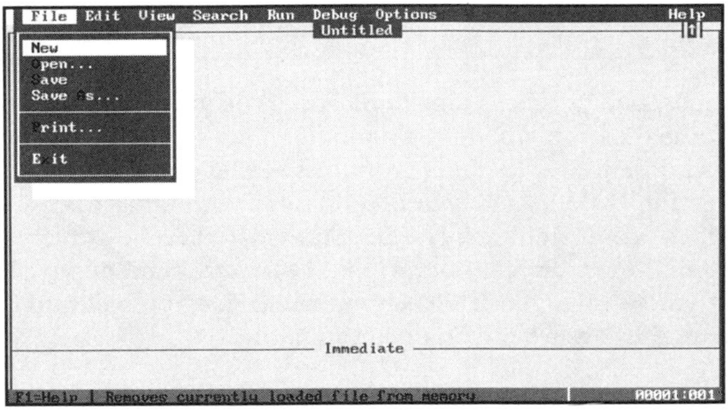

Figure 2.3. *Viewing the complete File pull-down menu.*

You can look at any of the menus by using either the mouse or
keyboard. To display a pull-down menu with the mouse, place the
mouse cursor on a menu bar item and click. Clicking on other
menu bar items displays the remaining pull-down menus.

Displaying a pull-down menu from the keyboard is just as easy.
Press the Alt key followed by the first letter of the menu. For instance, to display the Edit pull-down menu, press Alt-E. After you
are finished with a menu, press Esc to close it. You are, in effect,
escaping out of a command that you started.

Choosing an Option

After you open a pull-down menu and display its contents, you
can tell QBasic which command on the menu's list you want to
execute. For example, the File pull-down menu lists several commands. You can execute a command in any of three ways: by
clicking with the mouse, by moving to the command with the
arrow keys on the keyboard, or by pressing the command's highlighted letter. For example, to request the Open command, mouse
users can move the mouse cursor until it sits anywhere on the
Open option. One click of the mouse then chooses the Open command. Keyboard users can press the down-arrow key until the
Open command is highlighted. A subsequent press of the Enter
key then carries out the command. A shortcut for keyboard users
is to type the highlighted letter of the desired command. By pressing O, the Open command is executed.

> **TIP** The best way to get comfortable choosing from QBasic's pull-down menus is to experiment. As long as you do not save anything to disk, you will not harm QBasic program files or data.

Sometimes, one or more commands appear in gray and are not as readable as the others. This "grayed out" effect signifies that you cannot choose from these menu options at that particular point in the program. Later, you may be at a point in your QBasic session where these commands are practical; they will then be available and will no longer appear in gray. Even when they are not available for you to use, QBasic displays them so that you will remember where they are when you need them.

Menu Shortcut Keys

After you use QBasic for a while, you will become familiar with the commands on the pull-down menus. To help you select menu commands more quickly, QBasic offers *shortcut keys* for some of the commands.

Most of the function keys across the top of the keyboard execute menu commands when you press them. Table 2.2 lists these shortcut commands. For example, if you wanted to choose View, Output Screen, you could display the View pull-down menu, and then select Output Screen. However, the View, Output Screen menu option has an F4 listed to its right. That is the shortcut key for this menu option. Instead of opening the pull-down menu and then selecting the option, you can simply press F4 to immediately run the Output Screen command.

Table 2.2. QBasic menu shortcut keys.

Key	Menu Command
F1	Help
F2	SUBs...
F3	Repeat Last Find
F4	View Output Screen
F5	Run Continue
F8	Debug Step
F9	Debug Toggle Breakpoint

Key	Menu Command
F10	Debug Procedure Step
Del	Edit Clear (erase selected text)
Shift+F1	Help Using Help
Shift-F5	Run Start
Shift-Del	Edit Cut
Ctrl-Ins	Edit Copy
Shift-Ins	Edit Paste

Using Dialog Boxes

Not all menu commands execute as soon as you select them. Some commands are followed by an ellipsis (...), such as the File, Open... command. When you choose one of these commands, a *dialog box* appears in the middle of the screen and requests additional information from you before QBasic can carry out the command. This extra information might be a number, a word, a filename, or you might need to select between several options. Often, a dialog box needs a combination of several things from you.

Figure 2.4 shows the Options, Display... dialog box. This is a good time to practice both using a dialog box and changing QBasic's screen colors (assuming you have a color monitor). From the Options menu, select Display.... Notice that the three options on the left, Normal Text, Current Statement, and Breakpoint Lines, each have a set of parentheses beside them. One set of parentheses also contains a small dot. There are two lists of colors labeled Foreground and Background to the right. This dialog box controls the colors of the three kinds of text in QBasic.

The color of the characters on-screen is the foreground color; background color designates the color of the screen behind the characters. For instance, this book's printed page has black foreground characters on a white background.

To change the color of normal text on-screen, the circle beside Normal Text must be marked with a dot. To mark it and all similar dialog box selections, press the up-arrow or down-arrow key to move the dot between the selections until it marks Normal Text. It is even easier with a mouse—just point to the appropriate circle and click to mark it.

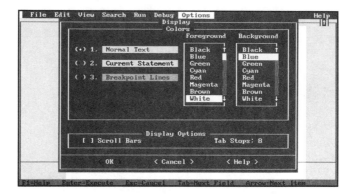

Figure 2.4. *Looking at the Options Display dialog box.*

Now, move to the Foreground color box by pressing Tab or by clicking with the mouse on one of the colors in the Foreground box. (You can use either method to move between sections of a dialog box.) Press the up-arrow or down-arrow key to highlight the foreground color you prefer. As soon as you move the bar to a particular color, you will see the text on-screen change to that color. There are more colors than can be displayed at one time inside the box, so continue to use the arrows on the keyboard to scroll through the list of additional colors.

As with most lists like these, you can select a color with a mouse click too. When you finish with the Foreground box, Tab to the Background box and again move the selection bar to choose a background color. When you type your QBasic programs, the text will appear on-screen in the colors you selected. You can, at any time, change the colors.

Notice the shaded bars to the right of the Background and Foreground boxes. These are called *scroll bars*. They show the relative position of the selected item in a list and are very useful if you have a mouse. If you point to the down arrow on one of the scroll bars and click the mouse, the list of colors moves upward so that you can see the colors toward the end of the list. Conversely, clicking on the up arrow of a scroll bar moves the list of colors downward so that you can see the colors toward the beginning of the list. This typically is faster than using the arrow keys on the keyboard to scroll through a list of items in a dialog box.

To see another type of dialog box selection, move (with Tab or the mouse) to the box marked Display Options. There are two options you can set here: Scroll Bars and Tab Stops. Whenever you see brackets to the left of a dialog box choice, you can only turn that choice on or off. An *X* inside the brackets turns the option on; an empty set of brackets indicates the option is off. For instance, to turn off the scroll bars in the program editing window, Tab or point to the brackets, and press Spacebar or click on the *X* with the mouse to remove the *X*. When you leave the dialog box, the scroll bar to the right of the program editing window disappears. (Because scroll bars are available for mouse users, keyboard users might not want the scroll bars to be visible on-screen.) Conversely, pressing the Spacebar, or clicking with the mouse when pointing to empty brackets beside a dialog box choice, marks that choice with the *X* and turns the scroll bar option on.

The **Tab Stops** option illustrates the last type of dialog box entry. When you write a QBasic program, you can designate the number of characters a Tab keypress will produce. The default is 8 (most programmers lower that to 3 or 4). If you want a different number, type it in place of the 8. When you leave the dialog box and start typing in a QBasic program, the Tab key will then produce that many spaces every time you press it.

Any time you need some assistance with the various choices you can make in the dialog box, click the **Help** button and an information screen appears. (For more information about the on-line help feature of QBasic, read the section titled "Getting Help.")

After you have made all necessary changes to a dialog box, press Enter or click the OK button to put the dialog box selections into effect. If you change your mind, even after altering some of the options, you can press Esc or click Cancel and the dialog box disappears, leaving the original options still in effect.

Getting Help

You can get help at any time in QBasic by using the on-line help feature. On-line help explains virtually every aspect of QBasic. Depending on your request, QBasic helps you with whatever you need and even offers sample programs that you can merge into your own programs.

The Help Survival Guide

QBasic's *Help Survival Guide* appears every time you start QBasic from the DOS prompt. After you get familiar with QBasic, you will bypass the Help Survival Guide by pressing Esc when it appears. However, new users of QBasic may find it very helpful. The opening copyright screen is the gateway to the Help Survival Guide.

After starting QBasic from the DOS prompt, you will see the copyright screen with the following message:

`<Press Enter to see the Survival Guide>`

Pressing Enter displays the Survival Guide's control screen shown in Figure 2.5.

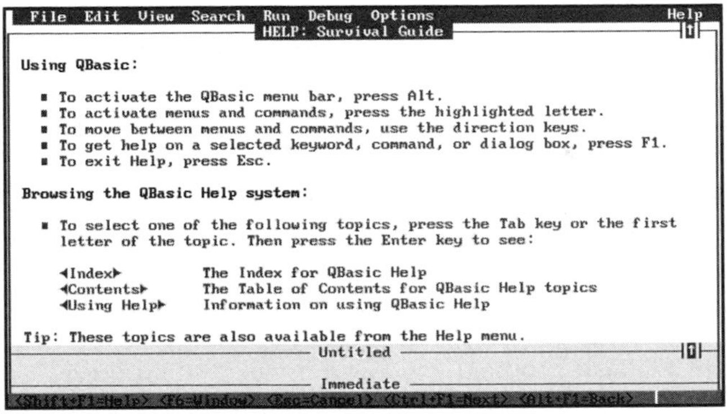

Figure 2.5. *The Help Survival Guide control screen.*

The top part of the Survival Guide screen explains how to choose from the menu bar, which you already learned about earlier in this chapter. The remainder of the screen explains the Help system in detail. You can access the three options, Index, Contents, and Using Help, from the **Help** pull-down menu as well as from elsewhere in the program. These options are explained in more detail in the next few sections. Feel free to browse through the Survival Guide. When you are through, press Esc to leave the Survival Guide and return to QBasic.

Help About Help

The QBasic on-line help system is so complete, it even gives you help on itself! The Survival Guide's Using Help option explains the many ways to get help from QBasic. If you select Using Help with a mouse click, or tab to it and press Enter, a screen appears that explains the help system. Clicking or tabbing on <Contents>, <Index>, or <Back>, moves you, respectively, to the help's table of contents, to the index of QBasic keywords, or back to the QBasic program editing window.

The Help Menu

You can display the Help pull-down menu by typing Alt-H. Notice that the Help menu contains three of the same commands as the Survival Guide: Index, Contents, and Using Help. You can also access the help Topic command from the Help menu (although pressing F1 is usually easier, as you will see).

Choosing Index from the Help menu displays a list of every command in QBasic. The index is more than just a list of command names. You can click on any command on the list or tab to any command, and a detailed explanation of that command appears, along with an actual QBasic program code example using that command. Selecting Help, Contents displays help on various parts of QBasic under these headings: Orientation, Keys, Using QBasic, and Quick Reference. As with all help screens, pressing Esc returns you to the program editing window.

Context-Sensitive Help

Once you become familiar with QBasic, you will find that the *context-sensitive help* feature relieves some programming frustration. Whenever you request context-sensitive help by pressing F1 or choosing Help, Topic, QBasic "looks" at what you are doing and gives you help with it. Suppose you are working on the QBasic PRINT statement, and the cursor is resting on the word PRINT when you press F1. QBasic will display help on the PRINT command. If you want help on a pull-down menu, you must press F1. You cannot choose from the Help menu while viewing another pull-down menu.

Loading a Program

Your DOS disks come with several QBasic programs. As with all QBasic filenames, these programs end in the .BAS extension, as in the following:

GORILLA.BAS   MONEY.BAS   NIBBLES.BAS

When you save and reload QBasic program files whose names end in .BAS, you don't have to specify the .BAS. When you supply the first part of the filename, with no .BAS extension, QBasic assumes the file has the .BAS extension.

Before you can run a QBasic program, you must load it from the disk into memory. Only one QBasic program at a time can be in memory. For example, to run the GORILLA.BAS game that comes with DOS, follow these steps:

1. Start QBasic.

2. Press Esc to clear the Survival Guide.

3. Select **File, Open** and a dialog box containing filenames is displayed. Either type **GORILLA.BAS** or use the arrow keys or horizontal scroll bar to scroll through the list of files until GORILLA.BAS is highlighted. After you highlight GORILLA.BAS, either click or press Enter and QBasic will load the file into the editor. Look through the program you see on-screen. By the end of this book, you should understand everything displayed there.

4. Select **Start** from the **Run** pull-down menu, or press Shift-F5. The game begins with a melody and then the start-up screen appears. Read through the game's instructions and play the game for a while to see what QBasic can do.

Stopping a QBasic Program

Most QBasic programs give you a chance to quit when you come to a logical stopping place. For example, GORILLA.BAS lets you exit the game after you play through and destroy a gorilla. Sometimes, however, you may need to stop a QBasic program in the middle of its execution.

Stopping a QBasic program while it is running is simple. When you press Ctrl-Break, the program stops and the program editing window appears. You can load another program, rerun the program you just exited by selecting **Run, Start** (Shift-F5), or exit to DOS.

> **TIP** If you stop a program with Ctrl-Break and decide you want to restart the program where it left off, select **R**un, **C**ontinue (F5) to resume the previous execution.

Using the Program Editor

One of QBasic's biggest improvements over its predecessors is the program editor. The program editor resembles a word processor: You can type a program, change it, move parts of it around, and

erase parts of it. Because you do most of these functions from the
menu bar, you don't have to remember command names.

Typing a Program

As you type a QBasic program, it appears in the program editor
window. After you type the program's instructions, you run it, ana-
lyze the results, and fix any problems that arise. Before you worry
about understanding the actual QBasic commands, however, you
have to understand how to move the cursor around in the window. Here are some quick editing hints:

- The cursor shows you where the *next* character you type will
  appear.

- Press Enter after each statement in the program.

- The Backspace key moves the cursor to the left and erases as
  it moves.

- Use the arrow keys and PageUp and PageDown to move the
  cursor left, right, up, and down the screen a character or a
  screen at a time.

- If you leave out a letter, word, or phrase, move the cursor to
  the location where you want to insert the missing text and
  type the text. Because QBasic's default is Insert mode, the
  rest of the line moves to the right to allow room for the inserted characters. If you want to overwrite existing text, press
  the Ins key. The blinking underline cursor becomes a block
  cursor, signifying that you are in Overtype mode. When you
  press Ins again, you are returned to Insert mode and the cursor reverts to a blinking underline.

- If you type an extra letter, word, or phrase, move the cursor
  over the extra text and press Del one or more times. The rest
  of the line moves to the left to fill in the gap left by the de-
  leted character.

- If the program is longer than a single screen, the program
  editing window scrolls upward to make room for the new
  text. If you want to see the text that has scrolled off the
  screen, press the up-arrow key or PageUp, or click on the top
  of the scroll bar with the mouse. The down-arrow key or
  PageDn, or clicking on the bottom of the scroll bar, rolls the
  bottom portion of the text back into view.

Table 2.3 provides a complete list of QBasic editing keys.

Table 2.3. The QBasic editing keys.

Description	Keystroke	Equivalent Keys
Cursor Movement		
Character left	Left Arrow	Ctrl-S
Character right	Right Arrow	Ctrl-D
One word left	Ctrl-Left Arrow	Ctrl-A
One word right	Ctrl-Right Arrow	Ctrl-F
One line up	Up Arrow	Ctrl-E
One line down	Down Arrow	Ctrl-X
Beginning of line	Home	Ctrl-Q, S
Start of next line	Ctrl+Enter	Ctrl-J
End of line	End	Ctrl-Q,D
Top of window		Ctrl-Q,E
Bottom of window		Ctrl-Q,X
Move to next window	F6	
Insert and overstrike	Ins	Ctrl-V
Text-Scrolling Keys		
Up one line	Ctrl-Up Arrow	Ctrl-W
Down one line	Ctrl-Down Arrow	Ctrl-Z
Up one page	PageUp	Ctrl-R
Down one page	PageDn	Ctrl-C
Text-Selection Keys		
Character left		Shift-Left Arrow
Character right		Shift-Right Arrow
Word left		Shift-Ctrl-Left Arrow
Word right		Shift-Ctrl-Right Arrow
Current line		Shift-Down Arrow
Preceding line		Shift-Up Arrow
Screen up		Shift-PageUp
Screen down		Shift-PageDn
To beginning of file		Shift-Ctrl-Home
To end of file		Shift-Ctrl-End

Description	Keystroke	Equivalent Keys
To Insert, Copy, and Delete		
Copy selected text to Clipboard		Ctrl-Ins
Delete selected text and copy it to Clipboard		Shift-Del
Delete current line and copy it to Clipboard		Ctrl-Y
Delete to end of line and copy it to Clipboard		Ctrl-Q, Y
Paste the contents of the Clipboard		Shift-Ins
Insert a blank line below the cursor position		End, Enter
Insert a blank line above the cursor position		Home, Ctrl-N
Insert special characters		Ctrl-P, Ctrl-key
Delete one character to the left of the cursor	Backspace	Ctrl-H
Delete one character at the cursor	Del	Ctrl-G
Delete the rest of the word the cursor is resting on		Ctrl-T
Delete selected text	Del	Ctrl-G
Delete leading spaces from selected lines	Shift-Tab	
Bookmark Keys		
Set as many as four bookmarks	Ctrl-K, 0-3	
Go to specific bookmark	Ctrl-Q, 0-3	
Window Commands		
Increase the size of the active window	Alt-Plus	
Decrease the size of the active window	Alt-Minus	
Zoom in/out of the active window	Ctrl-F10	
Move left one window	Ctrl-PageUp	
Move right one window	Ctrl-PageDn	

Your First Program

To get accustomed to the editor, type the following program into your program editing window. It takes up less than one screen, so it will not scroll.

Listing 2.1. Your first QBasic program.

```
REM My first QBasic program
REM
REM This program displays a message on the screen
REM
   CLS
   PRINT "Hello!  I am your computer."
   PRINT
   PRINT "Press the Enter key to clear the screen..."
   REM Wait for the Enter keystroke
   INPUT EN$
   CLS
END
```

Make sure you type it exactly as it appears in the listing. If you type the commands (shown in uppercase in the listing) in lowercase letters, the QBasic program editor will convert them to uppercase to make them easier to see.

You can see the results of this program by running it, just as you ran the GORILLA.BAS program earlier in this chapter. Select **Start** from the **Run** pull-down menu. Your screen will clear and you will see the output of the program.

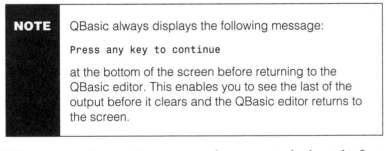

NOTE QBasic always displays the following message:

`Press any key to continue`

at the bottom of the screen before returning to the QBasic editor. This enables you to see the last of the output before it clears and the QBasic editor returns to the screen.

When you run (execute) a program, the computer looks at the first instruction and interprets it, followed by the second instruction, and so on.

This is a very simple program, but don't worry if you don't understand its contents. Just to whet your appetite, however, here is a description of the program listing. The first few lines beginning with REM contain *remarks* that QBasic completely ignores. The remarks are there just to document the program for the sake of anyone reading through it. CLS clears (erases) the screen. PRINT displays text and data on-screen. The INPUT statement waits for a keystroke from the keyboard. The Enter key always ends an INPUT action. Finally, the program ends after it clears the screen again.

Spacing in Programs

QBasic programs are *free-form*, which means that you can add spacing and blank lines as necessary to make a program more readable. Your computer ignores blank lines and spaces, so use them to make the program easier to read.

If There Are Errors...

If you misspell a word, leave out a quotation mark, or make another mistake, QBasic informs you with a dialog box that pops up in the middle of the screen. The word or line of the program where QBasic first spotted the error is highlighted. The most common error is a *syntax error*, which often means you've misspelled a command.

When you receive an error message, you can select **OK** to return to the program editor so you can fix the problem. If you don't understand the error, select **Help**; QBasic then displays an explanation of the error message.

Saving the Program

If you want to save programs to disk, you can do so. Use the File, Save As... command to save a program. After you choose File, Save As..., a filename dialog box appears. You can type a new filename, or to overwrite a file, you can type the name of a file that already exists. You also have the option of selecting a different disk drive or directory by selecting from the Dirs/Drives box.

A QBasic filename can contain from one to eight characters, including letters, numbers, and the underscore character. Additionally, a few special characters can be used, such as the exclamation point (!) and the pound sign (#). However, most QBasic programmers stick with letters, numbers, and the underscore.

The File, Save command saves the current program to disk under the most recent filename. For instance, if you load a file called MYFILE.BAS from disk and then make changes to it, File, Save stores it under the name MYFILE.BAS. This process is quicker than selecting File, Save As... and typing the filename every time.

Erasing the Program Editing Window

To clear the program editing window without saving the program (starting over with a "clean slate"), select File, New. QBasic warns you that you have not saved the program and gives you a chance to do so. The program then clears from the editing window.

For example, if you want to clear from memory the program you typed earlier, select File, New and then select No when QBasic asks if you want to save the file to disk. This clears your editing window.

Printing a Program

To print your program, select the File, Print... command, and the QBasic print dialog box appears. From the Print dialog box, choose one of the following three options:

- Selected Text Only—prints only the text that you have highlighted on-screen.

- Current Window—prints only the text from the window in which you were editing when you selected File, Print.

- Entire Program—prints your entire program.

Make sure your printer is on-line and has paper before choosing OK in this dialog box. If you want to cancel the File, Print command, press Esc or click Cancel.

Quitting QBasic

After finishing the QBasic session, you can exit QBasic and return to DOS by choosing File, Exit. If you add to or make changes to a QBasic program and then try to exit to DOS without saving those changes to disk, QBasic displays a warning message that asks if you want to save the file before exiting. Always remember to exit to DOS before powering off your computer so that you don't risk losing any of your most recent work.

Summary

This chapter familiarized you with the QBasic environment. The major advantage of QBasic over its predecessors is its screen menus and on-line help system. Now, you can use QBasic's built-in editor to enter your own programs and see their results.

Here are some of the things you learned in this chapter:

■ How to start QBasic from DOS. You now understand the names of the various areas of the QBasic screen.

■ Menu shortcut keys help you issue some commands much more quickly than either the pull-down menus or a mouse. The on-line help system is always available to answer your questions as you use QBasic. You can get help on any QBasic command, as well as help on using the QBasic environment.

■ How to load and run a QBasic program with just a few keystrokes.

■ The QBasic editor is easy to use and acts like a built-in word processor for the programs you write.

■ Using the **Run** pull-down menu, you can execute the programs you enter into QBasic.

■ You can print your programs to the printer using the **Print** command from the **File** pull-down menu.

Working with Data

To understand data processing with QBasic, you first must understand how QBasic creates, stores, and manipulates data. This chapter introduces variables and constants and also discusses how to create and name both numeric and string variables, how to assign values to variables, and how to view those results on-screen and on the printer.

Now that you have mastered the QBasic screen and program files, you can begin to write your own QBasic programs. Before you are done with this chapter, you will be writing QBasic programs from scratch!

QBasic Data

A QBasic program consists of commands and data. QBasic takes that data and processes it into meaningful results. The data is made up of *variables* and *constants*. As the name implies, a variable is data that can change (it is *variable*) as the program runs. A constant always remains the same. In real life, a variable might be your age or your salary. A constant could be your first name, because it remains with you throughout your life, or your social security number.

Numeric Variables

You can think of a QBasic variable as a small pocket in your computer that holds a number, special character, word, sentence, or an entire paragraph of text. You can have as many variables as your program requires to hold all data that can change. When you need a variable, you simply define it, and QBasic makes sure you get it.

Variables have characteristics. Because you are responsible for creating your own variables, you must understand these characteristics and make sure they fit the data. The characteristics of variables are as follows:

- Each variable has a name.

- Each variable has a type.

- Variables hold the values that you put in them.

To help you better understand these characteristics, the following sections explain each of them.

Naming Variables

You can have many variables in a single program. In order to keep track of them, you must assign them names. Variable names are unique, just as house addresses are unique. If two variables could have the same name, QBasic would not know which one you were requesting.

Variable names can be as short as a single letter or as long as 40 characters. Variable names must begin with a letter of the alphabet, but after the first letter they can contain letters, numbers, and the period (.).

> **TIP**   Because spaces are not valid in variable names, you can use a period to separate the parts of a variable name to make the name more readable.

The following variable names are all valid:

```
Salary    Aug91.Sales    I    index    AGE
```

You can use either uppercase or lowercase letters in a variable name. `Sales`, `SALES`, and `sales` all refer to the same variable. Variables cannot have the same name as a QBasic command or function.

The following variable names are all invalid:

```
81_SALES    Aug91+Sales    MY AGE    PRINT
```

(As you will learn later, `PRINT` is a QBasic command. Consequently, you cannot name a variable `PRINT`.)

TIP	Always use *meaningful* variable names. Give your variables names that help describe the values they are holding.

Variable Types

Variables can hold different *types* of numbers. Table 3.1 lists the different numeric types QBasic recognizes. For example, if a variable holds an integer, QBasic assumes that no decimal point or fractional part (the part to the right of the decimal point) exists for the variable's value.

Table 3.1. Numeric variable types in QBasic.

Type	Variable Suffix	Examples
Integer	%	12, 0, –765, 21843
Long Integer	&	32768, 99876
Single-Precision	!	1.0, 34.32345
Double-Precision	#	0.99999987654

Essentially, an integer is a number that has no decimal place (it is a whole number). Unless you specify otherwise, QBasic assumes that all variables are single-precision. If you put an integer into a variable, without overriding the default, QBasic converts that integer to a single-precision number.

Single-precision and double-precision variables are *real* numbers. They have decimal points and a fractional part to the right of the decimal. Single-precision variables accurately keep 6 decimal places, whereas double-precision variables keep accuracy to 14 places.

If you want QBasic to assume a specific type for a variable, add the variable suffix to the end of the variable's name. For example, if you store the distance between two cities (in miles) in a variable called `distance`, QBasic assumes the variable will always hold a single-precision number. However, if you want the mileage stored as an integer, you would refer to the variable by the name `distance%`. The percent sign (%) is not considered part of the name; it is simply a suffix you add to indicate which type of value the variable is to hold.

Once you use a variable's suffix to indicate its type, you must continue to use that variable suffix every time you refer to that variable. In QBasic, N!, N%, N&, and N#, all refer to different variables.

You might wonder why it is important to have so many types. The type of variable is very critical, and knowing which variable type to use is not as difficult as it may first appear. Table 3.2 lists the *ranges* of values each variable type can hold. Variables cannot hold just any value; they can only hold a value that falls within their own type and range of values. You could not, for instance, put a number larger than 32,767 into a variable defined as an integer. Only single- or double-precision or long integer variables can hold numbers over 32,767. Integers and single-precision numbers will be sufficient for most of your programming tasks. However, if you are working with very large or very small numbers, such as scientific computations, you may need the extra precision that the other types provide.

Table 3.2. The range of values for each variable type.

Type	Range of Values
Integer	−32,768 to +32,767
Long Integer	−2,147,483,648 to +2,147,483,647
Single-Precision	
Positive Numbers	3.402823×10^{38} to 2.802597×10^{-45}
Negative Numbers	$-2.802597 \times 10^{-45}$ to -3.402823×10^{38}
Double-Precision	
Positive Numbers	$1.79769313486231 \times 10^{308}$
	to $4.940656458412465 \times 10^{-324}$
Negative Numbers	$-4.940656458412465 \times 10^{-324}$
	to $-1.79769313486231 \times 10^{308}$

All variables used in this book will be integer or single-precision, unless otherwise noted. It is okay to put an integer number into a single-precision variable (remember that QBasic always assumes single-precision, unless you specify another variable suffix) because the range of regular integers falls within the range of single-precision numbers.

NOTE   As you will see later in this chapter, variables can hold character data as well as numeric data.

Assigning Values to Variables

Now that you know something about variables, you are probably wondering how to put values in them. You do so with the assignment statement.

Assigning Variables

The format of the assignment statement is

`[LET]` *variable* `=` *expression*

LET assigns values to variables. The *variable* is any valid variable name you create. The equal sign is required. The *expression* is a value, variable, or an expression that equates to a value (you will learn more about expressions in the next chapter).

Example

`LET a = 4 + 6`

LET is the command name and is optional. Assigning values to variables is so common in QBasic programs, the designers of the language decided that the actual command LET would be optional. Consequently, it is perfectly valid to write the example shown in the preceding syntax box as

```
a = 4 + 6
```

Perhaps you want to keep track of your current age, salary, and dependents. You can store these values in three QBasic variables, using variable names such as age, salary, and dependents, and insert the assignment statements into your program. Later in the program, these values may change if, for example, the program calculates a pay increase for you.

To assign values to these three variables, your program would resemble the following:

```
LET age = 32
LET salary = 25000
LET dependents = 2
```

You never have to put a decimal point in the value of the salary because QBasic assumes single-precision variables unless you override the type. Even though you are putting an integer value into these variables, QBasic changes them to single-precision (by adding a decimal point) for you.

The three-line program just shown doesn't do much. The code, however, is a complete program that illustrates naming and using variables and how to put numeric values in those variables.

> **NOTE**   Do not put commas in values you assign to variables. The following statement is invalid:
>
> LET salary = 25,000

Because the LET command is optional, you could rewrite this three-line program as

```
age = 32
salary = 25000
dependents = 2
```

Because a variable contains a value, you can even assign one variable to another, as shown in the following:

```
spouse.tax.rate = tax.rate
```

Whatever value you assigned to tax.rate would, at this point in the program, be copied to a new variable named spouse.tax.rate. The value in tax.rate still exists, however, even after the preceding line is executed.

The variable suffix indicates the variable data type you want QBasic to use. Suppose you want to keep your age in an integer variable, your salary in a single-precision variable, and your dependents in an integer variable. To designate the data type, add the type suffix to the end of the variable name, as follows:

```
age% = 32
salary! = 25000.00
dependents% = 2
```

> **NOTE**   QBasic initially puts a zero in each variable you use in a program. As soon as you assign a value to that variable, you replace the default zero.

QBasic Constants

Unlike a variable, a *constant* does not change; it always remains the same. You already have used constants in this chapter. The values that you have assigned to variables are constants; numbers are always constant. The number 7 always has the value of 7, and you cannot change it. You can, however, change a variable by putting another value into it.

Numeric constants can be positive or negative and have types just as variables do. Table 3.3 shows the available types of constants.

Table 3.3. The types of numeric constants.

Type	Suffix	Examples
Integer	None	158, 0, –86
Long Integer	None	21233343, –32889
Fixed Point	None	4.67, –0.08
Floating Point		
Single-Precision	!	3453.3!, 1.08E+8
Double-Precision	#	93045.65#, –1.8765456D–09

Numeric constants also have ranges, and it's important for you to be aware of them (see Table 3.4). Unlike variables, however, QBasic interprets the constants in your programs and decides which type to store them as. Generally, you don't have to worry about adding a suffix to a constant.

Table 3.4. Numeric constants and their ranges.

Type	Range
Integer	–32,768 to 32,767
Long Integer	–2,147,483,648 to 2,147,483,647
Fixed Point	Positive or negative numbers that have decimal points
Floating Point	
Single-Precision	-3.37×10^{38} to 3.37×10^{38}
Double-Precision	-1.67×10^{308} to 1.67×10^{308}

In your programs, remember not to use commas in constants.

Viewing Output

Now that you understand variables and constants, you have to learn how to display that data on-screen. A program with no output is useless. This section introduces one of the most important commands in the QBasic language: PRINT.

The *PRINT* Statement

The PRINT statement takes whatever is to the right of the word PRINT and sends it to the screen. (*Reminder:* The line-wrap icon (➡) indicates two lines that you should type as one in your program.)

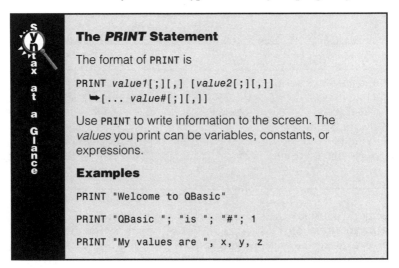

The *PRINT* Statement

The format of PRINT is

```
PRINT value1[;][,] [value2[;][,]]
  ➡[... value#[;][,]]
```

Use PRINT to write information to the screen. The *values* you print can be variables, constants, or expressions.

Examples

```
PRINT "Welcome to QBasic"

PRINT "QBasic "; "is "; "#"; 1

PRINT "My values are ", x, y, z
```

If you use a variable name as the *expression*, PRINT displays the contents of that variable on the screen. If you put a constant after PRINT, that constant is displayed. PRINT is actually a very complex command with lots of options. This chapter focuses only on the simpler PRINT options.

> **TIP** If you put PRINT on a line by itself, QBasic prints a blank line. You can use this to separate lines of screen output from each other.

You can print the three variables you typed in an earlier example, age, salary, and dependents, by adding three PRINT statements after them, for example:

```
age = 32
salary = 25000
dependents = 2

PRINT age
PRINT salary
PRINT dependents
```

Notice the blank line that separates the group of PRINT statements from the variable assignments? The blank line is not required, but it helps break the program into logical, more readable parts. If you were to type this program into the QBasic editor and then run it (with **Run, Start**), you would see this output:

```
32
25000
2
```

Notice that QBasic prints each of the variable's values on a separate line. If you can put constants to the right of a PRINT statement, the constants print exactly as you type them. For example, if you type and run the following program, the first three odd numbers will be displayed, followed by the first three even numbers. The odd numbers are stored in variables, and the even numbers are printed from constants.

```
odd1 = 1
odd2 = 3
odd3 = 5

PRINT odd1
PRINT odd2
PRINT odd3
PRINT 2
PRINT 4
PRINT 6
```

Here are the six lines of output from this program:

```
1
3
5
2
4
6
```

More About *PRINT*

There are many other things PRINT can do. In order to write more useful programs, you must learn how to access more of PRINT's options.

Printing String Constants

In QBasic, a *string constant* is one or more groups of characters enclosed by double quotation marks (" "). The following shows five examples of string constants:

```
"This is a string constant."
"ABC 123 $#@ —··· +=][ x"
"X"
"123.45"
"  "
```

Notice that even a single character, if it is between double quotation marks, is a string constant. (String constants are sometimes called *string literals*.) One question you may have about the preceding example is the number "123.45".

"123.45" is a string constant because it fulfills the definition of a string constant: one or more characters enclosed by double quotation marks. "123.45" is *not* a number, a numeric constant, or a variable. The double quotation marks always denote a string constant. You cannot use "123.45" in mathematical calculations because it is never viewed as a number in QBasic.

String constants are useful for printing names, titles, addresses, and messages on the screen and the printer. When you want your QBasic program to print a title or a word, you enclose the text in double quotation marks and place it after the PRINT command.

To print Widget, Inc.'s name and address on-screen, you would place the following section of code in your program:

```
' Prints a company's name and address on the screen
CLS                   .
PRINT "Widgets, Inc."
PRINT "307 E. Midway"
PRINT "Jackson, MI     03882"
```

When you run this program, QBasic prints the following on your screen:

```
Widgets, Inc.
307 E. Midway
Jackson, MI     03882
```

> **NOTE**   Whenever you print string constants, everything inside the double quotation marks prints exactly as it appears. This includes any and all spaces you typed between the quotation marks. The quotation marks, however, do not print.

Printing More Than One Value on a Line

You now know several ways to use PRINT, but there are even more things you can do with it. The PRINT statements you have seen so far have printed only one value—either a numeric constant, a variable, or a string constant—on a line. You can also print several values on a single line with one statement. To print more than one value on a line, you must separate the values with either a semicolon (;) or a comma (,). The choice depends on how closely you want the values printed to each other.

Using Semicolons with *PRINT*

To print two or more values—they can be variables, constants, or a combination of both—right next to each other on the same line, separate them with semicolons in the PRINT statement.

The following PRINT statement

```
age = 9
PRINT "I am"; age; "years old"
```

displays this output:

```
I am 9 years old
```

Space appears around the 9 in the preceding output line because a blank always prints on each side of a positive numeric constant or variable. If the value is negative, the minus sign takes the place of the leading blank.

Up to this point, every PRINT statement has caused the output to start on a new line. This is because QBasic automatically prints a carriage return-line feed sequence after each PRINT.

You can suppress the carriage return-line feed sequence by inserting a trailing semicolon at the end of a PRINT statement. The semicolon ensures that the next PRINT statement immediately follows the statement just printed. For example, the following short section of code prints all three names on the same line:

```
CLS
PRINT "Heath ";
PRINT "Jarrod ";
PRINT "Nick"
```

The output for this code is as follows:

```
Heath Jarrod Nick
```

The more you program in QBasic, the more likely it is you will have to *build* your output line. That is, you will print a little, make some computations, and then finish printing the rest of the line. The trailing semicolon enables you to finish the PRINT statement later in the program.

Using Commas with *PRINT*

If you want to print two or more values—again, variables, constants, or a combination of both—on the same line separated by several spaces, use commas (,) between the values. Using commas with the PRINT statement is very helpful if you want to print columns of output. QBasic assumes that there are five *print zones* on your screen, and a new print zone occurs every 14 columns. Each comma in your PRINT statement begins a new print zone. The following line

```
PRINT "Ed", "Julie", "Richard", "Sam"
```

prints Ed starting in the first column, Julie starting in column 15, Richard in column 29, and Sam in column 43 (each zone begins 14 columns to the right of the previous one). Notice that no matter how wide the name is, the next name begins at the start of the next print zone. The print zones are useful for printing columns of data when you want each column to begin in the same screen position.

You can insert two or more commas together to force printing in a farther print zone. The following PRINT statement prints QBasic in the fourth print zone:

```
PRINT ,,,"QBasic"
```

 **NOTE** If your data is longer than a print zone, it prints one additional print zone to the right. For instance, if you printed a name that had 20 letters in it, then followed the name with a comma and another name, the second name would start printing in column 29 (the third print zone), even though it was the second name printed.

Listing 3.1 illustrates the use of commas between PRINT values. The three lines print the animals in four columns. Even though the animal names vary in length, they all start in certain print zones. The comma always forces the next animal to be printed in the subsequent print zone.

Listing 3.1. Using commas with the *PRINT* statement.

```
' Uses the comma between printed values. Each comma
' forces the next animal into a new print zone
'
CLS
PRINT "Lion", "Whale", "Monkey", "Fish"
PRINT "Alligator", "Bat", "Seal", "Tiger"
PRINT "Dog", "Lizard", "Cat", "Bear"
```

Listing 3.1 produces this output:

```
Lion        Whale       Monkey      Fish
Alligator   Bat         Seal        Tiger
Dog         Lizard      Cat         Bear
```

Only string constants are printed in this example, but you can also print variables and numeric constants in print zones. Remember, all positive numbers print with at least one space before them.

Printing with *TAB( )*

Printing with commas is similar to using tabs. Each comma acts like a tab by moving the next value to the next print zone. Print zones, however, are not true tabs because you cannot change their location. Print zones always occur every 14 spaces. To print a table of values in columns that do not coincide with the print zones, you would use the TAB() command in your PRINT statement.

The tab value always goes in parentheses after TAB. Never use TAB by itself; always combine it with a PRINT statement. Notice that you can have several TAB() commands in a single PRINT statement.

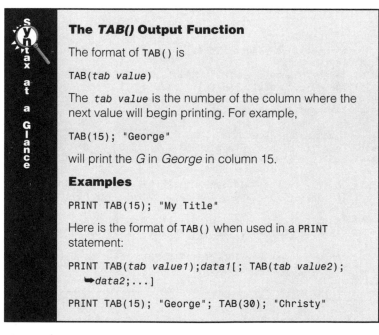

The *TAB()* Output Function

The format of TAB() is

TAB(*tab value*)

The *tab value* is the number of the column where the next value will begin printing. For example,

TAB(15); "George"

will print the *G* in *George* in column 15.

Examples

PRINT TAB(15); "My Title"

Here is the format of TAB() when used in a PRINT statement:

PRINT TAB(*tab value1*);*data1*[; TAB(*tab value2*);
➥*data2*;...]

PRINT TAB(15); "George"; TAB(30); "Christy"

The TAB() option is especially useful for tables of data. Even though words and values do not always take the same width on

the screen ("Alligator" is longer than "Dog"), you might want them
to begin printing in the same column.

> **TIP** You almost always see semicolons on both sides of a
> TAB( ). They let you know that the tab will occur
> immediately after the last value prints. Never use
> commas on either side of TAB( ); they force the cursor
> over to the next print zone, and *then* the TAB( ) takes
> effect. That next print zone may already be past the
> column you wanted to tab to.

Listing 3.2 prints a list of names and addresses on-screen. The
PRINT commands are lengthy, but by inserting TAB( )s between
them, the output is aligned in columns. Because some of the data
is longer than the 14-character print zones, printing them in print
zones, separated by commas, would not work.

Listing 3.2. Using *TAB()* to print a report.

```
' Uses the TAB() command to print a name and address report.
'
CLS

' Print underlined report titles
PRINT TAB(69); "ZIP"
PRINT TAB(5); "Name"; TAB(23); "Address"; TAB(48); "City";
PRINT TAB(60); "State"; TAB(69); "Code"
PRINT TAB(5); "----"; TAB(23); "------"; TAB(48); "----";
PRINT TAB(60); "----"; TAB(69); "----"

' Print the data values
PRINT TAB(5); "Michael Stapp"; TAB(23); "6104 E. 6th";
PRINT TAB(48); "Tulsa"; TAB(60); "Okla."; TAB(69); "74135"

PRINT TAB(5); "Jayne M. Wiseman"; TAB(23); "Elm and Broadway";
PRINT TAB(48); "Cleveland"; TAB(60); "Ohio"; TAB(69); "19332"

PRINT TAB(5); "Lou Horn"; TAB(23); "12 East Elm";
PRINT TAB(48); "Carmel"; TAB(60); "Indi."; TAB(69); "46332"

PRINT TAB(5); "Luke Ben Tanner"; TAB(23); "5706 S. Detroit";
PRINT TAB(48); "Salem"; TAB(60); "Mass."; TAB(69); "23337"
END
```

In this example, TAB( ) allowed the headings to align with the data
in the columns. Notice that a PRINT TAB( ) was required to print the
lone heading ZIP on a line by itself so it sits on top of Code on the

next line. The dashes (-) help underline each title to separate the title from the data. Here is the output from Listing 3.2:

```
                                              ZIP
Name               Address          City      State  Code
----               -------          ----      -----  ----
Michael Stapp      6104 E. 6th      Tulsa     Okla.  74135
Jayne M. Wiseman   Elm and Broadway Cleveland Ohio   19332
Lou Horn           12 East Elm      Carmel    Indi.  46332
Luke Ben Tanner    5706 S. Detroit  Salem     Mass.  23337
```

Printing to Paper

By now, you have made significant progress towards producing nice-looking output. Printing to the screen, however, is not always the best alternative. If you want to print a permanent copy of something, you would send that output to the printer. Printing to the printer is very easy with the LPRINT command.

LPRINT is identical to PRINT in every way, except the output goes to the printer and not to the screen.

Syntax at a Glance

The *LPRINT* Statement

The format of LPRINT is

```
LPRINT value1[;][,] [value2[;][,]]
    ➥[... value#[;][,]]
```

LPRINT writes information to the printer.

Examples

```
LPRINT "Welcome to QBasic"

LPRINT "QBasic "; "is "; "#"; 1

LPRINT "My values are ", x, y, z
```

Any program you write that uses PRINT statements can be redirected to the printer by substituting LPRINT for each occurrence of PRINT. The following statement

```
LPRINT "The cost is"; 34.67; "dollars."
```

prints this to the printer:

```
The cost is 34.67 dollars.
```

You can also use TAB() within LPRINT statements.

Clearing the Screen

If you have been running the examples so far in this chapter, you may have noticed an annoying problem with the output: the results of the *previous* output are still left on the screen when you run another QBasic program. To eliminate this, you can use the CLS command.

CLS is very easy to use. Whenever QBasic runs a program and gets to a line containing CLS, QBasic erases the output screen.

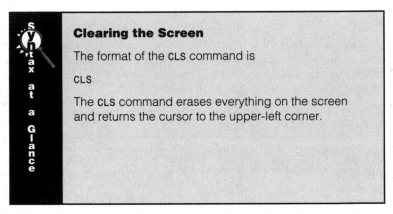

Clearing the Screen

The format of the CLS command is

CLS

The CLS command erases everything on the screen and returns the cursor to the upper-left corner.

Most QBasic programmers put CLS as the first line of every program so that the screen clears at the start of the program. This eliminates output from previous runs of the program, and the current program can start with a fresh screen. Listing 3.3 shows a program that clears the screen before printing values.

Listing 3.3. A program that clears the screen before printing.

```
CLS

LET age = 32
PRINT age

LET salary = 25000
PRINT salary

LET dependents = 2
PRINT dependents
```

Using the *END* Command

You can add the END command to the end of QBasic programs. END was required in earlier versions of BASIC but is optional in QBasic. Your computer knows when it reaches the end of a QBasic program, so only use END for compatibility with older versions of BASIC.

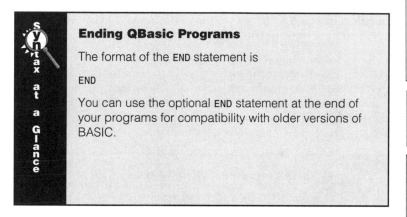

Ending QBasic Programs

The format of the END statement is

```
END
```

You can use the optional END statement at the end of your programs for compatibility with older versions of BASIC.

Although it is optional, some programmers end every program with an END statement, so that anyone reading the program knows for sure that he or she has reached the end of the program.

Listing 3.4 displays the program you saw in Listing 3.3, except an END statement has been added. (The extra blank lines between the PRINT statements also have been removed.)

Listing 3.4. The program from Listing 3.3 with an *END* statement.

```
CLS

LET age = 32
PRINT age
LET salary = 25000
PRINT salary
LET dependents = 2
PRINT dependents

END
```

In this book, the END statement is not used for small programs. In Chapter 10, "Modular Programming: Subroutines," the END statement is used with subroutines and with longer program sections so that the stopping point of each program or routine is very clear.

Program Remarks

By now, you know that a program provides instructions that the computer can read and interpret; as a programmer, you have to understand the programs you write. It isn't always easy to go back and make changes to a program you wrote earlier. It is even more difficult to revise a program written by someone else. Someday, computer languages may be written in ordinary English; until then, you have to learn to speak and understand the computer's language.

To help you document the purpose of each section of your program, QBasic provides the REM command. REM (short for *remark*) enables you to insert comments that are completely ignored by the computer. The only purpose of these comments is to make the program more easily understood by humans.

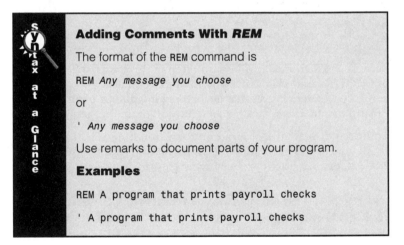

Adding Comments With *REM*

The format of the REM command is

REM *Any message you choose*

or

' *Any message you choose*

Use remarks to document parts of your program.

Examples

REM A program that prints payroll checks

' A program that prints payroll checks

You can have as many remarks in your program as you want. Many programmers scatter lots of them throughout a program. The command is completely ignored by the computer: no output is produced, no variables are stored, and no constants are required.

For instance, a QBasic program that produces a fancy colored box with your name inside and flashing lights around it (like a marquee) would take some cryptic QBasic commands. Before those commands, you might put a comment resembling the following:

REM The next few lines draw a colorful fancy boxed name

This does not tell QBasic to do anything, but it makes the next few lines of code more understandable to you and others. In plain English, it explains exactly what the program is getting ready to do.

REM statements are also useful for putting the programmer's name at the top of the program. In a large company with several programmers, this procedure makes it easier to track down the original programmer. If you need help changing his or her code, you will know who wrote it. Remember, a programmer's name inserted in a REM statement will not print that name when the program is run—printing requires a PRINT statement, not a REM statement. The name does appear in the program, however, for anyone looking at the program's listing.

You might also consider putting the filename of the program in a REM statement near the beginning of the program. For example, the following statement:

```
REM Programmer: Pat Johnston, Filename: PAYROL81.BAS
```

tells who the programmer is and gives the program's filename on disk. If you are looking through a bundle of printed program listings, you can quickly find the program you want by looking at the filename in the REM statement at the top of the listing. You can then load it and make any changes with the program editor .

Because REM statements appear so often in programs, the authors of QBasic supplied a shortcut for it. In place of REM, you can type a single apostrophe ('). Unlike REM, however, you can place a remark using the apostrophe to the right of a program line (on the same line) to help explain the line. REM statements, however, have to go on lines by themselves. Listing 3.5 shows a program with both types of remarks.

Listing 3.5. A program using both types of QBasic comments.

```
REM Filename: VARPRNT.BAS
REM
REM This program puts a few values in variables
REM and then prints those values to the screen.
REM
CLS
LET age = 32               'Stores the age
LET salary = 25000         'Yearly salary
LET dependents = 2         'Number of dependents

' Print the results

PRINT age
PRINT salary
PRINT dependents
```

Using Helpful Remarks

Make sure that the remarks you insert in your programs are helpful. Remember, remarks are there to *explain* to humans what the program code is doing. The following remark is not helpful:

```
REM Put the value 3 into the variable called NUM.KIDS
LET NUM.KIDS = 3
```

Even though it is rather wordy, the above remark does not explain why the value 3 is placed in NUM.KIDS. Consider the following improved comment:

```
REM Save the number of kids for dependent calculations
LET NUM.KIDS = 3
```

This gives a better idea of the purpose of the program's next statement. Anyone reading through the program trying to figure out what it does would appreciate the second remark much more than the first.

Many QBasic statements are completely clear without any remarks. It would be silly, for example, to use a remark to explain CLS. There is no ambiguity at all about what is going on; the screen clears.

Summary

This chapter explained the concepts of data variables and constants. You now know all about numeric variables, numeric constants, and string constants. In addition, you can now send data values to the screen or printer.

Here are some of the things you learned in this chapter:

- All variables have unique names.

- There are different types of numeric variables, and each type can hold a different range of numbers.

- The numeric variable or constant suffix symbol indicates the type of variable or constant.

- The PRINT command sends data to the screen. You can use the semicolon and the comma with PRINT to produce output with various spacing. PRINT can include a TAB() function that spaces to a specific column for the next item printed.

- LPRINT is the PRINT equivalent for your printer. TAB(), semicolons, and commas all work with LPRINT as they do with PRINT.

- The REM command (also denoted with ') is ignored by the computer and enables you to insert remarks that document what your program does.

Operators and String Variables

QBasic can do all your math for you, but you must know how to set up the calculations properly. This chapter introduces the QBasic math operators and shows you how they work. Numbers are useless by themselves; you must learn how to store strings of characters in *string variables* so that you can process both numeric and character data.

Once you complete this chapter, you will know almost all there is to know about the fundamental data types that QBasic supports.

The Math Operators

A QBasic math *operator* is simply a symbol used for addition, subtraction, multiplication, division, and other math operations. The operators are very similar to the ones you use when you do arithmetic. Table 4.1 displays the symbols for the QBasic math operators and their meanings.

The Four Primary Operators

The four primary QBasic operators, *, /, +, and ·, operate in ways that are probably familiar. Multiplication, division, addition, and subtraction, produce the same results as when you do these math functions with a calculator. Table 4.2 illustrates each of these simple operators.

Table 4.1. The QBasic operators.

Symbol	Meaning
*	Multiplication
/	Division
+	Addition
-	Subtraction
^	Exponentiation
\	Integer Division
MOD	Modulus

Table 4.2. Examples using the four primary operators.

Formula	Result
4 * 2	8
95 / 2	47.5
80 – 15	65
12 + 9	21

You must use an asterisk (*), not an *x*, for multiplication. QBasic would confuse an *x* with a variable called *x* and wouldn't know you wanted to multiply.

You can also use the addition and subtraction operators by themselves. When used in this way, they are called *unary* operators. For example, you can assign a positive or negative number to a variable, or you can assign a positive or negative variable to a variable by using the unary plus or minus, as shown in the following:

```
a = -25
b = +25
c = -a
d = +b
```

Integer Division and Exponentiation

Two of the remaining QBasic operators, integer division (\) and exponentiation (^), may be new to you. They are as easy to use as the other four operators you saw in the last section.

Use integer division to produce the integer, or whole number, result of a division. Integer division always produces an integer result and discards any remainder. You do not have to put integers on both sides of the \; you can use floating point numbers, integers, or a combination of both on each side of the \. Table 4.3 demonstrates how the integer division operator is used.

Table 4.3. Results using the integer division operator.

Formula	Result
8 \ 2	4
95 \ 2	47
95.0 \ 2	47
95 \ 2.0	47
95.0 \ 2.0	47

Use the exponentiation symbol (^) when you want to change the power of a number. The number to the left of the ^ is the base, and the number to the right is the power. You can put integers, floating point numbers, or a combination of both on each side of the ^. Table 4.4 shows the results of some exponentiation calculations.

Table 4.4. Results using the exponentiation operator.

Formula	Description	Result
2 ^ 4	2 raised to the 4th power (2^4)	16
16 ^ 2	16 raised to the 2nd power (16^2)	256
5.6 ^ 3	5.6 raised to the 3rd power (5.6^3)	175.616
144 ^ 0.5	144 raised to the .5 power ($144^{1/2}$)	12

If you want QBasic to provide you with the remainder, or modulus, in a division operation, you can apply a special operator called MOD. MOD combines division with integer division and returns the remainder of the integer division. To find the remainder of 10 divided by 3, you would use the following formula:

```
10 MOD 3
```

Assigning Formulas to Variables

Most of your QBasic programs use variables to store the results of these calculations. You have already seen how to assign values and variables to other variables. The true power of variables appears when you assign the results of formulas to them.

Listing 4.1 illustrates a payroll computation. First, the hours worked, the pay per hour (the *rate*), and the tax rate are assigned to three variables. Then, three new variables are created from calculations using these variables: the gross pay, the taxes, and the net pay.

Listing 4.1. A payroll computation program.

```
' Computes three payroll variables

hours.worked = 40          'Total hours worked
rate = 7.80                'Pay per hours
tax.rate = .40             'Tax rate percentage

gross.pay = hours.worked * rate
taxes = tax.rate * gross.pay
net.pay = gross.pay - taxes

CLS                        'Print the results
PRINT "The gross pay is"; gross.pay
PRINT "The taxes are"; taxes
PRINT "The net pay is"; net.pay
```

Here is the output from the program shown in Listing 4.1:

```
The gross pay is 312
The taxes are 124.8
The net pay is 187.2
```

> **NOTE** Chapter 5, "Advanced Input and Output," shows you how to print to two decimal places for the dollars and cents.

The Order of Operators

Knowing what the math operators represent is the first of two steps in understanding QBasic calculations. You also must understand the *order of operators*, sometimes called the *hierarchy of operators* or *operator precedence*. This order determines exactly how QBasic will compute a formula and is the same as what you remember from your high school algebra. To see how the order of operators works, try and determine the result of the following simple calculation:

```
2 + 3 * 2
```

If you said 10, you would not be alone; many people would respond with 10. However, 10 is only correct if you interpret the formula from left to right. If you calculate the multiplication first, you would compute the value of 3 * 2, get an answer of 6, and then add 2 to it. You would end up with the answer 8—exactly the answer that QBasic would compute!

QBasic always performs any exponentiation first, then multiplication and division, and, finally, addition and subtraction. Table 4.5 illustrates this order of operators.

Table 4.5. The order of operators.

Order	Operator
1	Exponentiation ($\wedge$)
2	Unary (+, −)
3	Multiplication, division, integer division (*, /, \)
4	Modulus (MOD)
5	Addition, subtraction (+, −)

It is easy to follow QBasic's order of operators if you follow the intermediate results one at a time. The following three complex calculations show you how to do this:

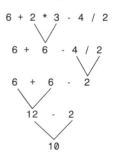

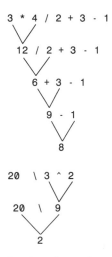

Looking back at the order of operations table again, you will notice that multiplication, division, and integer division are on the *same level*. This implies that there is no hierarchy on that level. If more than one of these operators appears in a calculation, QBasic performs the math from *left to right*. The same is true of addition and subtraction; the leftmost operation is performed first, as shown in the following example:

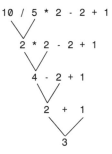

When division appears to the left of multiplication, the division is computed first because division and multiplication are on the same level.

Using Parentheses

If you want to override the order of operators, put parentheses in the calculation. Many times, the order of operator tables actually lists an extra level, before the others, with parentheses on that extra level. In other words, anything in parentheses, whether it is addition, subtraction, division, or whatever, is always calculated before the rest of the line. The rest of the calculations are performed in their normal, operator order.

The first formula in this chapter, 2 + 3 * 2, produced an 8 since the multiplication is performed before addition. However, by adding parentheses around the addition, as in (2 + 3) * 2, the answer becomes 10.

The following calculations illustrate how parentheses override the regular order of operators. These are the same three formulas shown in the last section, only their calculations are different because the parentheses override the order of operators.

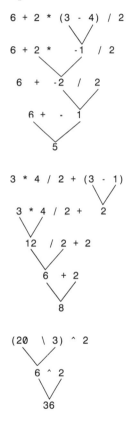

```
6 + 2 * (3 - 4) / 2
           \  /
            \/
6 + 2 *    -1   / 2
    \      /
     \    /
 6  +  -2  /  2
     \     /
      \   /
  6 +  -  1
    \    /
     \  /
      5


3 * 4 / 2 + (3 - 1)
             \  /
              \/
3 * 4 / 2 +    2
 \   /
  \ /
 12  / 2 + 2
   \   /
    \ /
   6  + 2
    \  /
     \/
     8


(20  \ 3)  ^  2
    \   /
     \ /
   6  ^  2
    \  /
     \/
     36
```

TIP	Use plenty of parentheses in your QBasic programs to make the order of operators clear, even when you do not *have* to override the order of operators. It sometimes makes the calculations easier to understand if you want to modify the program later.

Printing Calculations

You have seen how you can print variables and constants with
PRINT and LPRINT. These two statements can also print the values of
expressions. As long as the expression results in a valid value, you
can put the expression to the right of PRINT.

Do not confuse PRINT and LPRINT with the assignment statement.
The following PRINT is invalid:

```
PRINT sales = "are the sales"
```

QBasic gives you a syntax error if you use this line in a program.
PRINT and LPRINT require an expression to the right of PRINT. The
equal sign is reserved for the assignment statement. You first must
assign a value to sales and then print that value, as the following
example shows:

```
sales = 18750.43
PRINT sales; "are the sales."
```

You can compute payroll amounts and print them at the same
time. Listing 4.2 is a rewritten version of the payroll program you
saw earlier in this chapter. Listing 4.2 prints the results of the three
payroll expressions without storing the results in variables.

Listing 4.2. A payroll computation program that does not store results in variables.

```
' Computes and prints three payroll values

hours.worked = 40            'Total hours worked
rate = 7.80                  'Pay per hour
tax.rate = .40               'Tax rate percentage

CLS                          'Print the results
PRINT "The gross pay is"; hours.worked * rate
PRINT "The taxes are"; tax.rate * hours.worked * rate
PRINT "The net pay is";
PRINT (hours.worked * rate) - (hours.worked * rate * tax.rate)
```

This program is not necessarily better than the original one, but it
does illustrate that you can print variables, constants, *and* expressions. Notice that the parentheses are not required in the last expression, but they do make the meaning of the formula clearer: the
gross pay must be computed before the taxes are subtracted.

Although this program is shorter than the previous one, a shorter
program is not always better. A more readable program is generally the best kind. Being able to store the three values lets you use

them later in the program without having to recalculate their results. Also, the last expression is much less complicated if you had already calculated and stored the gross.pay and taxes, as you did in the first payroll program.

You can write simple programs to illustrate the operators in QBasic. Suppose you want to write a tutorial program that shows how each operator works. Listing 4.3 computes and prints the results of simple calculations using each QBasic operator. Be diligent with your double quotation marks around the string constants, so that you can maintain a clear difference between the formulas and the printed string constants.

Listing 4.3. A program demonstrating how each QBasic operator works.

```
' This program shows how each operator works

num1 = 7              'The variables to compute with
num2 = 4

CLS
PRINT "+num1 is"; num1
PRINT "+num2 is"; num2
ans = -num1                    'Unary minus
PRINT "-num1 is "; ans
ans = num1 - num2              'Subtraction
PRINT "num1 - num2 is"; ans
ans = num1 + num2              'Addition
PRINT "num1 + num2 is"; ans
ans = num1 * num2              'Multiplication
PRINT "num1 * num2 is"; ans
ans = num1 / num2              'Division
PRINT "num1 / num2 is"; ans
ans = num1 \ num2              'Integer Division
PRINT "num1 \ num2 is"; ans
ans = num1 ^ num2              'Exponentiation
PRINT "num1 ^ num2 is"; ans
END
```

Running the program in Listing 4.3 results in the following output:

```
+num1 is 7
+num2 is 4
-num1 is -7
num1 - num2 is 3
num1 + num2 is 11
num1 * num2 is 28
num1 / num2 is 1.75
num1 \ num2 is 1
num1 ^ num2 is 2401
```

String Variables

Chapter 3, "Working with Data," explained how to use string constants. Without string constants, you could not print messages to the screen or printer. Now, you are ready to see how to store string data in variables. String data consists of one or more characters *strung* together. A string variable can hold string data, just as integer variables can hold integers and double-precision variables can hold double-precision numbers. By storing strings of characters in variables, you can change the strings. This comes in handy if you keep track of names and addresses; when people move to another city, you simply change the string variable that holds that person's city.

By storing string data in string variables, you only have to type your string data once, even if you need to print it several times. After storing the string data in a string variable, you simply print the string variable from then on.

Creating String Variables

If computers only worked with numbers, they would be little more than calculators. True data processing occurs when you can process any type of data, including character string data. String variables can hold any character, word, or phrase that your PC can produce. There are two types of string variables: *variable-length string variables* and *fixed-length string variables*.

Most strings are variable-length strings, which means the size of the string data stored in the variable can be any length. If you put a short word in a variable-length string variable, and later replace it with a longer word or phrase, the string variable grows to hold the new, longer data.

On the other hand, the numeric variables you have been using have fixed lengths, or ranges of values, and you cannot exceed those stated ranges of numbers. Fixed-length string variables can hold only strings that are shorter or equal to the length you define. These strings are not as flexible as variable-length strings. Chapter 11, "Disk Files," addresses fixed-length strings and their uses.

> **NOTE**   String variables can hold strings as long as 32,767 characters.

Naming String Variables

As with numeric variables, it's up to you to provide names for your string variables. String variable names are easy to spot: they all end with a dollar sign ($). Whenever you see a variable whose name ends in a dollar sign, it is a string variable. For instance, the following are all valid string variable names:

```
MY.NAME$    month$    Customer.city$    X$    address$
```

When you are ready to store a name, address, or any other character, word, or phrase in a variable, create a name for the variable and end it with the $ suffix.

QBasic never treats a string of numbers in a string variable as numeric. Just as QBasic does not view string constants enclosed in double quotation marks as numbers, the dollar sign suffix of a string variable signifies to QBasic that no math can be performed on that data.

> **NOTE** Although it may be tempting, do not name a string variable DATE$ or NAME$. These are both reserved command names in QBasic (as is PRINT, LET, and so on), and you cannot use command names for variable names.

Suppose you wanted to keep track of a customer's name, address, city, state, ZIP code, and age in variables. You might use the following variable names:

```
cust.name$
cust.address$
cust.city$
cust.state$
cust.zip$
cust.age
```

Notice that the customer's age is numeric, so it is stored in a numeric variable and doesn't end with a $. You should only store data in numeric variables if you plan to perform math calculations with the data. Generally, this stipulation excludes data such as phone numbers, social security numbers, customer numbers, and so on. For instance, even though ZIP codes consist of numbers, you never will add or subtract them. They are best stored in string variables. You might use an age in an average age calculation, so it is best left in a numeric variable.

Remember that numeric variables have suffixes that describe their data types. If you want to keep track of an employee's salary, age, name, employee number, and number of dependents, you could use the following variable names:

```
emp.salary!
emp.age%
emp.name$
emp.number$
emp.dependents
```

Only the name and employee number should be stored in string variables. The salary should be stored in a numeric variable, and a single-precision variable is used here (signified by the ! suffix). If the salary is extremely large, however, a double-precision variable would be better. The age is stored in an integer variable, and the number of dependents is stored in a single-precision variable (the default variable type, if you do not specify a suffix).

Storing Data in String Variables

Use the assignment statement to put data into string variables, just as you do with numeric data and variables. You can put either a string constant or another string variable into a string variable with LET.

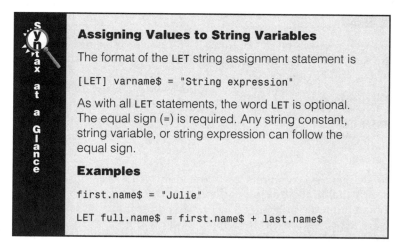

Assigning Values to String Variables

The format of the LET string assignment statement is

```
[LET] varname$ = "String expression"
```

As with all LET statements, the word LET is optional. The equal sign (=) is required. Any string constant, string variable, or string expression can follow the equal sign.

Examples

```
first.name$ = "Julie"

LET full.name$ = first.name$ + last.name$
```

Notice that if you put a string constant into a string variable name, you must enclose the string constant in double quotation marks ("). The quotation marks are not stored in the string; only the data between the quotation marks is stored there.

You can put an empty string, called a *null string*, into a string variable by placing two double quotation marks, with no space between them, after the equal sign. For example, the following assignment statement

```
LET E$ = ""
```

places an empty string, with zero length, into the string variable named E$. QBasic initializes all string variables to null strings before you use them. You might want to start with a null string when you are building strings a character at a time, such as when you receive data sequentially from a modem.

Suppose you are writing a program that manages a book inventory for a library, a collector, or a bookstore. To keep track of the title, author, and edition of a particular book, you might store the data in three string variables, as shown in the following:

```
LET book.title$ = "In Pursuit of Life"
LET book.author$ = "Francis Scott Key"
LET book.edition = "2nd"
```

Because LET is always optional in assignment statements, the string variables for these three books could be assigned as follows:

```
book.title$ = "In Pursuit of Life"
book.author$ = "Francis Scott Key"
book.edition = "2nd"
```

You can assign the value of a string variable to another string variable, as the second line illustrates in the next example:

```
LET emp.last.name$ = "Payton"
LET spouse.last.name$ = emp.last.name$
```

Printing String Variables

To print the data stored inside a string variable, put the string variable after PRINT or LPRINT, just as you did for numeric variables. You can combine numeric variables, string variables, string constants, semicolons, commas, and the TAB statement in PRINT and LPRINT statements if the output warrants it.

When you print a string variable next to another string variable or string constant (by using the semicolon), QBasic does not automatically print a separating space between them. Therefore, if you need to print any text before a string variable, be sure to add a space inside the description's closing double quotation marks so that the text will not bump into the variable:

```
PRINT "The highest-paid executive is: "; max.exe$
```

TIP If you must print a string constant several times throughout a program, it is easier to first store that string constant in a string variable and then print the string variable name. For example, if you have to print your company's name at the top of several checks and reports, store that name in a string variable, such as co.name$, and then simply print co.name$. This keeps you from having to repeatedly type the company name.

In order to print two string variables side-by-side and not have them running into each other, you must include a separating space, surrounded by double quotation marks. If you stored the names of three automobile makers in three string variables and then wanted to print them, you would want a space separating each name, as in:

```
PRINT auto1$; " "; auto2$; " "; auto3$
```

The output would look like this:

```
GM Ford Chrysler
```

Without the spaces, you would get run-on string output, which is difficult to read, such as the following:

```
GMFordChrysler
```

Listing 4.4 stores and prints the three book-related string variables mentioned in the preceding section.

Listing 4.4. Storing and printing the three book variables.

```
' Store and print three book-related variables

book.title$ = "In Pursuit of Life"
book.author$ = "Francis Scott Key"
book.edition$ = "2nd"

' Now, print them to the screen

CLS
PRINT book.title$
PRINT book.author$
PRINT book.edition$
```

By now, you know that printing the contents of variables, without first describing them, produces confusing output. To improve the preceding program, you could add a header, descriptive titles, and use the TAB statement to align the data in columns, as shown in Listing 4.5.

Listing 4.5. Improving the output of Listing 4.4.

```
' Store and print three book-related variables with a title

book.title$ = "In Pursuit of Life"
book.author$ = "Francis Scott Key"
book.edition$ = "2nd"

' Print a title
CLS
PRINT TAB(30);"Book Listing"
PRINT TAB(30);"---- -------"
PRINT                              ' Print two
PRINT                              ' blank lines

' Now, print the book data to the screen
PRINT "The book's title is"; TAB(24); book.title$
PRINT "The book's author is"; TAB(24); book.author$
PRINT "The book's edition is"; TAB(24); book.edition$
END
```

Here is the output of the preceding program. Even though the descriptions are three different lengths, the data all aligns in column 24 because of the values set in the TAB statements.

```
                    Book Listing
                    ---- -------


The book's title is    In Pursuit of Life
The book's author is   Francis Scott Key
The book's edition is  2nd
```

If you want the book data to go to the printer instead of to the screen, change the PRINT statements to LPRINT statements.

Listing 4.6 program adapts the payroll computation programs (shown earlier in Listings 4.1 and 4.2) to print a paycheck to the employee. Before running the program, make sure your printer is turned on and has paper.

Listing 4.6. The payroll computation program adapted to print a paycheck.

```
' Computes and prints a payroll check

' Initialize data variables
emp.name$ = "Larry Payton"
pay.date$ = "07/09/93"
hours.worked = 40           'Total hours worked
rate = 7.50                 'Pay per hour
tax.rate = .40              'Tax rate percentage

'Compute the pay

gross.pay = hours.worked * rate
taxes = tax.rate * gross.pay
net.pay = gross.pay - taxes

'Print the results on the format of a check
LPRINT TAB(40);"Date "; pay.date$
LPRINT                                 'Print a blank line
LPRINT "Pay to the Order of "; emp.name$
LPRINT
LPRINT "Pay the full amount of";gross.pay
LPRINT TAB(25);"---"                   'Underline the amount
LPRINT
LPRINT TAB(40);"----------------------"
LPRINT TAB(40);"Dan Chambers, Treasurer"
```

Here is what your printer will print if you run this program:

```
                                       Date 07/09/93

Pay to the Order of Larry Payton

Pay the full amount of  300
                        ---


                                       ---------------------
                                       Dan Chambers, Treasurer
```

Granted, this check does not have the amount spelled out, but it does illustrate some of the ways to print string variables and numeric data together in the same program.

At this point, you might be thinking it would be easier to type the check in a typewriter than write the program to compute and print it. In this case, that may be true. However, you are acquiring the groundwork you need to make QBasic do your tedious work for you. As you learn more of the language, you will see how writing the program becomes *much* faster than typing the data by hand, especially when you are working with large data files.

String Concatenation

You cannot perform any math calculations on string variables, even if they contain numbers. However, you can perform another type of operation on string variables called *concatenation*. Concatenation is combining two or more strings to make a single longer string. You can concatenate string variables, string constants, or a combination of both, and you can assign the concatenated strings to a string variable.

The string concatenation operator is the plus sign (+). By context, QBasic knows not to confuse the concatenation symbol with the addition symbol. If QBasic sees string data on either side of the plus sign, it knows to concatenate the strings.

> **NOTE** You can concatenate as many strings (variables and constants) as you like, as long as you do not exceed QBasic's 32,767 string variable limit.

Suppose you store an employee's first name in one string variable and his last name in a second string variable. You can print his full name by printing the two string variables next to each other, as the following example demonstrates:

```
first.name$ = "Bill"
last.name$ = "Cole"
PRINT first.name$;" ";last.name$
```

The problem with printing two individual variables is that every time you print them, you must specify both of them, separated by a space. It's easier to concatenate the two names into one string variable and then print that variable, as shown in the following:

```
LET first.name$ = "Bill"
LET last.name$ = "Cole"
LET full.name$ = first.name$ + " " + last.name$
PRINT full.name$
```

The extra space is a string constant you concatenate between the two strings. Otherwise, they would run together. Running this short section of code would produce

```
Bill Cole
```

Because you must include the line that concatenates the two variables, this method may seem to require more typing. However, if you have to print the name several times in the program, this method actually makes printing the full name easier.

If you want to print the full name with the last name first, you can do so by concatenating a comma between the names as in:

```
LET first.name$ = "Bill"
LET last.name$ = "Cole"
LET full.name$ = last.name$ + ", " + first.name$
PRINT full.name$
```

Running this section of code would produce

```
Cole, Bill
```

on your screen. The space after the comma is only there because in the third line of code it was concatenated in the string constant containing the comma.

Make Your Data Types Match

By now, you have seen examples of programs using these types of variables and constants:

   Integer

   Single-Precision

   Double-Precision

   String

You must be careful when you use the assignment statement. You can never put string data into a numeric variable or numeric data into a string variable.

CAUTION

This is critical: In an assignment statement, always make sure that both sides of the equal sign contain the same type of data and variables.

Table 4.6 shows you several assignment statements. You have seen many like them. They are valid because in each statement the variable on the left side of the equal sign is the same type as the expression, variable, or constant on the right side. Make sure that you understand why this entire table is valid before reading on.

Table 4.6. Valid assignment statements.

Variable = Expression	Assignment Statement
integer = integer	`distance = 175`
single-precision = single-precision	`salary = 45023.92`
double-precision = double-precision	`temp# = -123.43337689`
string = string	`a$ = "Candy"`

Each of the arbitrary assignment statements in the second column of the preceding table has the same type of variable, constant, or expression, on both sides of the equal sign. Table 4.7 presents a very different table. It shows many combinations of assignments that do not work because the types on either side of the equal sign do not match.

Table 4.7. Invalid assignment statements (types do not match).

Assignment	Problem Description
`greet$ = hello`	No double quotation marks around "hello."
`salary = "43234.54"`	Do not put string constants into numeric variables.
`avg.age$ = "100" / 2`	Cannot perform math with string constants.
`full.name$ = first + last`	No dollar sign after *first* and *last*. (QBasic will think these are two numeric variables called *first* and *last*.)
`weight% = pounds# + kilos#`	Cannot with accuracy put a double-precision number into an integer. (QBasic will round improperly.)
`month = month.name$`	Cannot put a string variable into a numeric variable.

If you attempt to mix types in an assignment statement, you will get a type mismatch error.

Summary

You should now understand most of the QBasic math operators. You must be able to follow the order of operator precedence before you will know how QBasic will calculate. QBasic also works well with string data, storing results in string variables that you can print and manipulate.

Here are some of the things you learned in this chapter:

- The four primary math operators are *, /, +, and -. The / (division operator) will return a whole number (integer) result only if the numbers on both sides of the / are integers. The modulus operator, MOD, returns the remainder of an integer division operation.

- The order of operator precedence determines how QBasic calculates an expression.

- Parentheses override the default order of precedence.

- The exponent operator (^) raises a number to a designated power.

- String variables hold string data (character data). String variable names always end in the $ suffix.

- The + performs string concatenation by merging one string onto the end of another.

Advanced Input and Output

You now understand about data and variables in QBasic. You have also seen several methods for outputting data with the PRINT and LPRINT statements. Nevertheless, there is one critical part of programming that you have not seen: using INPUT to enter data into your programs.

So far, every program you have seen has had no data input. All data you worked with was assigned to variables within the program. However, this is not the best way to get the data that your programs process; you rarely know what your data is going to be when you write your programs. Only when the programs are run are the data values known.

This chapter shows you how to make your programs ask the user for values. It also expands on the PRINT and LPRINT statements to show you how to produce better output.

The *INPUT* Statement

With INPUT, you can control the way your programs accept data from the keyboard. INPUT has several options.

When your program gets to the INPUT statement, it displays a question mark and waits for the user to type one or more values. If one variable follows INPUT, only one value is expected. If more than one variable follows INPUT, the user must type values separated by commas until each of the variables is filled up. Pressing Enter after typing values in response to INPUT informs QBasic that the user is finished typing values into the INPUT variables.

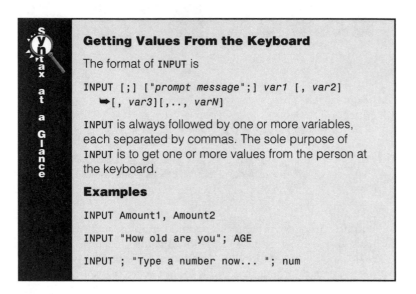

The format of INPUT is

```
INPUT [;] ["prompt message";] var1 [, var2]
➥[, var3][,.., varN]
```

INPUT is always followed by one or more variables, each separated by commas. The sole purpose of INPUT is to get one or more values from the person at the keyboard.

Examples

```
INPUT Amount1, Amount2

INPUT "How old are you"; AGE

INPUT ; "Type a number now... "; num
```

INPUT Fills Variables with Values

Both LET and INPUT fill variables with values. However, LET assigns specific values to variables *at programming time*. When you run a program with assignment statements, you know from the program listing exactly what values will go into the variables, because you wrote the program to store those values there. Every time you run the program, the results are exactly the same because the same values go into the same variables.

When you write programs that use INPUT, you have no idea what values will go into the INPUT variables, because their values are not known until the *program is run*. This makes for much more flexible programs that can be used by a variety of people. Every time the program is run, different results are output, depending on what is typed at the INPUT statements in the program.

If you want a program that computes a seven percent sales tax, you can use the INPUT statement to get the total sales, compute the tax, then print the results, as Listing 5.1 shows.

Listing 5.1. A program that calculates sales tax.

```
CLS

' Get the total sales
INPUT total.sales

' Calculate sales tax
stax = total.sales * .07
```

```
' Print the results
PRINT "The sales tax on"; total.sales; " is: "; stax
PRINT "Bringing the total needed to:"; (total.sales + stax)
END
```

When the user runs this program, the screen clears and a question mark appears. This signals that QBasic got to the INPUT statement and is waiting for the user to type a value. This value is stored in total.sales when the user types it. The user must always press Enter when finished typing values for INPUT. The program then computes the sales tax, prints the tax, and also prints the total for the sale with the sales tax added in.

Suppose you want to write a program that computes the average of three numbers. An averaging program would first ask the person running the program which three numbers to average. Then the program would print the average of those three numbers. Listing 5.2 does just that.

Listing 5.2. A program that computes the average of three numbers.

```
CLS

' Get three numbers from user
INPUT num1, num2, num3

' Calculate the average
avg = (num1 + num2 + num3) / 3

' Print the results
PRINT "The average of your three numbers is:"; avg
END
```

When you run this program, you see a question mark on the screen when QBasic gets to the INPUT statement. The program halts until you type three values, each separated by a comma. After you type three values and press Enter, the program continues from the INPUT statement, calculates the average, and prints the results.

> **NOTE** Only one question mark appears on the screen when you use INPUT, even if more than one variable appears after INPUT.

Improving the Use of *INPUT*

The preceding programs have flaws. These flaws are not exactly program bugs, but they do make the programs more difficult to run because the user sees only a single question mark. He or she has no idea exactly what kind of values or how many values to type.

You should always *prompt* the user for values to be typed in response to INPUT. Do not simply let the INPUT's question mark tell the user that values are needed; PRINT a message telling the user exactly what to type in response to INPUT's question mark.

Listing 5.3 averages three numbers entered by the user. A PRINT statement prompts the user for the values.

Listing 5.3. A program that averages three of the user's numbers.

```
CLS
' Prompt the user at the keyboard
PRINT "Please enter three numbers, separated by commas"

' Get the three numbers from user
INPUT num1, num2, num3

' Calculate the average
avg = (num1 + num2 + num3) / 3

' Print the results
PRINT "The average of your three numbers is:"; avg
END
```

Here is the output screen from this program:

```
Please ENTER three numbers, separated by commas
? 44, 64, 21
The average of your three numbers is: 43.33333
```

Some programmers prefer to print an example INPUT response to further ensure that the user knows exactly what to type. You could do this by adding additional PRINT statements, such as these:

```
PRINT "Please type three numbers, separated by commas"
```

```
PRINT "(For example, 4, 25, 70) and press Enter when done."
```

Let's say that you want to write a simple addition program for your seven-year-old daughter. Listing 5.4 prompts her for two numbers. The program then waits for her to figure out the answer. When she thinks she has it, she presses Enter to see the answer on-screen.

Listing 5.4. A program that prints the total of the user's two numbers.

```
' Program to help children with simple addition
'
' Prompt child for 2 values, after printing a title message
CLS
PRINT "*** Math Practice ***"
PRINT                      ' print 2 blank lines
PRINT
PRINT "Please enter the first number"
INPUT num1
PRINT "Please enter the second number"
INPUT num2

' Compute answer and give her a chance to wait for it
ans = num1 + num2
PRINT
PRINT "Press Enter when you want to see the answer..."
INPUT ent$              ' Nothing gets entered here

' Print answer after a blank line
PRINT
PRINT num1; "plus"; num2; "is"; ans
PRINT
PRINT "Hope you got it right!"
END
```

Figure 5.1 shows the result of running this program. Notice the blank INPUT statement toward the middle of the screen. This is a good way to make the computer wait on the user. By inputting nothing (because she only presses Enter to see the answer), she makes the computer wait at that point in the program while she figures out her own answer. When she is ready, she can verify her answer with the computer's by pressing Enter.

If you ask the user a question inside the prompt message, *two* question marks appear. The following section of code

```
PRINT "What is your name?"
INPUT full.name$
```

produces the following output:

```
What is your name?
?
```

If you left out the question mark in the printed prompt, the INPUT question mark would still appear on the next line. This makes answering questions with INPUT awkward. The trailing semicolon forces the cursor to remain on the line of the printed prompt.

By leaving a semicolon at the end of a prompt message, the next INPUT prints its question mark directly to the right of the prompt's question. The following pair of statements

```
PRINT "What is your name";
INPUT full.name$
```

produces this:

```
What is your name?
```

```
*** Math Practice ***

Please enter the first number
? 23
Please enter the second number
? 14

Press Enter when you want to see the answer...
?

  23 plus 14 is 37

Hope you got it right!




Press any key to continue
```

Figure 5.1. *The output from the addition program in Listing 5.4.*

Prompting with *INPUT*

The designers of QBasic knew that prompting for input is impor-tant. They added a shortcut to the typical PRINT-INPUT pair of statements; they designed INPUT so that you can print your prompt directly in the INPUT statement without needing a standalone PRINT before it. You can insert a *prompt message* after INPUT. This consid-erably shortens programs that use INPUT. By putting the prompt message directly inside INPUT, no PRINT is needed before INPUT.

The following program is a revised version of the three-number averaging program in Listing 5.3. Its INPUT statements contain prompt messages previously printed by PRINT statements.

```
CLS
' Prompt the user at the keyboard and INPUT numbers
INPUT "Enter 3 numbers, separated by commas"; num1, num2, num3
```

```
' Calculate the average
avg = (num1 + num2 + num3) / 3

' Print the result
PRINT "The average of your three numbers is:"; avg
END
```

Running this program produces the same results as before, but the prompting INPUT string streamlines it and all other programs that prompt before INPUT statements.

The following section of a program requests different types of data from the user: a number, a string, and another number. So many different data values are needed that it takes two PRINT statements, plus the message inside INPUT, to completely prompt for the three values.

```
PRINT "What is your age, hometown, and your weight (type"
PRINT "the three values, with commas between them, such"
INPUT "as: 35, Miami, 165)"; age, hometown$, weight
```

Inputting Strings

Although you may not have realized it, there is a character on the keyboard that you *cannot* INPUT with the INPUT statement: the comma. The comma is the delimiter that separates values from each other in the INPUT list of values. However, there are many times you need to enter data that contains commas. For example, if you were entering a full name, last name first, you could not put a comma between the names. INPUT would think two values were being entered.

To fix this problem, put double quotation marks around INPUT strings that contain commas. The quotation marks will not be part of the INPUT value; they serve only to enclose the full string, commas and all.

Listing 5.5 asks the user for a song title and prints the title to the screen.

Listing 5.5. A program that prompts for a song title and prints it.

```
' Get a song title and print it on the screen

CLS
PRINT "I need a song title enclosed in double quotation marks."
INPUT "What is the name of the song"; song.title$

PRINT "The title you entered is: "; song.title$
END
```

Only one string variable, song.title$, is input, and only one is printed. If the title contains a comma, the user has to enter that title enclosed in double quotation marks, as the prompt indicates. Here is a sample run with the user typing double quotation marks around the song title because the title includes a comma.

```
I need a song title enclosed in double quotation marks.
What is the name of the song? "My Town, My Home"
The title you entered is: My Town, My Home
```

Match the *INPUT* Variables

This chapter has stressed the need for good prompts for your INPUT statements. There is a one-to-one correlation between the number and types of your INPUT variables and the values the user types at the keyboard. Nevertheless, there will be a time when a user does not enter enough values, enters too many values, or enters the wrong type of values for the variables being INPUT.

Suppose your program needs the user to type three values. If the INPUT statement looks like this:

```
INPUT num1, num2, num3
```

but the user enters only *two* numbers, QBasic realizes that the user did not enter enough values for the INPUT statement. It would display this error message:

```
Redo from start
```

and prompt for the entire INPUT again.

The same error occurs if the user types too many values for the variables specified, or if the user enters values with the wrong type. This is most commonly due to the lack of double quotation marks around the INPUT strings. This error message continues to appear until QBasic is satisfied that the user has typed values that match the variables.

Eliminating the Question Mark

Although the INPUT question mark is almost always desired, QBasic offers a way for you to get rid of it when asking for keyboard values. If you follow the INPUT statement with a comma instead of a semicolon, no question mark appears. For example, the following INPUT statement:

```
INPUT "Please type your first name here -->", first.name$
```

does not produce a question mark. A question mark after the arrow (-->) would not look correct. The comma suppresses the question mark, but the value entered appears directly to the right of the prompt message.

The *LINE INPUT* Statement

Your application dictates the kind of string data your program requires. For example, what if you were writing a library book-cataloging program. The program would request book titles. Book titles often have commas in them. Earlier in this chapter, you saw that to INPUT commas, the user has to enclose the INPUT string inside double quotation marks.

There is another command, the LINE INPUT statement, that lets your user INPUT strings that contain commas without having to enclose them in double quotation marks. LINE INPUT allows INPUT that even contains double quotation marks *as part of the string.*

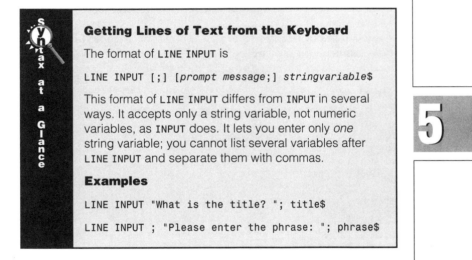

Getting Lines of Text from the Keyboard

The format of LINE INPUT is

```
LINE INPUT [;] [prompt message;] stringvariable$
```

This format of LINE INPUT differs from INPUT in several ways. It accepts only a string variable, not numeric variables, as INPUT does. It lets you enter only *one* string variable; you cannot list several variables after LINE INPUT and separate them with commas.

Examples

```
LINE INPUT "What is the title? "; title$

LINE INPUT ; "Please enter the phrase: "; phrase$
```

LINE INPUT also does *not* automatically display a question mark. If you ask a question with LINE INPUT's prompt message, you must put a question mark at the end of your prompt message.

Suppose you want your program to ask for a list of favorite quotes and their authors. LINE INPUT is the only way to INPUT those quotes into string variables, because they probably contain commas and quotation marks. Listing 5.6 clears the screen, then requests three of the user's favorite quotes. It then prints them back to the screen.

Listing 5.6. A program that requests three quotes and prints them on-screen.

```
' Request and display the user's favorite quotes
CLS
LINE INPUT "What is your first favorite quote? "; q1$
PRINT
LINE INPUT "What is the second? "; q2$
PRINT
LINE INPUT "What is the third? "; q3$
PRINT
PRINT "Quote 1:"
PRINT q1$
PRINT
PRINT "Quote 2:"
PRINT q2$
PRINT
PRINT "Quote 3:"
PRINT q3$
END
```

As you can see from the output that follows, each quote includes quotation marks and commas. LINE INPUT stored every character typed by the user into the three variables, q1$, q2$, and q3$.

```
What is your first favorite quote? "Italy, the spice of life!"

What is the second? "QBasic, language for all."

What is the third? "I see, don't you?"

Quote 1:
"Italy, the spice of life!"

Quote 2:
"QBasic, language for all."

Quote 3:
"I see, don't you?"
```

INPUT and *LINE INPUT* Cursor Control

There is one last option that is available when you are using INPUT and LINE INPUT. If you put a semicolon immediately after INPUT or LINE INPUT, the cursor remains on the same line as the INPUT prompt. If you insert a semicolon immediately after the command names, QBasic keeps the cursor where it ends up after the user inputs the data. In other words, if you answer the following INPUT statement

```
INPUT "What is your name"; full.name$
```

by typing Steve Austin and pressing Enter, QBasic places the cursor on the next line. Subsequent INPUT and PRINT statements begin on the next line. However, if the INPUT statement includes the semicolon, as in

```
INPUT ; "What is your name"; full.name$
```

subsequent INPUT or PRINT statements would begin immediately after the n in Steve Austin. This sometimes makes for more appropriate INPUT and LINE INPUT prompts, as is demonstrated in Listing 5.7.

Listing 5.7 asks for a first and last name and prints them back to the screen. By using the semicolon after INPUT, the INPUT prompts both appear on the same line.

Listing 5.7. A program that places both *INPUT* prompts on the same line.

```
' Program to demonstrate the extra semicolon in INPUT
'
CLS
INPUT ; "What is your first name"; first.name$
INPUT " What is your last name"; last.name$
PRINT first.name$; " "; last.name$
END
```

Here is the output from this program:

```
What is your first name? Joe What is your last name? Robbie
Joe Robbie
```

For the first time, here is a second INPUT statement's result appearing directly to the right of the preceding one. The extra space at the beginning of the second INPUT's prompt is needed. Without it, that prompt would print right next to the string from the first INPUT.

Producing Better Output

This section shows you ways to add pizzazz to your program's output. QBasic gives many more tools than just PRINT and LPRINT that improve the look of your program's output. With color screens, your programs will appeal to users. You can format your output so that two decimal places always appear; this is great for printing dollars and cents.

After learning the contents of this section, you will be able to print much more appealing output from QBasic. Many of the succeeding chapters include programs that use many of these powerful output statements.

The *PRINT USING* Statement

PRINT USING is a statement similar to PRINT that sends output to the screen. The corresponding LPRINT USING statement is identical to PRINT USING, except its output goes to the printer. PRINT USING is especially helpful for printing numbers. You can print dollars and cents, a plus or minus sign in front of or at the end of a number, and so on. These printed values are controlled by a *format string* inside the PRINT USING and LPRINT USING.

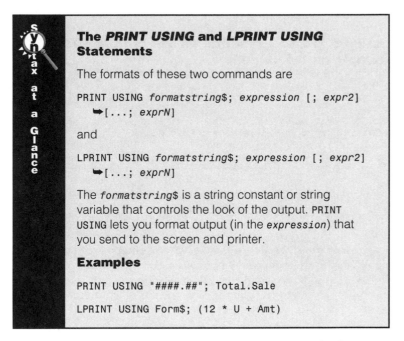

The *PRINT USING* and *LPRINT USING* Statements

The formats of these two commands are

PRINT USING *formatstring*$; *expression* [; *expr2*]
➡ [...; *exprN*]

and

LPRINT USING *formatstring*$; *expression* [; *expr2*]
➡ [...; *exprN*]

The *formatstring*$ is a string constant or string variable that controls the look of the output. PRINT USING lets you format output (in the *expression*) that you send to the screen and printer.

Examples

PRINT USING "####.##"; Total.Sale

LPRINT USING Form$; (12 * U + Amt)

It is in the format string that you specify output control information such as the decimal places. The rest of the statements are just like regular PRINT and LPRINT statements; the *expressions* are one or more variables or constants separated by semicolons.

> **NOTE** You can also use commas in place of the semicolons. Most programmers, however, do not do this, because the commas are misleading; they do not force the variables over to the next print zone because a PRINT USING statement's output is controlled solely by the format string.

Printing Strings with *PRINT USING*

Although you primarily use PRINT USING for numbers, there are four string control codes you can place inside the format string. They each print the characters in the string differently. Until now, you could only print strings and string constants exactly as they appear in memory. With the format string control codes shown in Table 5.1, you can print strings in more than one way. (Any character not listed in the control code table prints exactly as you type it.)

Table 5.1. *PRINT USING* string control codes.

Control Code	Explanation of Its Use
!	Requests that only the first character of the string constant or variable be printed.
\ \	Prints at least two characters of the string constant or variable—one character for each backslash and blank. If you insert one blank between the backslashes, the first three characters will print. Two blanks will print the first four characters, and so on.
&	Print the string as it would appear in a regular PRINT or LPRINT statement.
_	Literally prints whatever character follows the underscore. The only ways to print _, !, \, and & inside a format string are _ _, _!, _\, and _&.

Assume a customer's first and last names were stored in two variables called first.name$ and last.name$. You could print only the customer's initials with the following PRINT USING statement:

```
PRINT USING "!!"; first.name$; last.name$
```

If you want a space between the names, you have to add one to the format string, as follows:

```
PRINT USING "! !"; first.name$; last.name$
```

You do *not* need to put blanks between the actual variables. The format string controls all printing. You could print periods after each initial with

```
PRINT USING "!. !."; first.name$; last.name$
```

Because spaces, periods, and most other characters are not control codes for strings (see Table 5.1), they print exactly as they appear in the format string without controlling output as the !, \, and & do.

You can also put a format string into a string variable, as the following example shows:

```
LET fs$ = "!. !."
```

```
PRINT USING fs$; first.name$; last.name$
```

TIP   If you find yourself repeating the same format string throughout a program, put it in a variable. You can then use the variable name in subsequent PRINT USING statements instead of retyping the same format string repeatedly.

Assume you are printing the customer's first and last names on mailing labels. You don't have room to print a very long name. Therefore, you can limit the customer's first name to eight characters—regardless of how many characters are actually in the name—with the following LPRINT USING statement:

```
LPRINT USING "\      \ &"; first.name$; last.name$
```

You limit the first name to eight characters with the two backslashes and the six spaces between them (making a total of eight control codes). There is then a blank space printed between the two names. The blank space comes from the spaces inside the format string's slashes. Without the format string's blank space, the two names would print next to each other.

The ampersand lets the last.name$ variable print as it appears, regardless of its length. Without the ampersand, the last name is limited to eight characters because QBasic repeats control codes if there are more variables than control codes.

The length of the string you print with the backslash determines the way QBasic prints it. If you allow for six spaces (by typing four spaces between the backslashes) and the string is longer than six characters, only the first six print. This works like the previous examples. However, if the string variable or constant is shorter than six characters, QBasic adds spaces to the end of the string to make it take up the full six spaces. Therefore, the string is *left justified* within the six spaces.

The following program illustrates the use of each type of string format character for strings of three different lengths. Study Listing 5.8 and its output carefully to understand the format string control codes.

Listing 5.8. An illustration of each type of string format character for strings of three different lengths.

```
' Program to illustrate printing strings with
' PRINT USING's format string control codes.
'
CLS
' Initialize three strings with different sizes of data
s1$ = "Computers"
s2$ = "PC"
s3$ = "Disks"
' Print them with various format strings
PRINT USING "!!!"; s1$; s2$; s3$   ' 1st char of each
PRINT USING "!"; s1$; s2$; s3$     ' Format repeats
PRINT USING "&&&"; s1$; s2$; s3$   ' All three together
PRINT USING "& & &"; s1$; s2$; s3$ ' Separated by spaces
PRINT USING "&*&*&"; s1$; s2$; s3$ ' Separated by asterisks
PRINT USING "\   \"; s1$          ' 1st 5 characters of s1$
PRINT USING "\   \"; s2$          ' s2$ followed by 3 spaces
PRINT USING "\   \"; s3$          ' All 5 characters of s3$
PRINT USING "\   \"; s1$; s2$; s3$ ' All 3 printed in 5 spaces
END
```

The following is the output of Listing 5.8:

```
CPD
CPD
ComputersPCDisks
Computers PC Disks
Computers*PC*Disks
Compu
PC
Disks
CompuPC   Disks
```

Notice that the format string repeats, or is reused, if there are more variables than control codes. Any character that is not a proper control code, such as the spaces or the asterisks, prints as is. This also holds true for words inside the format string. For instance, the following PRINT USING statement prints a string inside another string:

```
PRINT USING "Her name, &, is Italian"; full.name$
```

This is equivalent to the following normal PRINT statement:

```
PRINT "Her name, "; full.name$; ", is Italian"
```

If you want to print an exclamation point or any of the other control codes, precede them with the underscore. To print an exclamation point after the first letter of each name, you use the following PRINT USING statement:

```
PRINT USING "!_! !_!"; first.name$; last.name$
```

This would create output such as:

```
G! P!
```

Printing Numbers with *PRINT USING*

There are more PRINT USING control codes for numeric constants and variables than there are for strings. You rarely want numeric data to print exactly as it appears inside memory. You will probably want control over the placement of the number's sign, decimal places, commas, and so on.

Table 5.2 presents every PRINT USING format control code for numbers along with their descriptions. As with strings, any character you include in the format string that is not a control code prints exactly as you type it. This enables you to output words and symbols around formatted numbers.

Table 5.2. *PRINT USING* numeric control codes.

Control Code	Explanation of Its Use
#	One number is printed for every pound sign in the format string. If the number contains fewer digits than the total number of pound signs, QBasic right justifies the number and pads it with spaces to the left.
. (period)	Ensures that QBasic prints a decimal point, even for whole numbers. QBasic rounds if needed.

Control Code	Explanation of Its Use
+	Forces the sign (+ or -) of the number to print, even if it is positive. If you put the + at the beginning of the format string, the sign (+ or -) is printed at the beginning of the number. Putting the + at the end of the format string forces the sign (+ or -) to print at the end of the number.
-	To print negative numbers with trailing minus signs (and no sign for positives), put the - at the end of the format string.
**	Prints asterisks to the left of the number. If the number does not take as many spaces as the total number of pound signs and asterisks, asterisks fill the extra spaces. This is called a *floating asterisk* because it prints one or more asterisks immediately to the left of the number, regardless of how many digits the number has.
$$	Prints a dollar sign to the left of the number. This is called a *floating dollar sign* because it prints immediately to the left of the number, regardless of how many digits the number has.
**$	Designed for printing check amounts. These three print positions force asterisks to fill from the left, followed by a dollar sign. If the number is negative, the minus sign prints directly to the left of the dollar sign.
,	You can put the comma in one of two places in a format string. A comma to the left of the decimal point (if there is one in the format) causes commas to print every third digit of the number. No commas print in the decimal portion of the number. Putting the comma at the end of the format string prints a comma at the end of the number.
^^^^	Prints the number in scientific notation, in the $E+xx$ format.
^^^^^	Prints the number in the expanded scientific notation, in the $E+xxx$ format.

If QBasic cannot fit the number inside your designated format string, a percent sign (%) prints to the left of the number. This lets you know that the number is not accurately printed. Unlike strings, printing only part of a number could easily cause errors. The preceding percent sign warns you that the printed number is not correct (you will see as much as QBasic could print, given the format string you specified).

Listing 5.9 is a rewrite of the payroll programs you have seen throughout this book. Now that you understand PRINT USING format strings, you can print each dollar amount with a dollar sign and two decimal places.

Listing 5.9. A program that prints dollar amounts with a dollar sign and two decimal places.

```
' Computes and prints payroll data
' Initialize data variables
emp.name$ = "Larry Payton"
pay.date$ = "01/09/92"
hours.worked = 40          'Total hours worked
rate = 7.5                 'Pay per hour
tax.rate = .4              'Tax rate percentage

'Compute the pay

gross.pay = hours.worked * rate
taxes = tax.rate * gross.pay
net.pay = gross.pay - taxes

'Print the results on the screen
CLS
PRINT "As of "; pay.date$
PRINT emp.name$; " worked"; hours.worked; "hours"
PRINT USING "and got paid $$##.##."; gross.pay
PRINT USING "After taxes of $$##.##,"; taxes
PRINT USING "his take-home pay was $$##.##."; net.pay
END
```

The following is the output from Listing 5.9:

```
As of 01/09/92
Larry Payton worked 40 hours
and got paid $300.00.
After taxes of $120.00,
his take-home pay was $180.00.
```

There is much to this program's simple-looking output; by mastering it, you are well on your way to understanding formatted output and QBasic.

No PRINT USING was needed when printing the date and the hours worked; there were no fixed decimal points to worry about. The last three lines of the program printed dollar amounts, so they required format strings. The words inside the strings print literally as they appear in the format string because they are not control codes. The double dollar signs, pound signs, periods, and commas, however, *are* control codes and they affect the way the variables print.

The gross.pay and net.pay variables can be as large as $999.99, because there are a total of seven places reserved for the dollar sign, amount, and decimal point. If a pay amount happens to be more than $999.99, QBasic prints as much of the number as it can, preceded by a percent sign to warn you that the number cannot fit in the specified format.

> **TIP** If you want to expand the field to hold a larger number, you will probably want to add both a pound sign *and* a comma (before the decimal point) so that the field can hold an amount as large as $9,999.99 and print the amount with the comma.

The commas and periods at the end of the format strings in the payroll program are not control codes; because they appear at the end, QBasic simply prints them literally.

Listing 5.10 illustrates each of the various numeric format strings available with PRINT USING. The output is shown after the listing.

Listing 5.10. A program that illustrates the numeric format strings available with PRINT USING.

```
' Program to demonstrate printing numbers with PRINT USING
'
CLS
PRINT USING "|######|"; 9146  ' Numbers print right-justified
PRINT USING "|######|"; 21
PRINT USING "#####.##"; 2652.2   ' Always prints 2 decimal
                                 ' places
PRINT USING "#####.##"; 2652.212  ' Rounds, if needed
PRINT USING "#####.##"; 2652.215
PRINT USING "+###"; 45      ' Always prints plus or minus
PRINT USING "+###"; -45
PRINT USING "###+"; 45       ' Prints the sign at the end
PRINT USING "###-"; 45       ' Only prints sign at end if
                             ' negative
```

continues

Listing 5.10. Continued

```
PRINT USING "###-"; -45
PRINT USING "**####.##"; 2.5    ' Left AND right fills with
                                ' asterisks
PRINT USING "$$####.##"; 2.5    ' Floating dollar sign
PRINT USING "**$###.##"; 2.5    ' Combine the two for checks
PRINT USING "######,.##"; 3234.54    ' A comma before decimal
PRINT USING "####,.##, "; 3234, 7832; 4326    ' Repeating format
                                              ' string
PRINT USING "#.##^^^^"; 0.00012    ' Scientific notation
PRINT USING "#.##^^^^^"; 0.00012   ' More precision
PRINT USING "###"; 43567.54    ' Not enough control codes
                               ' specified
PRINT USING "##.##"; 43567.54
PRINT USING "_#_###.##_#_#"; 32.45    ' Illustrates printing of
                                      ' literals
END
```

The following is the output of Listing 5.10:

```
!  9146!
!    21!
 2652.20
 2652.21
 2652.22
 +45
 -45
 45+
 45
 45-
 *****2.50
    $2.50
 ****$2.50
    3,234.54
 3,234.00, 7,832.00, 4,326.00,
 0.12E-03
 0.12E-003
 %43568
 %43567.54
 ##32.45##
```

Printing with *SPC()*

As with TAB, SPC goes inside a PRINT or LPRINT statement. SPC specifies how many spaces to skip. This keeps you from having to type a lot of string constants, filled with only spaces, in your output.

The *space value* is the number of characters to skip before printing the next value. The space value always goes in parentheses after SPC. Never use SPC by itself; always combine it with a PRINT or LPRINT statement.

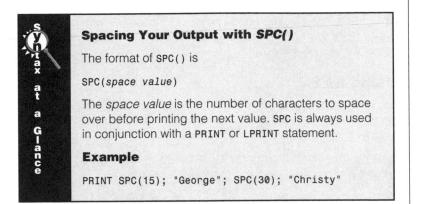

Spacing Your Output with *SPC( )*

The format of SPC() is

SPC(*space value*)

The *space value* is the number of characters to space over before printing the next value. SPC is always used in conjunction with a PRINT or LPRINT statement.

Example

PRINT SPC(15); "George"; SPC(30); "Christy"

As you can see, you can put more than one SPC inside a PRINT (or LPRINT). You can combine SPC with TAB, semicolons, and commas, as well. The following rule of thumb explains the difference between TAB and SPC: when you use TAB, the cursor always skips to a fixed position—the column number inside the TAB's parentheses. When you use SPC, the cursor skips over the number of spaces inside the SPC's parentheses.

If you always want a fixed number of spaces between numeric or string variables when you print them, use SPC rather than TAB. TAB forces the cursor to a fixed location, regardless of how wide the data is. Listing 5.11 shows you the difference between TAB and SPC.

Listing 5.11. A program that compares *TAB()* and *SPC()*.

```
CLS
a = 7865
b = 1
c = 6543.2

PRINT "Printing with TAB:"
PRINT a; TAB(7); b; TAB(14); c   ' The numbers are not aligned
PRINT
PRINT "Printing with SPC:"
PRINT a; SPC(7); b; SPC(7); c    ' There are 7 spaces between
                                 ' each
```

The following is the output of Listing 5.11:

```
Printing with TAB:
 7865  1      6543.2

Printing with SPC:
 7865         1             6543.2
```

Notice that with TAB, the numbers are not uniformly separated because they are different lengths. SPC solves this by spacing over an equal number of spaces.

Using *BEEP*

The BEEP command is a fun command that sounds the speaker. It has a very easy format: put BEEP on a line by itself whenever you want to beep (or buzz) the user.

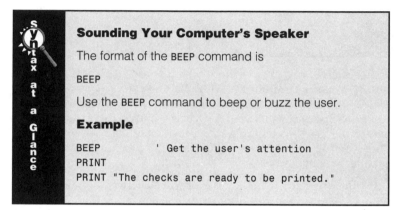

Sounding Your Computer's Speaker

The format of the BEEP command is

```
BEEP
```

Use the BEEP command to beep or buzz the user.

Example

```
BEEP          ' Get the user's attention
PRINT
PRINT "The checks are ready to be printed."
```

Printing Special Characters

Up to this point, you know how to print and store characters on the keyboard. There are several more characters that do *not* appear on the keyboard, that you might want to type as well. They include foreign characters, math symbols, line-drawing characters, and more.

Inside your computer is a table that includes every character your computer can represent. This table is called the *ASCII table*. The complete ASCII (pronounced *ask-ee*) table is located in the back of your DOS manual. Turn to your DOS manual now and glance at the table. You will see many special characters, only some of which are on the keyboard.

Your computer internally represents these ASCII characters by their ASCII numbers. There is a different number assigned to each character. These number assignments were arbitrarily designed, in a manner similar to the Morse code table. A unique number represents each character.

By having the ASCII table available, you can print any character by referring to its ASCII number. For instance, the capital letter *A* is number 65. The lowercase *a* is 96. Because you can type letters, numbers, and some special characters on your keyboard, the ASCII table is not needed much for these. However, you cannot use the keyboard to type the Spanish Ñ, or the cent sign (¢), under normal circumstances. You print these with the CHR$ function.

The *CHR$()* Function

The format of CHR$() is

CHR$(*ASCII number*)

Use CHR$() to create strings with special characters.

Example

```
PRINT "She said "; CHR$(34); "I will go.";
CHR$(34)
```

The *ASCII number* can be a numeric constant or a numeric variable. CHR$ is not a command, but a *function*. You have already seen two functions: TAB and SPC. As with TAB and SPC, you do not use CHR$ by itself. It is combined with other statements. If you combine CHR$ with a PRINT or LPRINT, the character matching the ASCII number in the parentheses will print. The following statement prints an up arrow on the screen:

```
PRINT CHR$(24)
```

You can also use the CHR$ function to store special characters in string variables. Many times, the concatenation character (+) enables you to insert a special character inside another string and store the complete string in a variable, as in the following:

```
message$ = "One-half is "; CHR$(171); " and one-fourth is ";
CHR$(172)
```

The first 31 ASCII codes represent *nonprinting* characters. Nonprinting characters cause an action to be performed, instead of producing characters. For instance, to form feed your printer paper, you could send the form feed ASCII code, like this:

```
LPRINT CHR$(12)
```

> **TIP** The higher ASCII codes are line-drawing characters. With a little practice, you can combine them to form shapes and boxes that enclose text on the screen.

Printing with *COLOR*

If you have a color monitor, you can add colors to output with the COLOR statement.

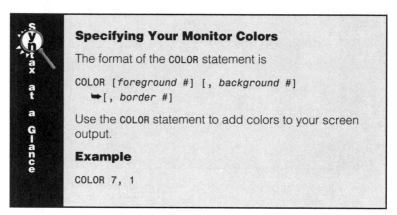

Syntax at a Glance

Specifying Your Monitor Colors

The format of the COLOR statement is

COLOR [*foreground* #] [, *background* #]
➡[, *border* #]

Use the COLOR statement to add colors to your screen output.

Example

COLOR 7, 1

The *foreground* # is a number from 0 to 31, representing the color of the characters on the screen. The *background* # is a number from 0 to 7 that represents the color of the screen behind the character's color. The *border* # is a number from 0 to 15 that represents the border drawn around the screen's edges.

Each of these options is optional, although the foreground and background colors are almost always specified. The border only works for CGA (Color Graphics Adapters) and is not supported for EGA, VGA, and MCGA monitors. The COLOR statement does not affect any text on the screen that was printed before the COLOR statement. COLOR affects only future PRINT statements.

Table 5.3 shows colors and their corresponding numbers. Although monochrome (noncolor) monitors do not produce colors, you can specify special screen attributes (such as underlining and blinking) on monochrome monitors.

If you add 16 to the color number, the characters blink in the color for that number, less 16. In other words, setting the foreground color to 28 (12 + 16), produces blinking light red text at the next PRINT statement.

Table 5.3. Color numbers for the *COLOR* statement.

Color monitors		Monochrome monitors	
Color	*Number*	*Color*	*Number*
0	Black	0	Black
1	Blue	1	Underline if foreground Black if background
2	Green	2	Standard foreground color Black if background
3	Cyan	3	Standard foreground color Black if background
4	Red	4	Standard foreground color Black if background
5	Magenta	5	Standard foreground color Black if background
6	Brown	6	Standard foreground color Black if background
7	White	7	Standard foreground color, even if used for background
8	Gray	8	Highlighted character
9	Light blue	9	Highlighted character
10	Light green	10	Highlighted character
11	Light cyan	11	Highlighted character
12	Light red	12	Highlighted character
13	Light magenta	13	Highlighted character
14	Yellow	14	Highlighted character
15	Bright white	15	Highlighted character

TIP Do not overdo the colors on the screen. Too many colors make the screen look too "busy" and not as readable.

To see the effects of different color combinations, Listing 5.12 prints several lines of text, each with a different color. This program illustrates the COLOR statement well, but shows you that too much color is too much to look at for normal applications.

Listing 5.12. A program that illustrates the *COLOR* statement.

```
' Print several lines of text in different colors
CLS
COLOR 15, 1
PRINT "Bright white characters on blue"
COLOR 1, 7
PRINT "Blue characters on white"
COLOR 4, 2
PRINT "Red characters on green"
COLOR 30, 2
PRINT "Blinking yellow characters on green"
COLOR 13, 0
PRINT "Light Magenta on black"
END
```

> **NOTE** To clear the screen in the colors you desire, place the CLS *after* the COLOR statement. For example, the following section of code clears the screen, setting the screen up with a blue background. Subsequent PRINT statements would print in bright yellow.
>
> ```
> COLOR 14, 1
>
> CLS
> ```

The *LOCATE* Statement

The screen is divided into 25 rows and 80 columns. You can use the LOCATE statement to place the cursor at any position at which you want to print.

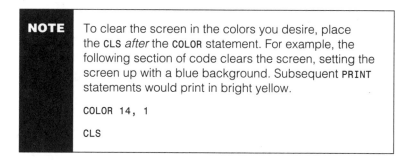

Locating the Cursor

The format of LOCATE is

```
LOCATE [row #] [, column #]
```

LOCATE moves the cursor to a specific location on the screen.

Example

```
LOCATE 10, 15
```

The *row* # has to be a number from 1 to 25. The *column* # must be a number from 1 to 80. LOCATE places the cursor at the row and column you specify. The next PRINT statement begins printing at the cursor's new location.

If you do not specify a row number, the cursor moves to the column number you indicate without changing rows. For instance, the following LOCATE command:

```
LOCATE , 40
```

moves the cursor to column 40 and does not change the row it was on.

Listing 5.13 prints "QBasic" in four different locations on the screen after setting the colors.

Listing 5.13. A program that prints QBasic in four different screen locations.

```
COLOR 15, 1      ' Bright white on blue screen
CLS
LOCATE 22, 60
PRINT "QBasic"
LOCATE 2, 5
PRINT "QBasic"
LOCATE 17, 25
PRINT "QBasic"
LOCATE 3, 40
PRINT "QBasic"
```

Summary

You can now accept INPUT from the keyboard. Before this chapter, you had to assign values to variables when you wrote the program. The variables can now be filled when the user runs the program by prompting the user for values when he or she runs the program. Depending on the needed data, you can use INPUT, LINE INPUT, or a combination of both.

Although it is easy to understand, the PRINT USING command has more options than any command you have seen so far. PRINT USING enables you to format your output of strings and numbers so that screens and printed results look the way you want them to. Combining PRINT USING with COLOR, BEEP, the ASCII table, TAB, and the SPC function enables you to control your screen and produce eye-catching displays.

Here are some of the things you learned in this chapter:

- The INPUT statement accepts values from the keyboard. Those values then go into variables to be processed by the program.

- You should always print a prompt message before each INPUT so that your user knows exactly what is needed. The expanded form of the INPUT statement lets you print the prompt from within the INPUT statement.

- There are many ways to output your data into whatever format you prefer. The PRINT USING statement can format your output values (for dollars and cents, for example), print initial letters of strings, and much more.

- If you have a color graphics monitor and color adapter, you can display your program's output in various colors using the COLOR statement.

- LOCATE moves the cursor so that you can print information wherever you want it on-screen.

Making Decisions with Data

Not every statement in your QBasic program should execute *every* time you run the program. Programs operate on data. They are known as *data-driven* programs. That is, the data should dictate what the program does. This chapter shows you how to create data-driven programs using the IF statement. These programs do not execute the same way every time they are run. Rather, they look at the constants and variables in the program, and operate based on what they find.

To teach you decision statements, this chapter takes a quick detour via the GOTO statement. GOTO is not highly recommended in most situations, but it is helpful when learning decision statements. Not only does this chapter introduce the decision commands, but it also explains two other methods QBasic offers for representing data: READ and DATA statements.

The *GOTO* Statement

The following sections require more program control than you have seen to this point. GOTO lets your program branch to a different location. Each program you have seen executes sequentially; GOTO lets you override that default execution.

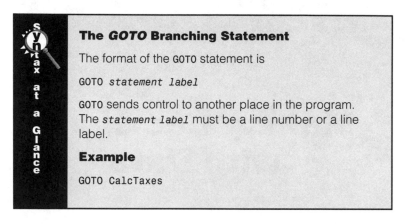

The *GOTO* Branching Statement

The format of the GOTO statement is

GOTO *statement label*

GOTO sends control to another place in the program. The *statement label* must be a line number or a line label.

Example

GOTO CalcTaxes

You have not seen statement labels in the QBasic programs so far, because none of the programs needed them. Statement labels are optional unless there is a GOTO in the program.

The following two statements both contain statement labels. Labels must be to the left of their lines. If your label is a word, separate it from the rest of the line with a colon (:). If you use a number for the label, it must be unique to the program.

```
PAY: PRINT "Place checks in the printer"
20 CLS
```

Labels give GOTO statements a tag to go to. When your program arrives at the GOTO, it branches to the statement labeled by the statement label. The program then continues to execute sequentially until the next GOTO changes the order again (or until the program ends).

> **NOTE** GOTO is not considered a good programming statement when overused. There is a tendency to include too many GOTOs in a program, especially for beginning programmers. Using a few GOTO statements is not necessarily a bad practice. To eliminate GOTO statements and write better, more structured programs, you must learn some control concepts covered in the next few chapters.

The program in Listing 6.1. is one of the worst-written programs ever! Do your best to follow it and understand that it prints the three letters *C*, *B*, and *A*. You will appreciate the fact that the rest of this book uses the GOTO statement only when it can make the program clearer.

Listing 6.1. A program overusing GOTO statements.

```
' Program demonstrates overuse of GOTO
CLS
GOTO Here

First:
    PRINT "A"
    GOTO Final
There:
    PRINT "B"
    GOTO First
Here:
    PRINT "C"
    GOTO There
Final:
    END
```

Comparison Operators

In addition to the math operators you learned earlier, there are also data comparison operators. These are called *relational operators*. Relational operators compare data; they tell how two variables or constants relate to each other. They let you know whether two variables are equal, not equal, or which one is less or more than the other. Table 6.1 lists the QBasic relational operators and their descriptions.

Table 6.1. The relational operators.

Operator	Description
=	Equal to
>	Greater than
<	Less than
>=	Greater than or equal to
<=	Less than or equal to
<>	Not equal to

The *IF* Statement

You incorporate relational operators in QBasic programs with the
IF statement. IF (sometimes referred to as the IF-THEN statement) is
called a *decision statement* because it tests a relationship—using
the relational operators—and makes a decision about which statement to execute next based on the result of that decision.

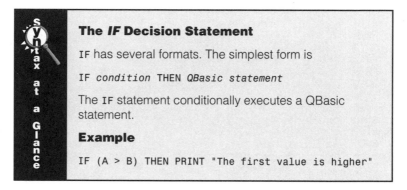

The *IF* Decision Statement

IF has several formats. The simplest form is

```
IF condition THEN QBasic statement
```

The IF statement conditionally executes a QBasic
statement.

Example

```
IF (A > B) THEN PRINT "The first value is higher"
```

IF is the first QBasic statement you have seen with two keywords:
IF and THEN. The condition can be any relational comparison. The
QBasic statement is any possible QBasic statement, such as LET or
PRINT. That statement will execute *only if the condition is True*. If
the condition is False, QBasic ignores the statement and executes
the next statement in the program following the IF.

For your first example of IF, the statement will be a GOTO followed
by a statement label. Limit your use of the IF-THEN-GOTO statement.
Get acquainted with this one for now; as your programs become
more sophisticated, you will see other formats.

You can read an IF-THEN-GOTO statement in the following way: "If
the condition is True, go to the statement labeled to the right of
GOTO. Otherwise, the condition must be False, so do *not* go to the
statement, but continue execution as though the IF statement did
not exist." Consider this IF statement:

```
IF sales > 5000 THEN GOTO Bonus
```

The value inside the variable sales determines what happens next.
If the value of sales is more than 5000, the next statement that
executes will be the one following the statement label Bonus. If,
however, sales is 5000 or less, the GOTO will not occur and the line
following the IF will execute. Here is another GOTO:

```
IF (age <= 21) THEN GOTO Minor
```

If the value in age is less than or equal to 21, the line at the label Minor will execute next. Notice that the parentheses help make the relational test more readable. You can include an expression in the IF, such as the following:

```
IF (pay * tax.rate < minimum) THEN GOTO Low.Salary
```

The program in Listing 6.2 requests an age and checks to make sure that age is less than 100 and more than 14. This is certainly not a foolproof test, as the user can still enter incorrect ages, but it takes care of the extremes.

Listing 6.2. An age verification program.

```
' Program section that helps ensure age values are reasonable
CLS
Start:
    PRINT
    INPUT "What is the student's age"; age

    IF (age > 14) THEN GOTO Over14    ' Age is at least 14
    BEEP
    PRINT "*** The age cannot be less than 14 ***"
    PRINT "Try again..."
    GOTO Start
Over14:
    IF (age < 100) THEN GOTO OkAge    ' Age is also less than 100
    BEEP
    PRINT "*** The age cannot be more than 100 ***"
    PRINT "Try again..."
    GOTO Start
OkAge:
    PRINT "You entered a valid age."
```

You can compare character string data with the IF as well as numeric data. This is very useful for alphabetizing, testing answers, comparing names, and much more. The order of the ASCII table determines how the comparison operates (*A* is less than *a* and so on).

The program in Listing 6.3 requests a password. It then checks the entered password with one stored in a variable. If they match, the program beeps once and a secret message appears. If they do not match, the program clears the screen and asks the user again. Only when a correct password is entered will the secret message appear.

Listing 6.3. A password program.

```
' Program to prompt for a password and
' check it against an internal one
stored.pass$ = "XYZ123"
COLOR 15, 1    ' Bright white characters on a blue screen
GetPass:
  CLS
  PRINT "What is the password";
  COLOR 0, 0    ' Blue on blue to hide the user input
  INPUT user.pass$
  COLOR 15, 1    ' Change the colors back
  IF (user.pass$ <> stored.pass$) THEN GOTO GetPass
  ' Control falls here if the user entered proper password
  BEEP
  CLS    ' Print the secret message for the valid user
  PRINT "You entered the correct password."
  PRINT "The cash safe is behind the picture of the ship."
END
```

Compound Logical Operators

There may be times when you need to test more than one set of variables. You can combine more than one relational test into a *compound relational test* by using the following logical operators:

AND   OR   XOR   NOT

Tables 6.2, 6.3, 6.4, and 6.5 show how each of the logical operators work. These tables are called *truth tables* because they show how to use the logical operators in an IF test to achieve True results. Take a minute to study the tables.

Table 6.2. The *AND* truth table—both sides must be True.

True AND True = True

True AND False = False

False AND True = False

False AND False = False

Table 6.3. The OR truth table—one or the other must be True.

True OR True = True

True OR False = True

False OR True = True
False OR False = False

Table 6.4. The *XOR* truth table—one or the other must be True, but not both.

True XOR True = False
True XOR False = True
False XOR True = True
False XOR False = False

Table 6.5. The *NOT* truth table—causes an opposite relation.

NOT True = False
NOT False = True

The True and False in these tables represent results of IF statements. For example, the following are valid IF tests that use logical operators (sometimes called *compound relational operators*):

IF ((A < B) AND (C > D)) THEN GOTO CalcIt

A must be less than B and, at the same time, C must be greater than D, for the CalcIt routine to execute.

IF ((sales > 5000) OR (hrs.worked > 81)) THEN GOTO OverPay

The sales must be more than 5000 or the hrs.worked must be more than 81, before the OverPay routine executes.

If ((bit2 = 0) XOR (bit3 <> 1)) THEN PRINT "Error"

The bit2 variable must be equal to 0 or bit3 must not be equal to 1, before the PRINT executes. However, if they *both* are True, the test fails (since XOR is used), the PRINT statement is ignored, and the next instruction is executed.

IF (NOT(sales < 2500)) THEN bonus = 500

If the sales variable is not less than 2500, the bonus variable is not initialized. This illustrates an important programming tip: Use NOT sparingly. It would be much clearer to rewrite this last example using a positive relational test:

```
IF (sales >= 2500) THEN bonus = 500
```

Now that you know about compound relations, you can improve upon the age verification program from Listing 6.2. That program ensured that the age fell between 14 and 100. The original program required two IF statements to validate input for reasonableness. The first IF statement checked to see if age was greater than 14, and the second checked to see if age was less than 100. Listing 6.4 uses a compound IF statement to perform both tests in a single statement.

Listing 6.4. The revised age verification program.

```
' Program that helps ensure age values are reasonable
CLS
Start:
   PRINT
   INPUT "What is the student's age"; age
   IF ((age > 14) AND (age < 100)) THEN GOTO OkAge  ' Age is
                                                    ' reasonable
   BEEP        ' Control falls here if age is out of the range
   PRINT "*** The age must be between 14 and 100 ***"
   PRINT "Try again..."
   GOTO Start
OkAge:
   PRINT "You entered a valid age."
```

Complete Order of Operators

The math order of operators you saw in Chapter 4, "Operators and String Variables," did not include the relational operators you learned in this chapter. You should be familiar with the entire order, presented in Table 6.6. As you can see, math operators take precedence over relational operators, and parentheses override any of these defaults.

Table 6.6. The entire order of operators.

Order	Operator
1	Parentheses
2	Exponentiation (^)
3	Negation (the unary −)
4	Multiplication, division, integer division (*, /, \)

Order	Operator
5	Modulus (MOD)
6	Addition, subtraction (+, -)
7	Relational Operators (=, <, >, <=, >=, <>)
8	NOT Logical Operator
9	AND
10	OR
11	XOR

You might wonder why the relational and logical operators are included. The following statement illustrates why:

```
IF (sales < min.sal * 2 AND yrs.emp > 10 * sub) ...
```

Without the complete order of operators, it would be impossible to determine how such a statement would execute. According to the operator order in Table 6.6, the preceding IF statement would execute as follows:

```
IF ((sales < (min.sal * 2)) AND (yrs.emp > (10 * sub))) ...
```

This might still be confusing, but it should be less so. The two multiplication statements are performed first, followed by the two relational statements (< and >). The AND operator is performed last because it is lowest in the order of operators.

> **TIP** To avoid such confusing statements, use ample parentheses. Even if you intend to follow the hierarchy order, do not combine too many expressions inside a single IF relational test.

READ and *DATA* Statements

Until now, you have seen two ways to put data values into variables: the assignment (LET) statement and the INPUT statement. You can also assign values to variables in QBasic with the READ and DATA statements.

READ and DATA statements are good to use when you know the data values in advance. But not all programs can use READ and DATA statements because many times you will not know the data value until the user runs the program. You learned INPUT so that the user can enter data at runtime.

The two statements, READ and DATA, never operate alone; you never see one without the other. A program that contains one or more READ statements must also contain at least one DATA statement. Although the program must contain both statements, these two statements need not be located close together in the program.

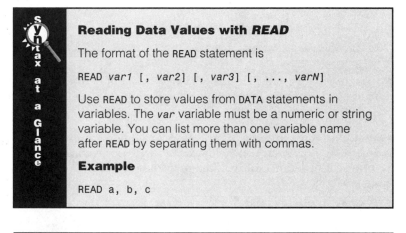

Reading Data Values with *READ*

The format of the READ statement is

```
READ var1 [, var2] [, var3] [, ..., varN]
```

Use READ to store values from DATA statements in variables. The *var* variable must be a numeric or string variable. You can list more than one variable name after READ by separating them with commas.

Example

```
READ a, b, c
```

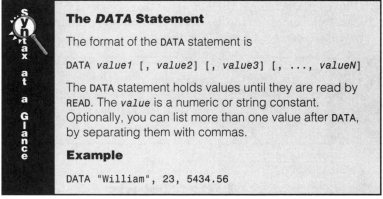

The *DATA* Statement

The format of the DATA statement is

```
DATA value1 [, value2] [, value3] [, ..., valueN]
```

The DATA statement holds values until they are read by READ. The *value* is a numeric or string constant. Optionally, you can list more than one value after DATA, by separating them with commas.

Example

```
DATA "William", 23, 5434.56
```

READ and DATA statements typically have a one-to-one correspondence to one another. Usually, if a READ statement has three variable names after it, the DATA statement (or statements) will be followed by three values.

READ is always followed by one or more variables—*never* by constants; DATA is always followed by one or more constants—*never* by variable names. READ reads DATA values into variables. Consider the following program statement. It is an assignment statement:

```
sales = 50000
```

The following READ and DATA statements do *exactly the same thing* as the preceding assignment statement:

```
READ sales
DATA 50000
```

Of the two statements, READ is always active and DATA is passive. DATA statements really do not execute. No matter where DATA statements fall in a program, QBasic ignores them until a READ statement is reached. When QBasic finally reaches the READ statement, it does the following:

1. Looks for the next DATA value that has yet to be read.

2. Assigns the value(s) in the DATA statement to the READ variable(s).

3. Remembers that the DATA statement was used, so it does not reuse it.

Because DATA statements are passive, they can go anywhere in the program—even at the beginning—without affecting the program's execution.

If a READ statement has a mixture of numeric and string variables after it, the DATA values being read into those variables must also be the same type mixture. It is up to you to ensure this as you write the DATA values into the program.

> **TIP** If QBasic ever gives you a "Syntax Error" on a READ statement, and the READ statement seems to be correct, check your data types. You are probably reading the wrong type of value, such as a string value, into a numeric variable.

Listing 6.5 is similar to the program in Listing 6.4, except there are more DATA statements. Listing 6.5 stores the inventory for a sporting goods company in DATA statements. This program produces a report of the inventory, including the inventory's total dollar value. Notice the program prints the inventory in a different order than it was read. The order of the READ and DATA values has nothing to do with what you do with those values. Once READ and DATA finish assigning variables, you can print and change them in any way you choose.

Unlike the previous lines, the final DATA line does not contain inventory information; rather, it is a *trailer* DATA *record* that contains *trigger* data. The IF conditional test knows it has read the last DATA line when it gets the trigger value of –99.

Listing 6.5. An inventory program.

```
' Program to produce an inventory listing on the printer
' and print the total value of the inventory.
total.inv = 0      ' Initialize the total variable
' Print titles on the printer
LPRINT "Inventory Listing"
LPRINT
LPRINT "Part No.", "Quantity", "Price", "Description"
LPRINT "--------", "--------", "-----", "-----------"

' Read the inventory, one DATA line at a time
ReadIt:
    READ part.no$, price, quantity, desc$
    IF (price = -99) THEN GOTO NoMore   ' If just read last
                                        ' record, quit
    LPRINT part.no$, quantity, price, desc$
    total.inv = total.inv + (price * quantity)
    GOTO ReadIt      ' get another inventory record

DATA "10112", 10.95, 13, "Widget"
DATA "21943", 14.78, 2, "Metal Wire #4"
DATA "38745", 10.91, 10, "Bolt Clip"
DATA "44335", 17.64, 43, "Fastener"
DATA "44336", 17.64, 56, "Long Fastener"
DATA "-99", -99, -99, "-99"

NoMore:
    ' Print the total and stop
    LPRINT
    LPRINT USING "& $$###,.##"; "Total inventory value is",
    ➥  total.inv
    END
```

The following is the output of this program. Notice that the titles are printed before the READ-GOTO loop begins. If the inventory changes, you only have to change the DATA statements in the program—not the program's logic.

```
Inventory Listing

Part No.      Quantity      Price        Description
--------      --------      -----        -----------
10112         13            10.95        Widget
21943         2             14.78        Metal Wire #4
38745         10            10.91        Bolt Clip
```

```
44335        43        17.64        Fastener
44336        56        17.64        Long Fastener
```

Total inventory value is $2,027.37

The *RESTORE* Statement

The RESTORE statement lets you override the way READ and DATA work.

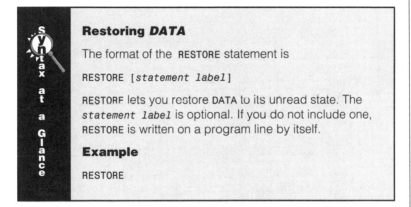

Restoring *DATA*

The format of the RESTORE statement is

RESTORE [*statement label*]

RESTORE lets you restore DATA to its unread state. The *statement label* is optional. If you do not include one, RESTORE is written on a program line by itself.

Example

RESTORE

When QBasic executes RESTORE, it resets all the internal DATA checking. A subsequent READ statement starts over at the very first DATA value. RESTORE causes the program to think it has never read any of the data before, so it starts over at the initial DATA value.

> **NOTE** If you include a *statement label* after RESTORE, the RESTORE statement only restores the DATA following *statement label*.

Listing 6.6 contains a revised inventory program. The only difference between this program and the original inventory program in Listing 6.5 is that this version asks the user if he or she wants to see the printed inventory report again. If yes, a form feed is sent to the printer, and a second report appears. This is made possible because the RESTORE statement resets the READ-DATA and allows the data to be read all over again.

Listing 6.6. The revised inventory control program.

```
' Program to produce an inventory listing on the printer
' Print titles on the printer
PrintRep:
    LPRINT "Inventory Listing"
    LPRINT
    LPRINT "Part No.", "Quantity", "Price", "Description"
    LPRINT "--------", "--------", "-----", "----------"
' Read the inventory, one DATA line at a time
ReadIt:
    READ part.no$, price, quantity, desc$
    IF (price = -99) THEN GOTO NoMore
    ' If just read last record, quit
    LPRINT part.no$, quantity, price, desc$
    GOTO ReadIt       ' get another inventory record
    DATA "10112", 10.95, 13, "Widget"
    DATA "21943", 14.78, 2, "Metal Wire #4"
    DATA "38745", 10.91, 10, "Bolt Clip"
    DATA "44335", 17.64, 43, "Fastener"
    DATA "44336", 17.64, 56, "Long Fastener"
    DATA "-99", -99, -99, "-99"
NoMore:

    INPUT "Do you want another copy (Y/N)"; ans$

    IF (ans$ = "N") THEN GOTO EndIt     ' User wants to quit
' Control gets to here only if user wants to see another report
    RESTORE
    LPRINT CHR$(12);   ' Print a form feed to ready a blank page
    GOTO PrintRep   ' Re-do entire report
Endit : END
```

The Block *IF-THEN-ELSE*

This section shows how you can build on the conditional IF statement to create truly well-written, structured programs. Any time
you sit down to write a program, you should always think about
making it easy-to-follow, well-ordered(rarely jumping from place to
place), and well-documented (with ample REM statements).

Multiple Statements on a Line

You can put more than one QBasic statement on a single line. To
do this, separate the statements with a colon (:). This has limited
use, but it can be used for variable initializations or for a couple of

statements following IF. Don't overuse the colon; putting too many statements on a single line makes the program unreadable.

The following short program takes only a single statement:

```
PRINT "Hello" : PRINT "QBasic" : PRINT "is" : PRINT "easy!"
```

The previous line is identical to the following four-line program:

```
PRINT "Hello"
PRINT "QBasic"
PRINT "is"
PRINT "easy!"
```

Even without remarks, the second version is the clearest—but the colon statement separator is not always a poor structure, and is not necessarily bad to use at times. The multiple-line separator is commonly used after an IF-THEN statement. Listing 6.7 shows two QBasic statements being executed after an IF, instead of a single statement as you saw in earlier examples.

Listing 6.7. A program demonstrating the multiline separator.

```
' Program that reads and prints high football
' teams and scores (those over 21 points) and
' prints the average of those high scores.

' Initialize total and count variables for average
ac = 0           ' Will hold the number of high scores
total = 0

' Read one at a time, print them, and add to total
CLS
GetScore:
   READ team$, score
   IF (team$ = "-99") THEN GOTO Finished
   ' Test for high score and use only those over 21
   IF (score > 21) THEN PRINT team$ : total = total + score :
      ➥ ac = ac + 1
   GOTO GetScore
Finished:
   PRINT
   PRINT "The average of the high scores is"; total / ac
   DATA "Tigers", 32, "Cyclones", 3, "Centurions", 21
   DATA "Pintos", 14, "Stars", 20, "Thunder", 24
   DATA "Okies", 56, "Surfers", 7, "Elks", 31
   DATA "-99", -99
END
```

The *ELSE* Statement

The ELSE statement is used in conjunction with the IF-THEN statement. This section introduces the ELSE statement by showing you the IF-THEN-ELSE compound statement in its simplest format.

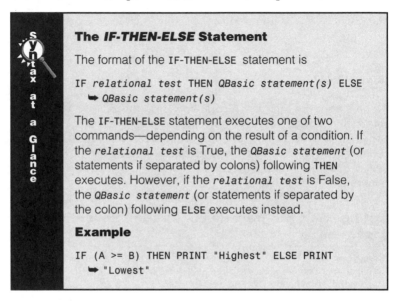

The *IF-THEN-ELSE* Statement

The format of the IF-THEN-ELSE statement is

```
IF relational test THEN QBasic statement(s) ELSE
➥ QBasic statement(s)
```

The IF-THEN-ELSE statement executes one of two commands—depending on the result of a condition. If the *relational test* is True, the *QBasic statement* (or statements if separated by colons) following THEN executes. However, if the *relational test* is False, the *QBasic statement* (or statements if separated by the colon) following ELSE executes instead.

Example

```
IF (A >= B) THEN PRINT "Highest" ELSE PRINT
➥ "Lowest"
```

The first part of this statement is identical to the IF-THEN statement, but the simple IF-THEN statement only determines what happens when the *relational test* is True. The IF-THEN-ELSE statement determines what happens if the *relational test* is True, *and* what happens if the *relational test* is False. No matter what the outcome is, the statement following the IF-THEN-ELSE executes next, unless one of the results of the *relational test* is a GOTO.

The following rule probably best describes the nature of the IF-THEN-ELSE statement: When the relational test is True, the statement following THEN executes; when the relational test is False, the statement following the ELSE executes.

The following program asks the user for a number. It then prints whether the number is greater than zero using an IF-THEN-ELSE statement:

```
' Program demonstrates IF-THEN-ELSE by printing whether
' an input value is greater than zero or not.
CLS
```

```
INPUT "What is your number"; num
IF (num > 0) THEN PRINT "More than 0" ELSE PRINT
  ➥ "Less or equal to 0"

' No matter what the number was, the following is executed
PRINT : PRINT "Thanks for your time!"
```

> **NOTE** The IF-THEN-ELSE can make for long statements, especially if you use the colon to execute more than one statement following THEN, ELSE, or both statements. This is one reason why IF-THEN-ELSE is best used for simple comparisons.

The Block

There will be many times when you want to perform several statements if the IF test is True. There also might be several statements you want performed if the ELSE portion is True. The one-line IF-THEN-ELSE statement you just saw was too limiting. Too much code can look squeezed on a single line. QBasic offers the block IF-THEN-ELSE to get around this problem.

In computer terminology, a *block* is generally one or more statements treated as a single statement.

The Block *IF-THEN-ELSE*

Here is the format of the block IF-THEN-ELSE:

```
IF relational test THEN
    A block of one or more QBasic statements
[ELSE
    A block of one or more QBasic statements]
END IF
```

The block IF-THEN-ELSE conditionally executes one or more groups of statements depending on a condition. If the *relational test* is True, the entire block of statements following IF is performed. If the *relational test* is False, the entire block of statements following ELSE is performed.

The Block *IF-THEN-ELSE* continued

Example

```
IF (sales < 5000) THEN
    PRINT "Get your sales up!"
ELSE
    PRINT "Congratulations!  You win the monthly
    ➥ sales award..."
    PRINT "You get an extra day off!"
END IF
```

The block `IF-THEN-ELSE` spans more than one line. Every QBasic statement between the `IF` and the `ELSE` makes up the block. The `ELSE` portion is optional; if you include one, `ELSE` can also be followed by one or more QBasic statements.

The block `IF-THEN-ELSE` statement lets you create truly well-structured programs. Instead of a True `IF` result branching off to a large section of code (with `GOTO`), you can keep it close to the `IF`.

The following code uses the block `IF` to test the user's response to a yes-or-no question. You could incorporate this code into your own programs. If the user answers the yes-or-no question with a **Y** or **N**, the program completes normally. (A typical program would execute certain code depending on the answer.)

```
' Checks the input using the block IF
'
CLS
' The following ensures that a proper input was typed
INPUT "What is your answer (Y/N)"; ans$
IF ((ans$ <> "Y") AND (ans$ <> "N")) THEN
    BEEP
    PRINT
    PRINT "You did not enter a Y or an N!"
    PRINT
ELSE
    PRINT "Thank you."
    PRINT
END IF
' Rest of program would go here
```

Notice the `END IF` statement. Without it, QBasic would have no idea where the block of statements ends. It knows where to go if the result is True because of the `ELSE`; however, if the result is False, it does not know where to go until the `END IF` statement.

Listing 6.8 is a complete payroll routine. It uses the block IF to compute overtime pay. The logic goes something like this: If an employee works 40 hours or fewer, he or she gets paid regular pay (the hourly pay times the number of hours worked). If the employee works between 40 and 50 hours, he or she gets one-and-a-half times the hourly rate for those hours over 40. The employee still gets regular pay for the first 40 hours. All hours over 50 are paid double-time pay.

Listing 6.8. A program to calculate overtime pay.

```
' Compute the full overtime pay possibilities
CLS
INPUT "How many hours were worked"; hours
INPUT "What is the regular hourly pay"; rate
' Compute pay here
' Double-time possibility
IF (hours > 50) THEN
    dt = 2 * rate * (hours - 50)
    ht = 1.5 * rate * 10      ' time + 1/2 for 10 hours
ELSE
    dt = 0   ' Either none or double for those hours over 50
END IF

' Time and a half
IF ((hours > 40) AND (hours <= 50)) THEN
    ht = 1.5 * rate * (hours - 40)
END IF

' Regular Pay
IF (hours >= 40) THEN
    rp = 40 * rate
ELSE
    rp = hours * rate
END IF

pay = dt + ht + rp    ' Add three components of payroll
PRINT
PRINT USING "& $$##,.##"; "The pay is"; pay
```

The *ELSEIF* Statement

The statements following the block IF can be anything. Even another IF statement can go inside the block IF. You also may need to perform another IF statement after the ELSE portion of the block IF. To do this, use an ELSEIF statement.

**S
y
n
t
a
x**

**a
t**

a

**G
l
a
n
c
e**

The Block *IF-THEN-ELSEIF* Statement

The format of the complete block IF-THEN-ELSEIF statement is

```
IF relational test THEN
   A block of one or more QBasic statements
[ELSEIF relational test
   A block of one or more QBasic statements]
END IF
```

The block IF-THEN-ELSEIF statement executes one of two statements depending on the result of the relational test. ELSEIF is actually an extension of the block IF-THEN statement.

Example

```
IF (Ans = 0) THEN
   RESTORE
   PRINT "I'm resetting the data"
ELSEIF (ANS = 1) THEN
   PRINT "No change is necessary"
END IF
```

The ELSEIF statement is useful for a number of reasons. A decision can have more than two choices. For example, you might ask for a "yes, no, or maybe" answer to a question. Depending on the answer, you might want to perform any one of three separate sections of code. As the following examples will show, ELSEIF is just an extension of the block IF statement, and simply adds power to an already powerful QBasic command.

TIP Be sure to type ELSEIF as one word, and not two. Otherwise, QBasic thinks you are starting another block IF-THEN without matching END IF statements.

Suppose you want to give an annual award to employees based on years of service to your company. The following program gives a gold watch to those with more than 20 years, a paper weight to those with more than 10 years, and a pat on the back to everyone else.

```
' Prints a message depending on years of service using
' the block IF-THEN-ELSEIF.
CLS
INPUT "How many years of service"; yrs

' Test for length of time and print matching message
IF (yrs > 20) THEN
   PRINT "Give a gold watch"
ELSEIF ((yrs > 10) AND (yrs <= 20)) THEN
   PRINT "Give a paper weight"
ELSEIF (yrs <= 10) THEN
   PRINT "Give a pat on the back"
END IF
```

The ELSEIF dictates what occurs—and does so in such a way that more than one decision can be made inside a single block IF statement without losing the meaning and the ease of readability.

You should probably not rely on the block IF-THEN-ELSEIF to take care of *too many* conditions, because more than 3 or 4 add to confusion (you get into messy logic such as: If this is true, then if this is true, then do something, else if this is true do something, else if this is true do something, and so on...) The SELECT CASE statement in the next section handles these multiple IF statements better than a long IF-THEN-ELSEIF.

The *SELECT CASE* Statement

SELECT CASE improves upon the block IF-THEN-ELSE by eliminating the "IF within an IF" construction. There are several forms of SELECT CASE, and the primary form is illustrated here. SELECT CASE is a little longer than the statements you have seen so far.

Selecting Possible Matches with
SELECT CASE

The format of the primary SELECT CASE is

```
SELECT CASE expression
CASE expression1
   Block of one or more QBasic statements
CASE expression2
   Block of one or more QBasic statements
   ⋮
[CASE ELSE
   Block of one or more QBasic statements]
END SELECT
```

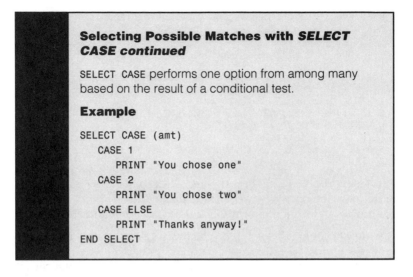

The number of CASE options that follow the SELECT CASE line is determined by your application. The *expressions* can be either text or numeric expressions (constants or variables). The *Block of one or more QBasic statements* is similar to the block of statements you saw for the block IF; one or more statements make up that block. The CASE ELSE line is optional—not all SELECT CASE statements require it. You must put the END SELECT line at the end of every CASE SELECT statement, otherwise, QBasic would not know where the last block of CASE statements end.

The SELECT CASE is easier to use than its format might lead you to believe. If the *expression* following SELECT CASE matches any of the *expressions* on a CASE line, the code following the matching CASE executes. If none of the CASE *expressions* match the SELECT CASE *expression*, the CASE ELSE code executes. If you do not supply a CASE ELSE, the next statement in the program executes next. You can use a SELECT CASE anywhere that you can use a block IF-THEN-ELSE—and it is usually easier to read.

The SELECT CASE is great for handling program *menus* (lists of options from which the user can select). The program in Listing 6.9 is a math tutorial that asks for two numbers and then asks the users what type of math operation they want to perform on those numbers.

Listing 6.9. A math tutorial program.

```
' Program to practice math accuracy
COLOR 7, 1      ' White characters on blue for a nice display
CLS
PRINT "Please type two numbers, separated by a comma"
PRINT "(For example, 8, 5) and press Enter"
INPUT num1, num2
PRINT     ' Prints a blank line
PRINT
PRINT "Choose your option:"
PRINT "1. Add"; num1; "to"; num2
PRINT "2. Subtract"; num1; "from"; num2
PRINT "3. Multiply"; num1; "and"; num2
PRINT "4. Divide"; num1; "by"; num2
PRINT "5. Quit"
PRINT
INPUT choice

SELECT CASE (choice)
    CASE 1
        PRINT num1; "plus"; num2; "is"; (num1 + num2)
    CASE 2
        PRINT num2; "minus"; num1; "is"; (num2 - num1)
    CASE 3
        PRINT num1; "times"; num2; "is"; (num1 * num2)
    CASE 4
        PRINT num1; "divided by"; num2; "is"; (num1 / num2)
    CASE ELSE
        PRINT "Thanks anyway!"
END SELECT
Endit: END
```

Here is the output from Listing 6.9:

```
Please type two numbers, separated by a comma
(For example, 8, 5) and press Enter
? 3, 7

Choose your option:
1. Add 3 to 6
2. Subtract 6 from 3
3. Multiply 3 and 6
4. Divide 3 by 6

? 3
 3 times 6 is 18
```

If you have to choose from a list of options, the SELECT CASE code is easier to read than the block IF-THEN-ELSE code.

Summary

You deserve a rest! You are now well on your way to mastering QBasic. This chapter presented several new means of processing the data within your programs. By using decision statements such as IF and SELECT CASE, you can write programs that perform actions based on input data.

Here are some of the things you learned in this chapter:

- The GOTO statement causes your program to execute in a different order from the top-to-bottom sequence. GOTO is best not over-used; it is helpful to know when learning the IF-THEN statement.

- The six comparison operators (=, >, <, >=, <=, and <>) determine how two values compare to one another.

- The IF statement is described as a decision statement because QBasic determines what to do (makes a decision) based on the IF statement's comparison.

- There are several forms of the IF statement, all of which are presented in this chapter. The IF-THEN-ELSE statement specifies which group of statements execute based on a True or False comparison.

- The SELECT CASE sometimes takes the place of complicated IF-THEN-ELSEIF statements. SELECT CASE is especially useful for menu selections.

- Many times, a block of statements can go in place of a single statement, such as after an IF or SELECT CASE.

Controlling Program Flow

The repetitive capability of the computer makes it a good tool for processing large amounts of information. The GOTO statement, which you were introduced to in the preceding chapter, provides one method of repeating a group of statements. You should use GOTO with care, however, because it can make a program difficult to follow. There are better ways to repeat sections of your program than simply using GOTO to branch forward and backward.

The FOR-NEXT, WHILE, and DO statements offer a way to repeat sections of your program conditionally. They create *loops,* which are the repeated execution of one or more statements.

The *FOR* and *NEXT* Statements

The FOR and NEXT statements always appear in pairs. If your program has one or more FOR statements, it will also have the same number of NEXT statements.

The FOR and NEXT statements enclose one or more QBasic statements, forming a loop that repeats a certain number of times. The programmer controls the number of times the loop repeats.

Looping with *FOR* and *NEXT*

The format of the FOR statement is

```
FOR counter = begin TO end [STEP increment]
```

FOR causes your program to loop a specific number of times. The *counter* variable, which helps control the body of the loop, is initialized to the value of *begin* at the beginning of the loop. *begin* is typically 1, but can be any numeric value. Every time the body of the loop repeats, the *counter* variable increments or decrements by the value of *increment*. If you do not specify a STEP value, an *increment* of 1 is assumed.

The value of *end* is a number or a variable that controls the end of the looping process. When *counter* is equal to or greater than *end*, QBasic does not repeat the loop, but continues at the statement following NEXT.

The format of the NEXT statement is

```
NEXT [counter] [, counter2] [, counterN]
```

NEXT is always the last statement in a FOR loop. Although the *counter* variable is optional, most programmers specify one. The *counter* variable is the same *counter* variable used at the top of the loop in the FOR statement. The remaining counter variables exist for those times when you want a single NEXT statement to terminate several FOR loops (instead of specifying a separate NEXT for each).

Here is the combined syntax of the FOR-NEXT statement:

```
FOR counter = begin TO end [STEP increment]
  One or more QBasic statements go here
NEXT [counter] [, counter2] [, counterN]
```

Use a FOR-NEXT loop when you can control a loop with a variable.

Example

```
total=0
FOR num = 1 to 25
    PRINT "I am adding the numbers from 1 to 25"
    total = total + num
NEXT num
```

To give you a glimpse of the FOR-NEXT loop's capabilities, look at the next two short programs. They both count from 1 to 5, printing the number each time the count increments. The first program contains a FOR-NEXT loop, and the next does not. Here is the first program, followed by its output:

```
FOR ctr = 1 to 5    ' Count from 1 to 5 each
   PRINT ctr        ' time through the loop
NEXT ctr
END


1
2
3
4
5
```

Here is the program without using FOR-NEXT statements:

```
ctr = 1
Again:
   IF (ctr > 5) THEN GOTO EndIt
   PRINT ctr
   ctr = ctr + 1    ; Add 1 to count
   GOTO Again
EndIt:
   END
```

The FOR-NEXT loop is a much cleaner way of controlling the looping process. The FOR-NEXT statements do several things that you previously had to accomplish with extra statements: the FOR statement initializes ctr to 1 (because 1 is the *begin* value), everything in the body of the loop (in this case, just the PRINT statement) executes, and the *counter* variable, ctr, is incremented by 1 automatically. As long as ctr is not more than 5 (the *end* value), the body of the loop repeats again.

The body of the FOR-NEXT loop certainly can contain more than one statement. Listing 7.1 reads and prints five pairs of data values. Notice that no trailer data record is needed. Because the FOR-NEXT loop counter counts only to 5, the READ statement does not read past the last data value.

Listing 7.1. Reading and printing data values inside a loop.

```
' Program that reads and prints data values inside a loop
CLS
PRINT "Name", "Age"
```

continues

Listing 7.1. Continued

```
FOR ctr = 1 to 5      ' ctr controls the number of iterations
    READ child.name$
    READ child.age
    PRINT child.name$, child.age
NEXT ctr

DATA "Susie", 6, "Bob", 8, "Jane", 10, "Tim", 7, "Joe", 9
```

Here is the output from Listing 7.1:

```
Susie        6
Bob          8
Jane         10
Tim          7
Joe          9
```

As mentioned, if you do not specify a STEP value, QBasic assumes a value of 1. You can increment the *counter* variable by any value, however. Listing 7.2 uses one loop to print the even numbers from 1 to 20, and another loop to print the odd numbers from 1 to 20. Both loops use a STEP value of 2, but note their different *begin* values.

Listing 7.2. Using two loops to print selected numbers.

```
' Prints the first few odd and even numbers
CLS
PRINT "Even numbers through 20"
' Start at 2 because it's the first even number
FOR num = 2 to 20 STEP 2
    PRINT num
NEXT num

PRINT "Odd numbers below 20"
FOR num = 1 to 20 STEP 2
    PRINT num
NEXT num
```

The body of each loop consists of a single PRINT statement. The CLS statement and the first PRINT statement are not part of either loop. (If they were, the screen would clear and the title would print before each number printed.)

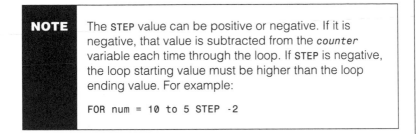

> **NOTE** The STEP value can be positive or negative. If it is negative, that value is subtracted from the *counter* variable each time through the loop. If STEP is negative, the loop starting value must be higher than the loop ending value. For example:
>
> ```
> FOR num = 10 to 5 STEP -2
> ```

Nested *FOR-NEXT* Loops

Any QBasic statement can go inside the body of a FOR-NEXT loop—even another FOR-NEXT loop! When you put a loop within a loop, you create a *nested loop*. The clock in a sporting event works like a nested loop. A football game counts down from 15 minutes to 0, four times. The first countdown can be thought of as a loop counting from 15 to 0 (for each minute). That loop is nested in another loop that counts from 1 to 4 (for each of the 4 quarters).

Any loop that must be repeated more than once is a good candidate for a nested loop. Figure 7.1 shows outlines of nested loops. In the example on the left, the FOR loop that counts from 1 to 5 is the inside loop. You can think of the inside loop as looping faster than the outside loop because the inside loop's Inner variable goes from 1 to 5 before the outside loop finishes its first iteration. The outside loop does not repeat until the NEXT Outer statement is reached. When the outside loop does iterate a second time, the inside loop starts all over again.

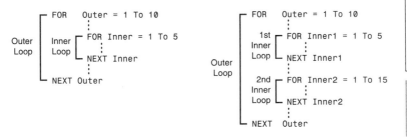

Figure 7.1. *Outlines of nested loops.*

The second nested loop outline shows two loops in an outside loop. Both of these loops execute in their entirety before the outside loop finishes its first iteration. When the outside loop starts its second iteration, the two inside loops repeat.

Notice the order of the NEXT variables in Figure 7.1. The inside loop *always* finishes before the outside loop; therefore, the inside loop's NEXT variable must come before the outside loop's NEXT variable. Figure 7.2 shows incorrect NEXT statements, in which the outside loop finishes before the inside loop or loops.

```
FOR Outer = 1 To 10              FOR Outer = 1 To 10
    :                                :
    FOR Inner = 1 To 5               FOR Inner1 = 1 To 5
        :                                :
    NEXT Outer  ◄── Invalid          NEXT Outer  ◄── Invalid
    :                                :
NEXT Inner  ◄── Invalid           FOR Inner2 = 1 To 15
                                     :
                                  NEXT Inner1  ◄── Invalid
                                     :
                                NEXT Inner2  ◄── Invalid
```

Figure 7.2. *Incorrect nested loops.*

NOTE In nested loops, the order of the NEXT variables should be the opposite of the order of the FOR variables. In this way, the inside loop (or loops) complete before the outside loop's next iteration.

Listing 7.3 contains a loop within a loop—a nested loop. The inside loop counts and prints from 1 to 4. The outside loop counts from 1 to 3. Therefore, the inside loop repeats, in its entirety, three times. In other words, the program prints the values 1 to 4 and does so three times.

Listing 7.3. Counting and printing with a nested loop.

```
' Uses a nested loop to print the numbers
' from 1 to 4 three times

CLS
FOR times = 1 TO 3        ' Outside loop
    FOR num = 1 TO 4      ' Inside loop
        PRINT num
    NEXT num
NEXT times
```

The program's indentation follows the standard used with FOR loops—each statement in a loop is indented three spaces. Because

the inside loop is already indented, its body is indented another
three spaces.

Here is the output from Listing 7.3:

```
1
2
3
4
1
2
3
4
1
2
3
4
```

In Listing 7.3, the outside loop's *counter* variable changes each
time through the loop. In Listing 7.4, the outside loop's counter
variable is also used as one of the inside loop's control variables.

Listing 7.4. An inside loop controlled by the outer loop's counter variable.

```
' An inside loop controlled by the outer loop's
' counter variable
CLS
FOR outer = 5 TO 1 STEP -1
   FOR inner = 1 TO outer
      PRINT inner;  ' Semicolon keeps cursor on same output
line
   NEXT inner
   PRINT         ' Print a blank line. Forces cursor to next line
NEXT outer
```

Here is the output from Listing 7.4:

```
1 2 3 4 5
1 2 3 4
1 2 3
1 2
1
```

The inside loop repeats, in its entirety, five times (as outer counts
from 5 to 1), printing one less number with each iteration of the
outer loop.

Table 7.1 traces the two variables through this program. Sometimes it helps to "play computer" when learning a new concept
such as nested loops. You can reproduce this table by executing
the program a line at a time and writing each variable's contents.

Table 7.1. Tracing the program's output.

Variable Values

outer	inner
5	1
5	2
5	3
5	4
5	5
4	1
4	2
4	3
4	4
3	1
3	2
3	3
2	1
2	2
1	1

The *EXIT FOR* Statement

The FOR-NEXT loop was designed to execute a loop a specified number of times. In rare instances, however, the FOR-NEXT loop should quit before the FOR *counter* variable has reached its *end* value. You can use the EXIT FOR statement to quit a FOR loop early.

The EXIT FOR statement goes in the body of a FOR loop. Although the EXIT FOR statement can appear on a line by itself, it generally does not. The EXIT FOR statement almost always follows the true condition of an IF test. If the EXIT FOR statement were on a line by itself, the loop would always quit early, defeating the purpose of the FOR-NEXT statements.

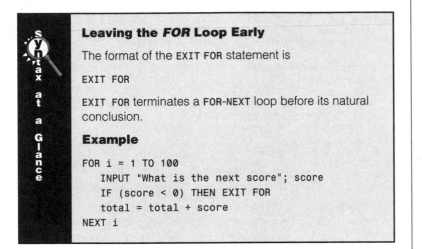

Leaving the *FOR* Loop Early

The format of the EXIT FOR statement is

```
EXIT FOR
```

EXIT FOR terminates a FOR-NEXT loop before its natural conclusion.

Example

```
FOR i = 1 TO 100
    INPUT "What is the next score"; score
    IF (score < 0) THEN EXIT FOR
    total = total + score
NEXT i
```

Listing 7.5 shows what can happen when QBasic encounters an unconditional EXIT FOR statement, that is, one *not* preceded by an IF statement:

Listing 7.5. A program illustrating an unconditional *EXIT FOR* statement.

```
' A FOR-NEXT loop defeated by the EXIT FOR statement
CLS
PRINT "Here are the numbers from 1 to 20"
FOR num = 1 TO 20
    PRINT num
    EXIT FOR     ' Will exit the FOR loop immediately
NEXT num         ' Never gets looked at
PRINT "That's all, folks!"
```

You can tell from the following output that EXIT FOR forces an early exit from the loop, which would normally loop twenty times. The EXIT FOR ends the FOR loop immediately, before it has gone through one cycle. The FOR-NEXT loop might as well not be in this program.

```
Here are the numbers from 1 to 20
 1
That's all, folks!
```

Listing 7.6 is an improved version of the last example. It asks the user if he or she wants to see another number. If so, the FOR-NEXT loop continues its next iteration. If not, the EXIT FOR statement terminates the FOR loop.

Listing 7.6. An improved version of Listing 7.5.

```
' A FOR-NEXT loop running at the user's request
CLS
PRINT "Here are the numbers from 1 to 20"
FOR num = 1 TO 20
    PRINT num
    INPUT "Do you want to see another (Y/N)"; ans$
' Exits the FOR loop if user wants to
    IF (ans$ = "N") OR (ans$ = "n") THEN EXIT FOR
NEXT num
PRINT "That's all, folks!"
END
```

The FOR-NEXT loop prints 20 numbers, as long as the user does not type N or n. Otherwise, the EXIT FOR takes over and terminates the FOR loop early. The statement after NEXT always executes next if the EXIT FOR occurs, providing the user did not type N or n.

> **NOTE** If you nest one loop inside another, the EXIT FOR terminates the "most active" loop, that is, the innermost loop in which the EXIT FOR resides.

> **TIP** The conditional EXIT FOR (an EXIT FOR preceded by an IF) can be useful when you are processing data that might be incomplete. When you start processing data files, or large amounts of user input, you might expect 100 input numbers, for example, but get only 95. You could use an EXIT FOR to terminate the FOR-NEXT loop before it cycles through its 96th iteration.

Other Loop Statements

The combined FOR and NEXT statements are only one way to control a loop. Although a FOR-NEXT loop is great for loops that must execute a specific number of times, WHILE-WEND and DO loops enable your program to execute a loop as long as (or until) a true or false condition is met. There are several ways to program a DO loop. This sections shows you all of them.

The *WHILE* and *WEND* Statements

Like the FOR and NEXT statements, the WHILE and WEND statements operate as a pair. A WHILE statement must be followed somewhere in the program with a WEND statement. The WHILE and WEND statements enclose a repeating loop, just as the FOR and NEXT statements. Whereas the FOR-NEXT loop is controlled by a specified number of iterations, however, the WHILE-WEND loop is controlled by a relational test.

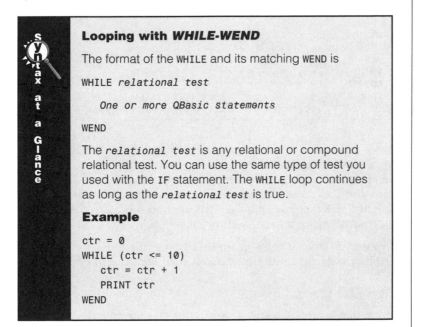

Looping with *WHILE-WEND*

The format of the WHILE and its matching WEND is

```
WHILE relational test
    One or more QBasic statements
WEND
```

The *relational test* is any relational or compound relational test. You can use the same type of test you used with the IF statement. The WHILE loop continues as long as the *relational test* is true.

Example

```
ctr = 0
WHILE (ctr <= 10)
    ctr = ctr + 1
    PRINT ctr
WEND
```

You can put one or more statements between a WHILE-WEND. Because WHILE and WEND enclose a loop, you should indent the body of the loop, as you did with the body of the FOR-NEXT loop.

Because the WHILE-WEND loop repeats (that is, the body of the loop executes) as long as the *relational test* is true, the body of the loop *must* modify one of the variables being tested in the *relational test*. Otherwise, the loop repeats indefinitely.

The WHILE-WEND loop tests for the relational condition at the top of the loop. Therefore, if the test initially is false, the loop will not execute, even once. (Later in the chapter, you see a loop that always executes at least once.)

Listing 7.7 should help clarify your understanding of the WHILE-WEND loop. This program checks the user's input to make sure Y or N was entered.

Listing 7.7. Ensuring a correct user response with *WHILE-WEND.*

```
' Input routine to ensure that the user types a
' correct response
' This routine could be part of a larger program
CLS
INPUT "Do you want to continue (Y/N)"; ans$
WHILE ((ans$ <> "Y") AND (ans$ <> "N"))
    BEEP
    PRINT "You must type a Y or an N"
    PRINT
    INPUT "Do you want to continue (Y/N)"; ans$
WEND    ' The input routine quits when the user types Y or N
```

Notice that two INPUT statements do the same thing. The first INPUT, outside the WHILE loop, gets an answer that the WHILE loop can check. If the user types something other than Y or N, the program prints an error message, asks for another answer, then loops back to check the answer again. This method is preferred over the IF-THEN-GOTO process for data-entry validation.

Because you cannot know in advance how many times the WHILE-WEND loop will cycle, WHILE-WEND is called an *indeterminate loop.*

The *DO* Loop

A loop that is more flexible than WHILE-WEND is the DO loop. The DO loop is similar to the WHILE-WEND loop, except the DO loop allows the *relational test* to be either true or false; you can loop on either condition. The DO loop also can test the relation at the top *or* the bottom of the loop. If you test at the bottom of the loop, you can ensure that the loop always executes at least once.

The DO loop has four forms, each of which is described in this section.

The *DO WHILE-LOOP* Statements

DO WHILE-LOOP is similar to WHILE-WEND. It tests at the top of the loop (so the loop might not execute at all) using only a positive *relational test*. As long as the test is true, the loop executes.

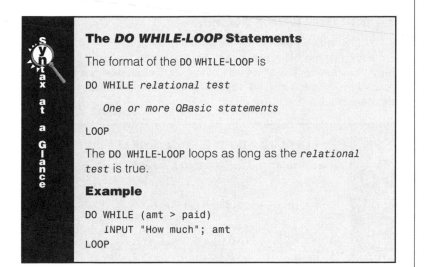

The **DO WHILE-LOOP** Statements

The format of the DO WHILE-LOOP is

DO WHILE *relational test*

   One or more QBasic statements

LOOP

The DO WHILE-LOOP loops as long as the *relational test* is true.

Example

DO WHILE (amt > paid)
   INPUT "How much"; amt
LOOP

As with all the other loops in this chapter, the *relational test* does not have to be enclosed in parentheses, but most programmers use parentheses around tests. Notice that the way DO loops work is identical to the way the WHILE-WEND works. If you become familiar with the DO WHILE-LOOP, you will find it easier to learn the other types of DO loops.

Listing 7.8 is just like the first program you saw for the WHILE-WEND statements, except it uses a DO WHILE-LOOP set of statements. Because DO WHILE-LOOP statements are more flexible than WHILE-WEND statements, you probably will use DO WHILE-LOOP more often. QBasic retained the WHILE-WEND statements only for compatibility with previous versions of BASIC.

Listing 7.8. The program from Listing 7.7 using a *DO WHILE-LOOP*.

```
' Input routine to ensure that the user types a
' correct response
' This routine could be part of a larger program
CLS
INPUT "Do you want to continue (Y/N)"; ans$
DO WHILE ((ans$ <> "Y") AND (ans$ <> "N"))
   BEEP
   PRINT "You must type a Y or an N"
   PRINT
   INPUT "Do you want to continue (Y/N)"; ans$
LOOP     ' The input routine quits when the user types Y or N
```

The *DO-LOOP WHILE* Statements

The DO-LOOP WHILE statements are similar to the DO WHILE-LOOP statements, except the *relational test* occurs at the *bottom* of the loop. This ensures that the body of the loop executes at least once. It uses a positive *relational test*; as long as the test is true, the loop continues to execute.

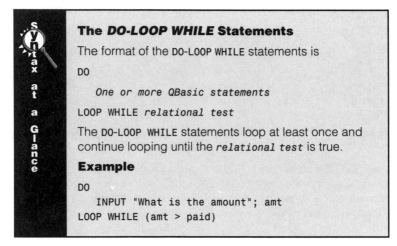

The *DO-LOOP WHILE* Statements

The format of the DO-LOOP WHILE statements is

```
DO

    One or more QBasic statements

LOOP WHILE relational test
```

The DO-LOOP WHILE statements loop at least once and continue looping until the *relational test* is true.

Example

```
DO
    INPUT "What is the amount"; amt
LOOP WHILE (amt > paid)
```

Checking at the bottom of the loop can be an advantage. For example, you might want a loop to execute once, then execute again depending on the results of the first loop.

Listing 7.9 makes the input-checking routine shown previously a little clearer. Because the body of the loop always executes at least once, this program requires only one INPUT statement.

Listing 7.9. The program from Listing 7.7 using *DO-LOOP WHILE.*

```
' Input routine to ensure that the user types a
' correct response
' This routine could be part of a larger program
CLS
INPUT "Do you want to continue (Y/N)"; ans$
IF ((ans$ <> "Y") AND (ans$ <> "N")) THEN
    DO
        BEEP
        PRINT "You must type a Y or an N"
        PRINT
        INPUT "Do you want to continue (Y/N)"; ans$
    LOOP WHILE ((ans$ <> "Y") AND (ans$ <> "N"))
END IF
        ' The input routine continues until the user types Y or N
```

The INPUT statement is not required before the loop starts because it is the first statement in the loop and will always execute at least once. This gives the user a chance to enter the answer. If the answer to the prompt is Y or N, the LOOP WHILE *relational test* fails (at the bottom of the loop) and the rest of the program continues from there.

The *DO UNTIL-LOOP* Statements

The DO UNTIL-LOOP statements cycle through the body of the loop until the *relational test* is true.

> ### The *DO UNTIL-LOOP* Statements
>
> The format of the DO UNTIL-LOOP statements is
>
> ```
> DO UNTIL relational test
>     One or more QBasic statements
> LOOP
> ```
>
> The DO UNTIL-LOOP statements loop until the *relational test* is true.
>
> ### Example
>
> ```
> DO UNTIL (sales > 2000)
>     sales = sales + 400
> LOOP
> ```

The DO UNTIL-LOOP statements check for a false *relational test* at the top of the loop. Therefore, if the condition is false to begin with, the loop never executes.

Being able to check for a false *relational test* makes the data-validation routine even easier. The "not equal to" symbols are changed to "equal" symbols, making the *relational test* easier to read, as shown in Listing 7.10.

Listing 7.10. The program from Listing 7.7 using a *DO UNTIL-LOOP.*

```
' Input routine to ensure that the user types a
' correct response
' This routine could be part of a larger program
CLS
```

continues

Listing 7.10. Continued

```
INPUT "Do you want to continue (Y/N)"; ans$
DO UNTIL ((ans$ = "Y") OR (ans$ = "N"))
   BEEP
   PRINT "You must type a Y or an N"
   PRINT
   INPUT "Do you want to continue (Y/N)"; ans$
LOOP    ' The input routine quits when user types Y or N
```

Listing 7.11 requests a list of numbers. As the user types numbers, the program adds them to a total and counts them. When the user enters 0, the program computes the final total and average. The 0 is not part of the list—it signals the end of input. A DO UNTIL-LOOP tests the input for a 0.

Listing 7.11. Using a *DO UNTIL-LOOP* to test the input for 0.

```
' Program that accepts a list of numbers, then counts
' and averages them
'
total = 0      ' Initialize total and count variables
count = 0
' Get input until a 0 is entered
CLS
INPUT "What is your number (0 ends the input)"; num
DO UNTIL (num = 0)
   total = total + num
   count = count + 1
   INPUT "What is your number (0 ends the input)"; num
LOOP

' Control goes here when the user has entered the last number
PRINT
PRINT "The total is"; total
IF (count <> 0) THEN
   PRINT "The average is"; (total / count)
ELSE
   PRINT "The average is 0"
END IF
```

Notice that the program would work correctly even if the user entered 0 as the first number. The check at the top of the loop, right after the initial INPUT, makes this possible. The INPUT statement also tells the user how to end the input.

The DO UNTIL-LOOP statements can also be used to process READ-DATA statements. Listing 7.12 reads city names and their average summer temperatures, and then prints the names of the cities whose temperatures average more than 90 degrees. In Chapter 6, "Making Decisions with Data," IF-THEN was used to test for the trailer data record. In the following program, the check for the trailer data record is embedded in the DO UNTIL-LOOP.

Listing 7.12. Using a *DO UNTIL-LOOP* to process *READ-DATA* statements.

```
' Reads city names and temperatures, then prints high temp
' cities
' Initialize screen with titles
CLS
PRINT "List of high temperature cities:"
PRINT
PRINT "City Name"; TAB(20); "Temperature"

READ city$, temp     ' Initial READ to start data checking
DO UNTIL (city$ = "-99")   ' temp = -99) would work too
   IF (temp > 90) THEN PRINT city$; TAB(20); temp
   READ city$, temp
LOOP    ' The bottom of the cycle

DATA "Memphis", 90, "Miami", 94, "Salem", 86
DATA "Tulsa", 97, "San Francisco", 83, "Dallas", 98
DATA "Bangor", 76, "Juno", 65, "Chicago", 89
DATA "-99", -99
```

Even though the DO UNTIL-LOOP reads every data value, only selected values are printed. Here is the output from Listing 7.12:

```
List of high temperature cities:

City Name       Temperature
Miami           94
Tulsa           97
Dallas          98
```

If you wanted to add more city and temperature combinations, you would put them before the trailer data record. The IF-THEN statements ensure that only the high cities are printed by filtering the low temperature cities from the output.

The *DO-LOOP UNTIL* Statements

The DO-LOOP UNTIL statements, like DO UNTIL-LOOP, cycle through the body of a loop, repeating the loop's statements, until the *relational test* is true. The difference between the statements is the position of the *relational test*. The DO UNTIL-LOOP statements test at the top of the loop, but the DO-LOOP UNTIL statements test at the *bottom* of the loop, which means that the loop executes at least once.

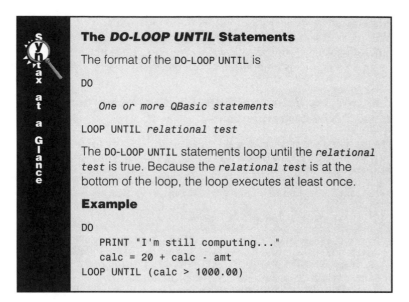

The DO-LOOP UNTIL Statements

The format of the DO-LOOP UNTIL is

```
DO

    One or more QBasic statements

LOOP UNTIL relational test
```

The DO-LOOP UNTIL statements loop until the *relational test* is true. Because the *relational test* is at the bottom of the loop, the loop executes at least once.

Example

```
DO
    PRINT "I'm still computing..."
    calc = 20 + calc - amt
LOOP UNTIL (calc > 1000.00)
```

Listing 7.13 is a brief, familiar example of the DO-LOOP UNTIL.

Listing 7.13. A counting program using *DO-LOOP UNTIL*.

```
' Program to count down to a blast-off using DO-LOOP UNTIL
'
CLS
count = 10      ' Begin the count...
DO
    PRINT count
    count = count - 1
LOOP UNTIL (count = 0)   ' Do not loop past 1
PRINT "*** Blast off! ***"
```

The *EXIT DO* Statement

Previously in this chapter, you learned how to exit the FOR loop early with the EXIT FOR statement. Likewise, you can exit a DO-LOOP early with the EXIT DO statement.

EXIT DO can be used in the body of any variation of the DO loop. It usually is preceded by the IF statement. As with the EXIT FOR statement, putting EXIT DO on a line by itself makes the program unconditionally exit the DO loop, thus defeating its purpose.

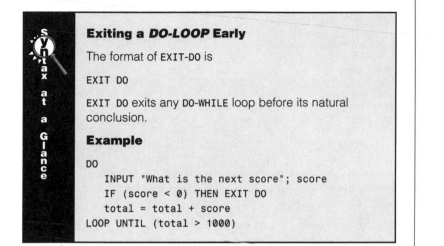

Exiting a *DO-LOOP* Early

The format of EXIT-DO is

EXIT DO

EXIT DO exits any DO-WHILE loop before its natural conclusion.

Example

```
DO
    INPUT "What is the next score"; score
    IF (score < 0) THEN EXIT DO
    total = total + score
LOOP UNTIL (total > 1000)
```

Listing 7.14 is the high-temperature city program changed so that only the first three cities with temperatures over 90 degrees are printed. When three city names and temperatures are printed, the EXIT DO takes control and forces the end of the DO-LOOP. If the end of data is reached before three values are printed, the DO-LOOP ends naturally at the DO-UNTIL.

Listing 7.14. A *DO-LOOP* illustrating the *EXIT DO* statement.

```
' Reads city names and temperatures, then prints
' the first three high temperature cities

city.count = 0
' Initialize screen with titles
CLS
PRINT "List of high temperature cities:"
PRINT
PRINT "City Name"; TAB(20); "Temperature"

READ city$, temp      ' Initial READ to start data checking
DO UNTIL (city$ = "-99")   ' (temp = -99) would work too
    IF (temp > 90) THEN
        PRINT city$; TAB(20); temp
        city.count = city.count + 1
    END IF
    IF (city.count > 2) THEN EXIT DO ' Quit if 3 have been
                                     ' printed
    READ city$, temp
```

continues

Listing 7.14. Continued

```
LOOP    ' The bottom of the cycle

DATA "Memphis", 90, "Miami", 94, "Salem", 86
DATA "Tulsa", 97, "San Francisco", 83, "Dallas", 98
DATA "Bangor", 76, "Juno", 65, "Chicago", 89
DATA "New York", 88, "Atlanta", 95, "Burbank", 79
DATA "New Orleans", 93, "Boston", 84, "Phoenix", 98
DATA "-99", -99
```

As you can see from the output of Listing 7.14, six cities have temperatures over 90, but only the first three are printed because of the EXIT DO statement:

```
List of high temperature cities:
City Name        Temperature
Miami            94
Tulsa            97
Dallas           98
```

Summary

You can now control your programs using FOR-NEXT statements and WHILE-WEND and DO WHILE loops. Loops enable you to perform repetitive tasks such as reading data, calculating totals, and printing reports.

Here are some of the things you learned in this chapter:

■ The FOR-NEXT loop offers a way for you to control how many times a set of statements executes.

■ With FOR-NEXT loops, you can count up or down depending on the FOR statement's STEP value.

■ You can nest FOR-NEXT loops within each other, compounding the effect of single FOR-NEXT statements.

■ WHILE-WEND control statements provide a way to control a series of statements as long as a specific relational test is true. QBasic offers WHILE-WEND to maintain compatibility with programs written for older versions of BASIC.

■ QBasic provides four DO statements that provide more flexibility and program control than the WHILE-WEND statements. These statements are DO WHILE-LOOP, DO-LOOP WHILE, DO UNTIL-LOOP, and DO-LOOP UNTIL.

Data Structures

This chapter begins a new approach to an old concept for storing data. In other chapters, you stored data in memory variables. In this chapter, you learn how to store data in array variables.

Conquering arrays is your next step toward understanding advanced uses of QBasic. This chapter's examples are some of the longest programs you have seen in the book. Arrays are not difficult, but their power makes them more suited to advanced programs.

What Is an Array?

An *array* is a list of more than one variable with the same name. Not every list of variables is an array. For example, the following list of four variables is *not* an array:

```
sales       bonus.92       first.name$       ctr
```

This is a list of variables (four of them) but not an array because each variable has a different name. You might wonder how more than one variable can have the same name—this seems to violate the rules of variables. If two variables have the same name, how does QBasic know which one you want?

A numeric *subscript* differentiates the variables (also called *elements*) of an array. Before discussing definitions, however, an example might help.

Good Array Candidates

Suppose you want to keep track of 35 people in your neighborhood association. You might want to track their names and their monthly dues. Their dues are fixed, and are different for each person because they joined the association at different times and bought houses with different prices.

Without arrays, you would have to store each person's name in a different variable and each person's dues in a different variable. That would make for a complex and lengthy program! To enter the data, you would have something like this:

```
INPUT "What is the name of the 1st family"; family1$
INPUT "What are their dues"; dues1
INPUT "What is the name of the 2nd family"; family2$
INPUT "What are their dues"; dues2
                  :      ' Remaining INPUTs go here
INPUT "What is the name of the 35th family"; family35$
INPUT "What are their dues"; dues35
```

Every time you had to print a list of members, calculate average dues, or use any of this data, you would have to scan at least 35 variable names. This would quickly become tiring. (Imagine if the neighborhood grew to 500 residents!) Arrays were developed because creating and processing different variable names for similar data is too cumbersome and requires too much time.

Arrays let you store similar data in a single variable. In effect, each data value has the same name. You use a numeric subscript to differentiate the values (the elements in the array).

For example, we started out using a different variable name—`family1$`, `dues1`, `family2$`, `dues2`, and so on—for the neighborhood association data. Instead, you can give similar data the same variable name—`family$` and `dues`—and differentiate them with subscripts, as shown in Table 8.1.

Table 8.1. Using arrays to store similar data.

Old Names	Array Names
family1$, dues1	family$(1), dues(1)
family2$, dues2	family$(2), dues(2)
⋮ ⋮	⋮ ⋮
family35$, dues35	family$(35), dues(35)

"Where is the improvement?" you might ask. The column of array names has a major advantage over the old variable names. The number inside parentheses is the *subscript number* of the array. Subscript numbers differentiate one array element from another (and are always enclosed in parentheses). They are never part of an array name.

> **NOTE** Because the subscript number (the only thing that differentiates one array element from another) is not part of the array name, you can use a FOR-NEXT loop or any other counter variable to input, process, and output any or all elements in an array.

How many arrays are listed in Table 8.1? If you said 2, you are correct. There are 35 elements in each array. How many nonarray variables are there in Table 8.1? There are 70 (35 family name variables and 35 dues variables). The difference between array and nonarray variables is very important when you consider how they can be processed.

For instance, to input every family name and their dues when each had a different name, you would need 70 statements. Now, using the 2 arrays, you need only 4 statements, as follows:

```
FOR sub = 1 to 35
   INPUT "What is the name of the 1st family member";
     ➡ family$(sub)
   INPUT "What are their dues"; dues(sub)
NEXT sub
```

This is a major advantage! Notice that the FOR-NEXT loop keeps incrementing sub throughout the data input of all 70 values. The first time through the loop, sub is equal to 1, so the user enters a value into family$(1) and dues(1). The loop then increments sub to 2 and the input process begins for the next two variables. The FOR-NEXT loop could not be used to process a group of differently named variables, even if their names contained numbers, as in the first method.

These four lines of code are much easier to write and maintain than the previous seventy lines, and they do the same thing. This code uses two arrays of 35 elements, rather than two groups of 35 different variable names.

8

Any time you work with a list of similar data, an array works best. Arrays make your input, process, and output routines much easier to write. QBasic initializes all array elements to 0 (and initializes all string arrays to null strings).

Using *DIM* to Set Up Arrays

When you set up an array, you must tell QBasic that you are going to use a specific number of array elements. To do this, you use the DIM (which means *dimension)* statement. In the last example, you would have to dimension 35 string array elements called family$ and 35 single-precision array elements called dues.

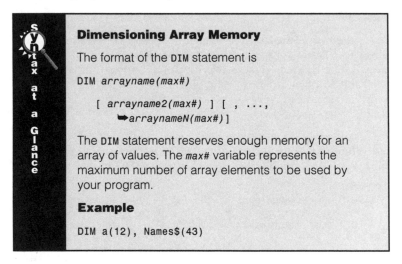

Dimensioning Array Memory

The format of the DIM statement is

```
DIM arrayname(max#)

    [ arrayname2(max#) ] [ , ...,
        ➥arraynameN(max#)]
```

The DIM statement reserves enough memory for an array of values. The *max#* variable represents the maximum number of array elements to be used by your program.

Example

```
DIM a(12), Names$(43)
```

If you want to declare a data type for an array, make sure you put the proper symbol after the array's name and before the opening parenthesis. For example, to dimension the family$ and dues arrays, you would type the following:

```
DIM family$(35), dues(35)
```

The dollar sign follows family because it must be a character string array. There is no symbol after dues because it defaults to a single-precision array. Remember: All elements in an array must be the same type (such as string or integer), and that type is determined when you dimension the array.

Typically, programmers dimension all arrays as early in the program as possible. A good location is after the opening remarks. The first subscript is always 0 (later you see a way to override this). The highest subscript (the maximum number of elements in the array) is determined by the DIM statement. You can dimension a maximum of 32,767 elements in an array. This should be more than enough for most purposes.

 **NOTE** Arrays contain one more element than the DIM statement reserves because the first usable subscript in an array is 0. Most QBasic programmers ignore this 0 element and begin subscripting at 1. The choice to start subscripting at 0 is up to you.

Because all the elements in an array have the same type, you can use them in calculations, just like you use nonarray variables. For example:

```
dues(5) = dues(4) * 1.5
```

Table 8.2 consolidates reserving arrays into a meaningful format. Study the table before going further. If you have forgotten the variable type symbols for single precision, double precision, and integers, review Chapter 3.

Table 8.2. Array declarations and subscripts.

DIM Statement	Type	Array Name	First Element	Last Element
DIM months(12)	single	months	months(0)	months(12)
DIM names$(5)	string	names	names$(0)	names$(5)
DIM temp#(300)	double	temps	temps#(0)	temps#(300)
DIM sales!(20)	single	sales	sales(0)	sales(20)
DIM ages%(10)	integer	ages	ages(0)	ages(10)

You can dimension a maximum of 32,767 elements in an array. This should be more than enough for most purposes.

8

To further illustrate the way an array works, suppose you dimensioned an array called ages to 8 elements, as follows:

```
DIM ages(8)
```

The elements are numbered ages(0) through ages(8), as shown in Figure 8.1. The values of each element are filled in when the program runs with INPUT, assignment, or READ-DATA statements.

ages

ages(0)
ages(1)
ages(2)
ages(3)
ages(4)
ages(5)
ages(6)
ages(7)
ages(8)

Figure 8.1. *The nine elements, ages[0] to ages[8], of the ages array.*

In the examples that follow, array elements are filled by INPUT and READ-DATA statements. Most programs, however, get their input data from disk files. When your array will be storing large amounts of data, you do not want to type that data into the variables every time you run a program. In addition, READ-DATA statements are not efficient statements to use for extremely large amounts of data. For now, concentrate on how arrays operate. In an upcoming chapter, you see how they can be initialized from data on a disk drive.

Listing 8.1 is the full program that dimensions two arrays for the neighborhood association's 35 family names and their dues. It prompts for all the neighborhood data, then prints it. If you enter this program, you might want to change 35 to 5 or so to reduce the amount of typing.

Listing 8.1. Neighborhood association program for 35 families.

```
' Program to gather and print 35 names and dues
DIM family$(35)    ' Reserve the array elements
DIM dues(35)
CLS
FOR subsc = 1 TO 35
   INPUT "What is the next family's name"; family$(subsc)
   INPUT "What are their dues"; dues(subsc)
NEXT subsc

subsc = 1     ' Initialize the first subscript
DO
   PRINT "Family"; subsc; "is "; family$(subsc)
   PRINT "Their dues are"; dues(subsc)
   subsc = subsc + 1
LOOP UNTIL (subsc > 35)      ' Prints all the input data
```

Notice that the program inputs and prints all these names and dues with simple routines. The input routine uses a FOR-NEXT loop and the printing routine uses a DO-LOOP. The method you use to control the loop is not critical. The important thing to see at this point is that array subscripts make it possible to input and print lots of data, without writing lots of code.

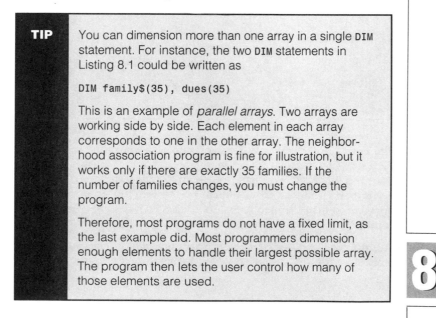

TIP You can dimension more than one array in a single DIM statement. For instance, the two DIM statements in Listing 8.1 could be written as

```
DIM family$(35), dues(35)
```

This is an example of *parallel arrays*. Two arrays are working side by side. Each element in each array corresponds to one in the other array. The neighborhood association program is fine for illustration, but it works only if there are exactly 35 families. If the number of families changes, you must change the program.

Therefore, most programs do not have a fixed limit, as the last example did. Most programmers dimension enough elements to handle their largest possible array. The program then lets the user control how many of those elements are used.

8

Listing 8.2 is similar to Listing 8.1, except it dimensions 500 elements for each array. This reserves more than enough array elements for the association. The user then inputs the required number (from 1 to 500). The program is flexible, allowing a variable number of members to be input and printed each time the program runs (up to a limit of 500 members).

Listing 8.2. Neighborhood association program for up to 500 families.

```
' Program to gather and print up to 500 names and dues
DIM family$(500), dues(500)    ' Reserve the array elements
CLS
subsc = 1     ' Initial subscript to get loop started
' The following loop asks for family names and dues until the
' user presses ENTER without typing a name. Whenever a null
' input is given (just an ENTER keypress), the DO-LOOP exits
' early with sub holding the number input to that point.
DO
    PRINT "Please type the family's name"
    INPUT "(Press ENTER without typing a name if you are
    ➥finished"; family$(subsc)
    IF (family$(subsc) = "") THEN subsc = subsc -1 EXIT DO
' Preceding line triggers early exit
    INPUT "What are their dues"; dues(subsc)
    subsc = subsc + 1      ' Add one to the subscript variable
LOOP UNTIL (subsc > 500)

' When the last loop finishes, sub holds the number input

FOR ctr = 1 to subsc      ' Loop through each family just
                          ' entered
    PRINT "Family"; ctr; "is "; family$(ctr)
    PRINT "Their dues are"; dues(ctr)
NEXT ctr                  ' Prints all the input data
```

The empty Enter keypress is a good way to trigger the early exit of the loop. Just because 500 elements are reserved for each array does not mean that you have to use all of them. Dimensioning more than enough array elements is common, but do not go overboard. Too many array dimensioned elements could cause your computer to run out of memory.

You do not have to access an array in the same order as it was entered. In addition, later sections of this chapter show you how to change the order of an array. You can use the subscript to select items from a list (array) of values.

Listing 8.3 requests salary data for the last twelve months. It then waits until a user requests a certain month's salary data, and prints the requested data. This is how you could begin to build a search program to find requested data—store the data in an array or on a disk file that can be read into an array (as you will soon see), then wait for a request from the user to see specific pieces of that data.

Listing 8.3. Monthly salary program.

```
' Store 12 months of salaries, and print selected ones
'
DIM salary(12)  ' Reserve enough elements for the 12 salaries
CLS
FOR subsc = 1 TO 12
   PRINT "What is the salary for month"; subsc;
   INPUT salary(subsc) ' The trailing semicolon keeps the
                       ' question mark after the prompt
NEXT subsc
' Clear the screen, and wait for a requested month
CLS
PRINT "*** Salary Printing Program ***"
PRINT "Prints any salary from the last 12 months"
PRINT
' Request the month number
DO
   PRINT "You want to see a salary for which month (1-12)"
   INPUT "(Type 0 to end the program)"; month.num
   PRINT
IF month.num = 0 THEN EXIT DO
   PRINT "The salary for month"; month.num; "is";
      ➥salary(month.num)
   INPUT "Do you want to see another (Y/N)"; ans$
LOOP WHILE (ans$ = "Y")
```

After the 12 salaries are entered into the array, any or all of them can be requested one at a time, simply by supplying the month number (the number of the subscript).

Listing 8.4 shows some of the calculations you can perform on arrays. The program asks the user to input a temperature, until the user enters –99 to signal that there are no more temperatures. The program then computes the average temperature by adding each entry and dividing by the total number of entries.

Listing 8.4. Temperature averaging program.

```
' Prompt the user for a list of temperatures and average them

DIM temp(100)    ' Up to 100 temperatures can be entered
total.temp = 0   ' Holds totals as the user enters the temps
CLS

' Prompt user for each temperature
FOR temp.sub = 1 TO 100    ' Maximum limit
   PRINT "What is temperature number"; temp.sub
   INPUT "(type -99 to end the input)"; temp(temp.sub)
   ' If user wants to stop, decrease total count by 1
   ' and exit loop
   IF (temp(temp.sub) = -99) EXIT FOR
   total.temp = total.temp + temp(temp.sub)   ' Add to total
NEXT temp.sub
temp.sub = temp.sub -1

avg.temp = total.temp / temp.sub
PRINT
PRINT "The average temperature was"; avg.temp
```

The *OPTION BASE* Statement

Until now, every array's first element was 0. This is the QBasic default. However, you can change the default to 1 with the OPTION BASE statement.

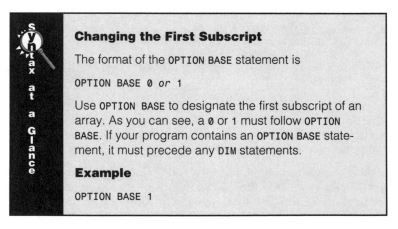

Changing the First Subscript

The format of the OPTION BASE statement is

OPTION BASE 0 *or* 1

Use OPTION BASE to designate the first subscript of an array. As you can see, a 0 or 1 must follow OPTION BASE. If your program contains an OPTION BASE statement, it must precede any DIM statements.

Example

OPTION BASE 1

The first subscript of any array is always 0, unless you change it to 1 with OPTION BASE 1. As mentioned, most QBasic programmers ignore the 0 subscript. If you precede the DIM statement with OPTION BASE 1, QBasic will not use the 0 subscript and will reserve storage locations only for subscripts 1 through the dimensioned number.

Listing 8.5 reads day names into 7 variables. The program does not contain an OPTION BASE statement, so only 6 elements have to be dimensioned because you can use subscript 0.

Listing 8.5. Days-of-the-week program without the *OPTION BASE* statement.

```
DIM days$(6)        ' For elements days(0) through days(6)
FOR ctr - 0 TO 6
   READ days$(ctr)
NEXT ctr
DATA "Sunday", "Monday", "Tuesday", "Wednesday", "Thursday"
DATA "Friday", "Saturday"
' Print them out
FOR ctr = 0 to 6
   PRINT "Day"; ctr; "is "; days$(ctr)
NEXT ctr
```

Putting an OPTION BASE 0 statement in this program would be redundant because QBasic always assumes that arrays are zero based.

Listing 8.6 is like Listing 8.5, except an OPTION BASE statement has been added. It informs QBasic that the base subscript (the first one) will be 1. Therefore, 7 elements must be dimensioned.

Listing 8.6. Days-of-the-week program with the *OPTION BASE* statement.

```
OPTION BASE 1
DIM days$(7)        ' For elements days(1) through days(7)
FOR ctr = 1 TO 7
   READ days$(ctr)
NEXT ctr
DATA "Sunday", "Monday", "Tuesday", "Wednesday", "Thursday"
DATA "Friday", "Saturday"
' Print them out
FOR ctr = 1 to 7
   PRINT "Day"; ctr; "is "; days$(ctr)
NEXT ctr
```

8

Searching and Sorting Arrays

Arrays are the primary means by which data is stored in QBasic programs. As mentioned, array data is usually read from a disk. Chapter 11 explains disk processing. For now, you should understand how to manipulate arrays so that you see the data exactly the way you want to see it.

The original order of an array is not always the best order for your application. For instance, suppose that a school uses a QBasic program for enrollment information. A clerk at the computer types each student's name as he or she enrolls, until all the names are in the computer, stored in a string array.

What if the school wants a listing of each student's name in alphabetical order? The students did not enroll in name order, so you cannot write a FOR-NEXT loop to print the elements from 1 to the total number of students.

You need a method for *sorting* an array in a specific order. When you sort an array, you put the array in a specific order, such as alphabetical or numerical. For example, a dictionary and a phone book are sorted. You can also reverse the order of a sort and do a *descending sort*. For instance, in a list of all employees in descending salary order, the highest paid employees are printed first.

Learning how to search an array for a value is a preliminary step in learning to sort. What if a student marries and wants her name changed? Neither the student nor the clerk knows which element the student's name is stored under. As the following section shows, however, the computer can search for the name.

Searching for Values

You don't need to know any new commands to search an array for a value—just use the IF-THEN and FOR-NEXT statements. To search an array for a value, simply look at each element in that array and use IF-THEN to compare the value with the element to see if they match. If they do, you have found the value. If they do not, keep searching down the array. If you run out of array elements before finding the value, the value is not in the array.

You can perform several kinds of searches. You might need to find the highest or lowest value in a list (array) of numbers. This is informative when you have lots of data and want to know the extremes of the data (such as the highest and lowest sales region in your division).

The following programs illustrate some of these array searching techniques. This example prints the highest sales of a company's sales staff.

To find the highest number in an array, you compare each element to the first one. If you find a higher value, it becomes the basis for the rest of the array. Continue until you reach the end of the array and you will have the highest value, as the Listing 8.7 shows.

Listing 8.7. Program to compute the highest sales.

```
' Find the highest sales total in the data
' Reserve room for up to 25 sales values
DIM sales(25)
' Read all the data into the array
subsc = 1     ' Array subscript
DO
    READ sales(subsc)
    subsc = subsc + 1
LOOP UNTIL (sales(subsc - 1) = -99)
high.sales = sales(1)     ' Store first sales value
FOR ctr = 2 TO subsc      ' And compare all others to it
    ' Store current sales if it is higher than high sales so
far
    IF sales(ctr) > high.sales THEN
        high.sales = sales(ctr)
    END IF
NEXT ctr
PRINT "The highest sales were"; high.sales
DATA 2900, 5400, 3429, 3744, 7678, 4585, -99
```

Notice that no ELSE or ELSEIF is needed because you save the high sales information only if you find a higher value than the one you are comparing. Finding the smallest value in an array is just as easy. However, make sure you compare to see if each succeeding array element is less than the lowest value found so far.

Sorting Arrays

Many times, you need to sort one or more arrays. Suppose you had a group of names, each on a separate piece of paper, and threw them in the air. The steps you would take to alphabetize the names—changing the order of the pieces of paper—are similar to what your computer does when it sorts numbers or character data.

Because sorting arrays requires exchanging values of elements, it helps to learn a new command in QBasic called the SWAP command.

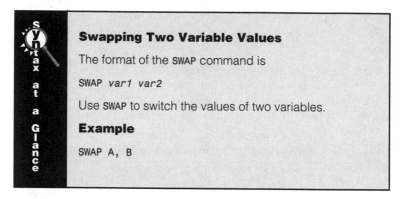

Swapping Two Variable Values

The format of the SWAP command is

SWAP *var1 var2*

Use SWAP to switch the values of two variables.

Example

SWAP A, B

You can sort arrays in several ways, such as the *bubble sort*, the *quicksort*, and the *shell sort*. The basic goal in each method is to compare each array element to another array element and swap them if necessary to put them in order.

The theory behind these sorts is beyond the scope of this book. The bubble sort, however, is one of the easiest to follow. Values in an array are compared a pair at a time, and swapped if they are not in order. The lowest value eventually "floats" to the top of the list, like a bubble in a glass of water.

Listing 8.8 reads 15 random numbers into an array and prints them in sorted order.

Listing 8.8. Sorting and printing numbers using the bubble sort.

```
' Sort and print a list of numbers
DIM number(15)
CLS
PRINT "Here are the unsorted numbers:"
FOR ctr = 0 TO 14
    READ number(ctr)
    PRINT number(ctr);
NEXT ctr

DATA 4, 3, 17, 5, 23, 44, 54, 8, 7, 54, 33, 22, 42, 48
DATA 90

FOR ctr1 = 0 TO 14
    FOR ctr2 = ctr1 TO 14  ' Each element is compared to its
                           ' predecessor
```

```
          IF number(ctr1) >= number(ctr2) THEN
              SWAP number(ctr1), number(ctr2)    ' "Float" the lowest
                                                 ' to the top
          END IF
      NEXT ctr2
  NEXT ctr1

  ' Print them to show that they are sorted
  PRINT
  LINE INPUT "Press Enter to see the sorted numbers..."; ans$
  FOR ctr = 0 TO 14
      PRINT number(ctr);
  NEXT ctr
```

Here is the output from Listing 8.8:

```
Here are the unsorted numbers:
 4  3  17  5  23  44  54  8  7  54  33  22  42  48  90
Press Enter to see the sorted numbers...
 3  4  5  7  8  17  22  23  33  42  44  48  54  54  90
```

Notice that even the two numbers that are the same (54) sort next to each other as they should. Listing 8.9 is similar to listing 8.8, except it prints the list of numbers in descending order:

Listing 8.9. Sorting and printing numbers in descending order using the bubble sort.

```
' Sort and print a descending list of numbers
DIM number(15)
CLS
PRINT "Here are the unsorted numbers:"
FOR ctr = 0 TO 14
    READ number(ctr)
    PRINT number(ctr);
NEXT ctr

DATA 4, 3, 17, 5, 23, 44, 54, 8, 7, 54, 33, 22, 42, 48
DATA 90

FOR ctr1 = 0 TO 14
    FOR ctr2 = ctr1 TO 14
        IF number(ctr1) < number(ctr2) THEN
            SWAP number(ctr1), number(ctr2)
        END IF
    NEXT ctr2
NEXT ctr1
```

continues

Listing 8.9. Continued

```
' Print them to show that they are sorted
PRINT
LINE INPUT "Press Enter to see the sorted numbers..."; ans$
FOR ctr = 0 TO 14
    PRINT number(ctr);
NEXT ctr
```

You can also sort character data. The computer uses the ASCII table to decide how the characters sort. Listing 8.10 reads and sorts a list of names.

Listing 8.10. Sorting and printing names using the bubble sort.

```
' Sort and print a list of names
DIM names$(15)
CLS
PRINT "Here are the unsorted names:"
FOR ctr = 0 TO 14
    READ names$(ctr)
    PRINT names$(ctr); " ";
NEXT ctr

DATA "Jim", "Larry", "Julie", "Kimberly", "John", "Mark",
➡"Mary", "Terry"
DATA "Rhonda", "Jane", "Adam", "Richard", "Hans", "Ada",
➡"Robert", "-99"

FOR ctr1 = 0 TO 14
    FOR ctr2 = ctr1 TO 14
        IF names$(ctr1) > names$(ctr2) THEN
            SWAP names$(ctr1), names$(ctr2)
        END IF
    NEXT ctr2
NEXT ctr1

' Print them to show that they are sorted
PRINT
LINE INPUT "Press Enter to see the sorted names:"; ans$
FOR ctr = 0 TO 14
    PRINT names$(ctr); " ";
NEXT ctr
```

Ada sorts before *Adam*, as it should. Remember the goal of a sort is to reorder the array but not change the contents of the array elements. The subscripts change in a sort, but the data values do not change.

The *ERASE* Statement

The ERASE statement erases the contents of an array. It does this by zeroing all elements in a numeric array or by putting null strings into each element of a character string array.

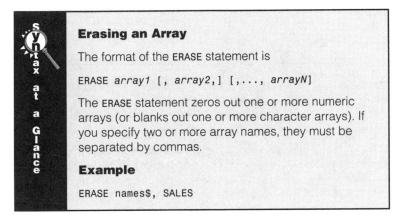

Erasing an Array

The format of the ERASE statement is

ERASE *array1* [, *array2*,] [,..., *arrayN*]

The ERASE statement zeros out one or more numeric arrays (or blanks out one or more character arrays). If you specify two or more array names, they must be separated by commas.

Example

ERASE names$, SALES

There is no reason to use the ERASE statement immediately after dimensioning an array, because QBasic automatically clears all elements when an array is dimensioned. However, if you must replace the values in an array with a different set of values, the ERASE statement is a quick way to clear the array. This beats the older BASIC method of writing a loop to clear out each element in the array.

An Array as a Table

Suppose a softball team wants to keep track of its players' hits. There are 8 players on the team, and they played 6 games. Table 8.3 shows the team's hit record.

Table 8.3. A softball team's hit record.

Player Name	Game 1	Game 2	Game 3	Game 4	Game 5	Game 6
Adams	2	1	0	0	2	3
Berryhill	1	0	3	2	5	1
Downing	1	0	2	1	0	0
Edwards	0	3	6	4	6	4
Franks	2	2	3	2	1	0

continues

Table 8.3. Continued

Player Name	Game 1	Game 2	Game 3	Game 4	Game 5	Game 6
Grady	1	3	2	0	1	5
Howard	3	1	1	1	2	0
Jones	2	2	1	2	4	1

Note that the softball table is a two-dimensional table. It has rows (the first dimension) and columns (the second dimension). Therefore, you would call this a two-dimensional table with 8 rows and 6 columns. Generally, the number of rows is specified first.

Each row has a player's name, and each column is associated with a game number, but these are not part of the data. The data consists only of 48 values (8 rows times 6 columns equals 48 data values). The data in a table, like the data in an array, is always the same type of data (in this example, every value is an integer). If the table contained names, it would be a string table, and so on.

The number of dimensions corresponds to the dimensions in the physical world. The first dimension represents a line. The single-dimensional array is a line, or list, of values. Two dimensions represent length and width. You write on a piece of paper in two dimensions; two dimensions represent a flat surface. Three dimensions represent length, width, and depth. You may have seen a three-dimensional movie. Not only do the images have width and height, but they also (appear to) have depth.

It is difficult for us to visualize more than three dimensions. You can, however, think of each dimension after three as another occurrence. In other words, a list of one player's season hit record could be stored in a single-dimensional array. The team's hit record (as shown previously) is two-dimensional. The league, made up of several team's hit records, would represent a three-dimensional table. Each team (the depth of the table) would have rows and columns of hit data. If there is more than one league, leagues could be considered another dimension.

Although QBasic can store up to 60 dimensions, real world data rarely requires more than two or three dimensions.

Dimensioning Multidimensional Arrays

You use the DIM statement to reserve multidimensional tables. Rather than putting one value in the parentheses, you enter a value for each dimension in the table.

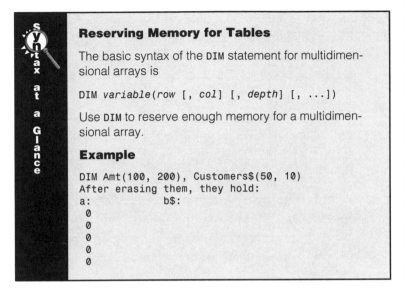

Reserving Memory for Tables

The basic syntax of the DIM statement for multidimensional arrays is

```
DIM variable(row [, col] [, depth] [, ...])
```

Use DIM to reserve enough memory for a multidimensional array.

Example

```
DIM Amt(100, 200), Customers$(50, 10)
After erasing them, they hold:
a:            b$:
0
0
0
0
0
```

Nothing is printed below the b$: column because null strings (sometimes called *empty strings*) contain nothing, not even a 0.

Multidimensional Arrays

Some types of data fit in lists; other data is better suited to a table of information. The previous sections introduced *single-dimensional arrays*, which are arrays with only one subscript.

A *multidimensional array* is an array with more than one subscript. Multidimensional arrays, sometimes called *tables* or *matrices*, have rows and columns. If you understand single-dimensional arrays, you should have no trouble understanding multidimensional ones.

A single-dimensional array is a list of values, whereas a multidimensional array simulates a table of values, or even multiple tables of values. The most commonly used table is a two-dimensional table (an array with two subscripts).

For example, to reserve the team data from Table 8.3, you would use the following DIM statement:

```
DIM teams(8, 6)
```

This requires a two-dimensional table with 48 elements. Figure 8.2 shows the subscript for each element (assuming an OPTION BASE of 1).

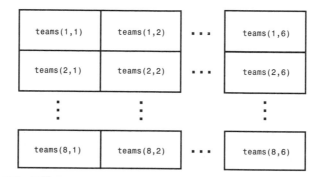

Figure 8.2. *Subscripts for the softball team table.*

If you needed to track three teams, and each team had 8 players and played 6 games, you could dimension the table as follows:

```
DIM teams(8, 6, 3)
```

This statement dimensions three occurrences of the team table shown in Figure 8.2.

When dimensioning a table, always put the maximum number of rows first and the maximum number of columns second. Because QBasic always assumes a starting subscript of 0, unless you override it with the OPTION BASE command, the two-dimensional DIM statement shown previously—DIM teams(8, 6)—actually stores up to 9 rows (numbered 0 through 8) and 7 columns (numbered 0 through 6).

Most programmers, however, ignore the 0 subscript. If you want to keep the total number of rows and columns the same as that in the DIM statement, be sure to use the OPTION BASE statement to set the starting subscript to 1, as in

```
OPTION BASE 1
DIM teams(8, 6)
```

OPTION BASE sets the starting value for both subscripts to 1 or 0. You cannot set only one of them with OPTION BASE.

If you are keeping track of complex subscripted data, you can use the TO option of the DIM statement to dimension a table with different starting and ending subscripts. The following statement dimensions a three-dimensional table. The first dimension (the number of rows) subscripts from –5 to 6. The second dimension (the number of columns) subscripts from 200 to 300. The third dimension (the number of depth values, or the number of sets of rows and columns) is subscripted from 5 to 10.

```
DIM ara1(-5 TO 6, 200 TO 300, 5 TO 10)
```

Using different starting and ending subscripts can be confusing, and it's not always much more useful than simply using the default subscript values. Therefore, you rarely see this complex type of DIM statement for multidimensional arrays.

You can combine several DIM statements into one. For instance, the following line reserves storage for three multidimensional arrays:

```
DIM ara1(10, 20), ara2(4, 5, 5), ara3(6, 10, 20, 30)
```

Assuming an OPTION BASE of 1, the first multidimensional array, ara1, reserves 200 elements. The second array reserves 100 elements (4 times 5 times 5). The third reserves 36,000 elements (6 times 10 times 20 times 30). As you can see, the number of elements adds up quickly.

Be careful that you do not reserve so many array elements that you run out of memory for storing them. If you run out of memory, you receive the following error message:

```
Subscript out of range
```

NOTE	As with single-dimensional arrays, QBasic always initializes numeric table values to 0 and string table values to null strings.

Tables and *FOR-NEXT* Loops

As you will see in the programs that follow, nested FOR-NEXT loops are good candidates for looping through every element of a multi-dimensional table. For instance, this section of code:

```
FOR row = 1 to 2
   FOR col = 1 to 3
      PRINT row, col
   NEXT col
NEXT row
```

8

produces the following output:

```
1          1
1          2
1          3
2          1
2          2
2          3
```

These are the subscripts, in row order, for a two-row-by-three-column table that is dimensioned in the following statement:

```
DIM table(2, 3)
```

Notice that there are as many FOR-NEXT statements in the code as there are subscripts in the DIM statement (two). The outside loop represents the first subscript (the rows), and the inside loop represents the second subscript (the columns).

INPUT statements can be used to fill a table, but programmers rarely do so. Most multidimensional array data comes from READ and DATA statements or, more often, data files from the disk. Regardless of what method you use to store values in multidimensional arrays, nested FOR-NEXT loops are excellent control statements to step through the subscripts.

Listing 8.11 is a comprehensive program that reads in the softball team hits shown in Table 8.3. The values are read from DATA statements. This program shows the usefulness of arrays. Instead of simply printing the complete table, it processes the table's raw data into meaningful information by supplying the following information:

A list showing each player's total hits for the season

The name of the player with the most hits

The name of the player with the fewest hits

The game with the most hits

The game with the fewest hits

The player names cannot be stored in the table with the hit data because the names are string data and the hits are stored as integers. Therefore, a separate single-dimensional array that holds the player names is read. When the numbers of the rows with the most and fewest hits are known, those two player's names are printed from the player name array using the row number.

Listing 8.11. Softball league statistics program.

```
' Program to display stats from the team's softball league
' Reserve storage for hits and player names
OPTION BASE 1
DIM hits(8, 6), player$(8)
CLS
' Read the data into a table
FOR row = 1 TO 8    ' First read the hit data
   FOR col = 1 TO 6
      READ hits(row, col)
   NEXT col
NEXT row

FOR ctr = 1 TO 8    ' Now read the player names
   READ player$(ctr)
NEXT ctr

' Find and print each player's total hits
' and find highest and lowest
highest = 0    ' Ensure that first player's hits
               ' are more than highest
lowest = 999   ' and less than lowest to start
               ' the ball rolling
PRINT "Name", "Total Hits"
FOR row = 1 TO 8
   total = 0       ' Initialize before each player's hit total
   FOR col = 1 TO 6
      total = total + hits(row, col)
   NEXT col
   PRINT player$(row), total
   IF (total > highest) THEN high.row = row: highest = total
   IF (total < lowest) THEN low.row = row: lowest = total
NEXT row
PRINT
PRINT player$(high.row); " had the highest number of hits ";
PRINT "at"; highest
PRINT player$(low.row); " had the lowest number of hits ";
PRINT "at"; lowest
highest = 0    ' Ensure first game's hits are more than highest
lowest = 999   ' and less than lowest to start the ball rolling
FOR col = 1 TO 6   ' Step through columns to add game totals
   total = 0       ' Initialize before each game
   FOR row = 1 TO 8
      total = total + hits(row, col)
   NEXT row
   IF (total > highest) THEN high.game = col: highest = total
   IF (total < lowest) THEN low.game = col: lowest = total
NEXT col
PRINT
PRINT "Game number"; high.game; "had the highest number of ";
PRINT "hits at"; highest
```

continues

Listing 8.11. Continued

```
PRINT "Game number"; low.game; "had the lowest number of ";
PRINT "hits at"; lowest

DATA 2, 1, 0, 0, 2, 3, 1, 0, 3, 2, 5, 1
DATA 1, 0, 2, 1, 0, 0, 0, 3, 6, 4, 6, 4
DATA 2, 2, 3, 2, 1, 0, 1, 3, 2, 0, 1, 5
DATA 3, 1, 1, 1, 2, 0, 2, 2, 1, 2, 4, 1
DATA Adams, Berryhill, Downing, Edwards
DATA Franks, Grady, Howard, Jones
```

Here is the output from Listing 8.11:

```
Name           Total Hits
Adams          8
Berryhill      12
Downing        4
Edwards        23
Franks         10
Grady          12
Howard         8
Jones          12

Edwards had the highest number of hits at 23
Downing had the lowest number of hits at 4

Game number 5 had the highest number of hits at 21
Game number 1 had the lowest number of hits at 12
```

Summary

This chapter covered a lot of ground. You learned about arrays and multidimensional tables. By stepping through the values of an array or table, your program can quickly scan, print, sort, and calculate a large number of values. You now have the tools to sort lists of names and numbers, as well as search for values in a table.

Here are some of the things you learned in this chapter:

- The DIM statement reserves memory for arrays and matrices.

- Nested FOR-NEXT loops make working with multidimensional arrays easy.

- The OPTION BASE command changes the subscript's starting value from its 0 default.

- ERASE erases the elements of an array or table.

- QBasic enables you to create tables of up to 60 dimensions. DIM statement options enable you to specify which subscripts are used in tables.

Built-In Functions

You have already seen several methods of writing routines that
make your computer work for you. This chapter shows you
ways to increase QBasic's productivity. It shows you the ways
to use the many built-in routines that work with numbers and
strings. These are called *functions*. By learning the functions,
you can let QBasic manipulate your mathematical and string
data.

This chapter explores several built-in functions. After you
learn about the built-in functions, Chapter 10 teaches you how
to write your own functions.

Although some of the built-in functions are highly technical,
many of them are used daily by QBasic programmers who do
not use much math in their programs. Most of the built-in
functions reduce your programming time. Instead of having to
"reinvent the wheel" every time you need QBasic to perform a
numeric or string operation, you might be able to use one of
the many built-in functions to do the job for you.

Overview of Functions

Functions are built-in routines that manipulate numbers,
strings, and output. You have already seen two functions that
manipulate output: the TAB() and SPC() functions inside the
PRINT and LPRINT statements. By putting a number in parentheses after the function name, you space output by a tab stop
or by a certain number of spaces.

You have also seen the string function CHR$(). By putting a
number inside the parentheses, you can print the character
that corresponds to that number in the ASCII table.

Each of these functions illustrates what all functions (numeric, string, and output) have in common: the function name is always followed by parentheses. The value in the parentheses determines what the function does. It is called an *argument*. Without the argument, the function has no parameters on which to work.

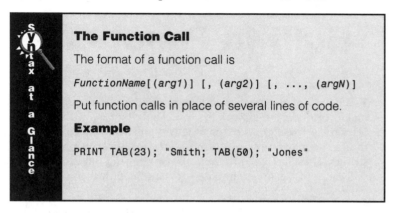

The Function Call

The format of a function call is

```
FunctionName[(arg1)] [, (arg2)] [, ..., (argN)]
```

Put function calls in place of several lines of code.

Example

```
PRINT TAB(23); "Smith; TAB(50); "Jones"
```

Notice that a function can have no arguments, one argument, or more than one argument, depending on how it is defined. A function never stands by itself on a line; you always combine functions with other statements (assignment statements, output statements, and so on).

A function always *returns* a value as well. Output functions always perform a cursor movement. Numeric and string functions return either a number or a string based on the argument you send to them. When a numeric function returns a value, you must do something with that value: print it, assign it to a variable, or use it in an expression. Because the purpose of a function is to return a value, you cannot put a function on the left side of an assignment statement.

Math Functions

There are several functions supplied by QBasic that perform math routines, and this section introduces you to those functions. Using these functions can save you much code. There are several integer and mathematical functions, and they are easy to use.

Integer Functions

The following functions work only with integer data. There are times when you need to round values to whole values, such as when you compute counts and totals. QBasic supplies integer functions to round values in either direction—up or down.

Syntax at a Glance

The Integer Functions

The formats of the integer functions are

```
INT(numeric value)
```

```
FIX(numeric value)
```

```
CINT(numeric value)
```

```
CLNG(numeric value)
```

The integer functions modify the numeral you pass to them in some way, usually by a form of rounding.

Examples

```
PRINT INT(45.2)

S = FIX(Sales)

x = x + CINT(71.23 + a)

Num = CLNG(x + 12.3 * y)
```

One of the most common integer functions is the INT() function. It returns the integer value of the number you put in the parentheses. If you put a single-precision or double-precision number inside the parentheses, INT() converts it to an integer. For example,

```
PRINT INT(8.93)
```

prints an 8 (the function's return value) on-screen. INT() returns a value that is equal to or less than the argument in the parentheses. INT() does not round numbers up.

NOTE As with all math functions, you can—and normally should—use a variable or expression as the function's argument.

The following three expressions all print 8:

```
num = 8.93
PRINT INT(num)
```

```
num = 8
PRINT INT(num + 0.93)

num1 = 8.93
num2 = INT(num1)
PRINT num2
```

INT() works for negative arguments as well. The following line of code:

```
PRINT INT(-7.6)
```

prints -8. This might surprise you until you learn the complete definition of INT(). It returns the highest integer that is less than or equal to the argument in parentheses. The highest integer less than or equal to −7.6 is −8.

FIX() returns the *truncated* whole number value of the argument. Truncation means that the fractional part of the argument is taken off the number. FIX() always returns an integer value. The line

```
PRINT FIX(4.93)
```

prints the value of 4. With positive numbers, FIX() and INT() work identically. With negative numbers, FIX() and INT() return very different values. FIX() simply drops the fractional part of the number—whether it is positive or negative—from the argument. Therefore,

```
PRINT FIX(-8.93)
```

and

```
PRINT FIX(-8.02)
```

both print -8. INT() would return -9 in both examples because it returns the closest integer less than or equal to the argument.

INT() and FIX() both return whole numbers, but they return the whole numbers in single-precision format. For practical purposes, you can assume that INT() and FIX() return integers, because it appears that they do. Because they actually return whole-number, single-precision values, however, you can use them for much larger or smaller arguments than those that the integer data type can hold.

CINT() returns the closest rounded integer to the value of the argument. For positive numbers, if the fractional portion of the argument is less than or equal to one-half (.5), CINT() rounds down to the nearest whole number. Otherwise, it rounds upward. For negative numbers, CINT() rounds to the closest integer. For instance:

```
PRINT CINT(-8.1), CINT(-8.5), CINT(-8.5001), CINT(-8.8)
```

produces the following output:

```
-8           -8           -9           -9
```

`CINT()` has a limitation: it is limited to return values that fall within the range of –32,768 to 32,767 because it returns only the integer data type. Unlike with `INT()` and `FIX()`, you must use a different function if you want to round values outside these two extremes.

Use `CLNG()` (for *convert long integer*) if you need to round numbers outside `CINT()`'s extremes. If you attempt to use `CINT()` to round numbers larger or smaller than its extreme values, you get an error message that says `Overflow`. `CLNG()` rounds integers within the range of –2,147,483,648 to 2,147,483,647.

Listing 9.1 summarizes each of the four integer functions. It prints the return values of each integer function using several different arguments. Notice how each function differs for both positive and negative numbers.

Listing 9.1. A summary of each of the four integer functions.

```
' The four integer functions
CLS
PRINT "Argument", "INT()", "FIX()", "CINT()", "CLNG()"
PRINT "--------", "-----", "-----", "------", "------"
num = 10
PRINT num, INT(num), FIX(num), CINT(num), CLNG(num)
num = 10.5
PRINT num, INT(num), FIX(num), CINT(num), CLNG(num)
num = 10.51
PRINT num, INT(num), FIX(num), CINT(num), CLNG(num)
num = .1
PRINT num, INT(num), FIX(num), CINT(num), CLNG(num)
num = .5
PRINT num, INT(num), FIX(num), CINT(num), CLNG(num)
num = .51
PRINT num, INT(num), FIX(num), CINT(num), CLNG(num)
num = -.1
PRINT num, INT(num), FIX(num), CINT(num), CLNG(num)
num = -.5
PRINT num, INT(num), FIX(num), CINT(num), CLNG(num)
num = -.51
PRINT num, INT(num), FIX(num), CINT(num), CLNG(num)
num = -10
PRINT num, INT(num), FIX(num), CINT(num), CLNG(num)
num = -10.5
PRINT num, INT(num), FIX(num), CINT(num), CLNG(num)
num = -10.51
PRINT num, INT(num), FIX(num), CINT(num), CLNG(num)
END
```

The following is the output of Listing 9.1:

```
Argument    INT()      FIX()      CINT()     CLNG()
--------    -----      -----      ------     ------
   10        10         10         10         10
   10.5      10         10         10         10
   10.51     10         10         11         11
    .1        0          0          0          0
    .5        0          0          0          0
    .51       0          0          1          1
   -.1       -1          0          0          0
   -.5       -1          0          0          0
   -.51      -1          0         -1         -1
  -10       -10        -10        -10        -10
  -10.5     -11        -10        -10        -10
  -10.51    -11        -10        -11        -11
```

Other Common Math Functions

You don't have to be an expert in math to use many of the mathematical functions that come with QBasic. Often, even in business applications, the following functions come in handy:

Common Math Functions

The formats of the common math functions are

SQR(*numeric value*)

ABS(*numeric value*)

SGN(*numeric value*)

These functions are used to calculate a square root, find the absolute value, or determine a sign (positive or negative), respectively.

Examples

PRINT SQR(64)

x = ABS(-237)

IF (SGN(x)<>0) THEN PRINT "Turn on the printer."

SQR() returns the square root of its argument. The argument can be any positive data type. The square root is not defined for negative numbers. If you use a negative value as an argument to SQR(), you get an illegal function call error. The line

PRINT SQR(4), SQR(64), SQR(4096)

produces the following output:

```
2        8            64
```

The ABS() function, called the *absolute value* function, can be used in many programs as well. ABS() returns the absolute value of its argument. The absolute value of a number is simply the positive representation of a positive or negative number. Whatever argument you pass to ABS(), its positive value is returned. For example, the following line of code:

```
PRINT ABS(-5), ABS(-5.76), ABS(0), ABS(5), ABS(5.76)
```

produces the following output:

```
5        5.76         0            5           5.76
```

The SGN() function returns the following:

-1 if the argument is negative

0 if the argument is zero

+1 if the argument is positive

The SGN() function (called the *sign* function) determines the sign of its argument.

The *LEN()* Function

The LEN() function (which stands for *length*) is one of the few functions that can take either numeric or string variables as arguments. LEN() returns the number of bytes needed to hold a variable. The variable can be any data type. LEN() returns the length of the integer variable, single-precision variable, or double-precision variable. Most programmers do not care what internal size each variable takes. If you are preparing to dimension a single-precision array of 200 elements and you want to see how much memory the array will take, you can use the program in Listing 9.2.

Listing 9.2. A program to see how much memory it will take to dimension an array.

```
test! = 0      ' A sample single-precision variable
PRINT "The 200 element single-precision array will take"
PRINT (LEN(test!) * 200); "bytes of storage."
```

Listing 9.2 prints the following output:

```
800 "bytes of storage"
```

Each single-precision number takes four bytes of internal storage. You will see how to apply this function to string data later in this chapter.

String Functions

QBasic's string functions work in a manner similar to numeric functions. When you pass them an argument, they return a value you can store or print. String functions enable you to print strings in ways you never could before, as well as look at individual characters from a string.

The string-handling functions are what make QBasic excel over other computer languages. Few languages offer the string manipulation that QBasic does.

ASCII String Functions

You have already seen one of the ASCII string functions, the CHR$() function. When you enclose an ASCII number inside the CHR$() parentheses, QBasic substitutes the character that matches that ASCII value. Three additional string functions work with the ASCII table.

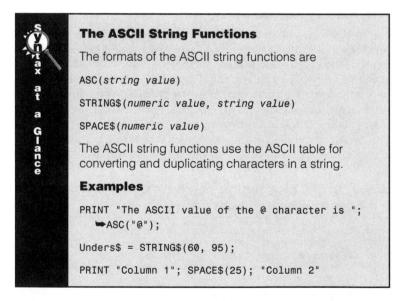

The ASCII String Functions

The formats of the ASCII string functions are

ASC(*string value*)

STRING$(*numeric value, string value*)

SPACE$(*numeric value*)

The ASCII string functions use the ASCII table for converting and duplicating characters in a string.

Examples

```
PRINT "The ASCII value of the @ character is ";
   ➥ASC("@");

Unders$ = STRING$(60, 95);

PRINT "Column 1"; SPACE$(25); "Column 2"
```

ASC() returns the ASCII number of the character argument you give it. The argument must be a string of one or more characters.

If you pass ASC() a string of more than one character, it returns the ASCII number of the first character in the string. For example, the statement

```
PRINT ASC("A"), asc("B"), asc("C")
```

produces the following output:

```
65          66          67
```

You can look at the ASCII table to see that these three numbers are the ASCII values for A, B, and C. You can also use string variables as arguments:

```
letter1$ = "A"
letter2$ = "B"
letter3$ = "C"
PRINT ASC(letter1$), ASC(letter2$), ASC(letter3$)
```

This produces the same output as the previous example produces.

If you pass a string with more than one character to ASC(), it returns the ASCII value of only the first character. Therefore, the statement

```
PRINT ASC("Hello")
```

prints 72 (the ASCII value of H). This is a better method of testing for input than you have seen so far. Look at the following example:

```
INPUT "Do you want to see the name"; ans$
IF ((ASC(ans$) = 89) OR (ASC(ans$) = 121)) THEN
    PRINT "The name is "; a.name$
ENDIF
```

The user can answer the prompt with y, Y, Yes, or YES. The IF-THEN test works for any of those input values because 89 is the ASCII value for Y and 121 is the ASCII value for y.

The STRING$() function also uses the ASCII table to do its job. This function is generally used to create strings for output and storage. The STRING$() function requires two arguments: an integer followed by a character, a character string, or another integer. STRING$() replicates its second argument.

The best way to learn the STRING$() function is to see it used. Consider the following statement:

```
PRINT STRING$(15, "a")
```

This prints the lowercase letter a 15 times, as in

```
aaaaaaaaaaaaaaa
```

STRING$() is useful for drawing boxes around text, or for putting a string of dashes under words on the screen. You can also assign the return result of STRING$() to a string variable, as in

```
underline$ = STRING(30, "_")
```

You can also use STRING$() in output to insert spaces:

```
PRINT "Apples"; STRING$(10, " "); "Oranges"
```

This line prints the following:

```
Apples          Oranges
```

You saw another function in an earlier chapter that produced spaces: the SPC() function. There is a third function in QBasic that also produces spaces: the SPACE$() function. SPACE$() returns the number of spaces specified by its integer argument. The following PRINT statements do exactly the same thing:

```
sp$ = STRING$(40, " ")
sp$ = SPACE$(40)
```

String Conversion Functions

As with numeric functions, there are several string functions that convert string data from one form to another. Two of them, VAL() and STR$(), convert data from numeric to string and back.

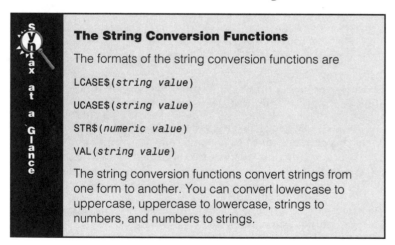

The String Conversion Functions

The formats of the string conversion functions are

LCASE$(*string value*)

UCASE$(*string value*)

STR$(*numeric value*)

VAL(*string value*)

The string conversion functions convert strings from one form to another. You can convert lowercase to uppercase, uppercase to lowercase, strings to numbers, and numbers to strings.

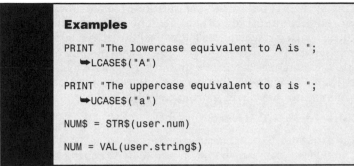

Examples

```
PRINT "The lowercase equivalent to A is ";
    ➡LCASE$("A")

PRINT "The uppercase equivalent to a is ";
    ➡UCASE$("a")

NUM$ = STR$(user.num)

NUM = VAL(user.string$)
```

The first two string functions convert strings to and from their native cases. LCASE$( ) converts its string argument to lowercase letters. If the argument contains only lowercase letters, no conversion is done. UCASE$( ) converts its string argument to uppercase letters. If the argument contains only uppercase letters, no conversion is done.

These functions are straightforward. Each can convert a string variable, constant, or expression (such as two strings concatenated together) to the indicated case. Listing 9.3 explains both functions.

Listing 9.3. An illustration of *LCASE$()* and *UCASE$()*.

```
up$ = "HELLO"
lc$ = "goodbye"
mixed$ = "Hello, Goodbye"
PRINT LCASE$(up$), LCASE$(lc$), LCASE$(mixed$)
PRINT UCASE$(up$), UCASE$(lc$), UCASE$(mixed$)
```

Listing 9.3 produces the following output:

```
hello      goodbye       hello, goodbye
HELLO      GOODBYE       HELLO, GOODBYE
```

There are many uses for these two string functions. When you ask the user a question, such as a yes-or-no question, you can ensure that the answer is in lowercase (or uppercase) and perform an IF-THEN. For example,

```
IF (UCASE$(ans$) = "YES")) THEN ...   ' Rest of code follows
```

Without the UCASE$( ) function, you would have to test for each of the following possible answers:

```
YES     YEs     YeS     yES     yEs     yeS     yes
```

The STR$() and VAL() functions are mirror-image functions. These two functions convert string data to numeric data and numeric data to string data, respectively. The STR$() function converts the numeric variable, constant, or expression inside the parentheses to a string. If the number is positive, the string will have a leading space. The following statement is not a valid statement because you cannot put a number in a string variable:

```
s$ = 54.6    ' This is invalid
```

You can avoid this Type Mismatch error by first using STR$() to convert the number to a string before assigning it to a string variable, as in

```
s$ = STR$(54.6)    ' This works
```

If you print s$, you see 54.5 (with a space before it where the imaginary plus sign is). You must realize, however, that QBasic does not recognize this as a number; it is simply a string of characters with a period in the middle that looks like a number when it is printed. You cannot perform any math with s$ because it is not a number.

There might be times when you want to combine numbers and words into a string. You can enclose the number inside the STR$() function and concatenate it with other strings to build the longer string.

VAL() converts the string variable, constant, or expression inside the parentheses to a number. The argument (the string in the parentheses) must start with a string of characters that looks like a valid number (integer, single-precision, or any other data type). VAL() ignores any spaces at the beginning of the string (called *leading blanks*). If there is no valid number at the beginning of the string (not including the leading zero), VAL() converts the string to the number 0. Listing 9.4 illustrates the VAL() function.

Listing 9.4. An illustration of the *VAL()* function.

```
s1$ = "44 bottles"
n1 = VAL(s1$)    ' Ignores everything after the number
PRINT n1
s2$ = "00012.5"
n2 = VAL(s2$)    ' Converts the string to single-precision
PRINT n2
s3$ = "Sam is 68 years old"    ' No valid number at
s3$ = VAL(s3$)                 '    beginning of string
PRINT s3$
```

The following output is produced by Listing 9.4:

```
44
12.5
0
```

String Character Functions

There are several more string functions that manipulate strings in many ways. They enable you to break one string into several smaller strings by removing portions of it. You can trim the leading spaces from strings and change the middle of a string without changing the rest of the string.

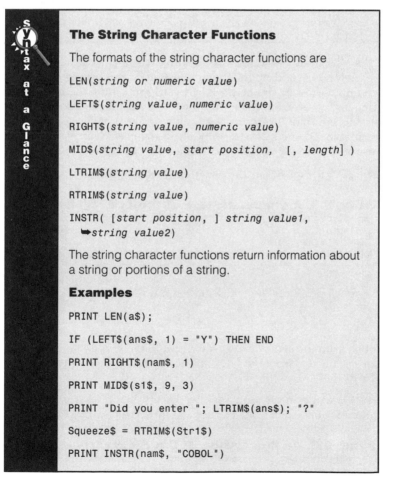

The String Character Functions

The formats of the string character functions are

LEN(*string or numeric value*)

LEFT$(*string value, numeric value*)

RIGHT$(*string value, numeric value*)

MID$(*string value, start position,* [, *length*])

LTRIM$(*string value*)

RTRIM$(*string value*)

INSTR([*start position,*] *string value1,*
➠*string value2*)

The string character functions return information about a string or portions of a string.

Examples

```
PRINT LEN(a$);

IF (LEFT$(ans$, 1) = "Y") THEN END

PRINT RIGHT$(nam$, 1)

PRINT MID$(s1$, 9, 3)

PRINT "Did you enter "; LTRIM$(ans$); "?"

Squeeze$ = RTRIM$(Str1$)

PRINT INSTR(nam$, "COBOL")
```

The LEN( ) function can tell you the length of a string. You saw this
function used earlier in this chapter with numeric values. LEN( )
also works with strings. LEN( ) returns the length (number of characters) of the string variable, constant, or expression inside its
parentheses. The following PRINT statement:

```
PRINT LEN("abcdef")
```

produces 6 as its output.

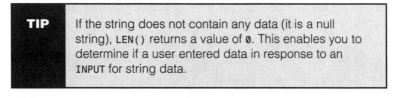

TIP   If the string does not contain any data (it is a null
       string), LEN( ) returns a value of ø. This enables you to
       determine if a user entered data in response to an
       INPUT for string data.

LEFT$( ) requires two arguments, a string variable, a constant, or an
expression followed by an integer constant or variable. The integer
determines how many characters are "stripped" from the left of the
string and returned. RIGHT$( ) requires two arguments also: a string
variable, constant, or expression, followed by an integer constant
or variable. The integer determines how many characters are
"stripped" from the right of the string and returned.

Listing 9.5 demonstrates the use of the LEFT$( ) function.

Listing 9.5. A demonstration of the *LEFT$()* function.

```
a$ = "abcdefg"
PRINT LEFT$(a$, 3)
PRINT LEFT$(a$, 20)
```

Listing 9.5 produces the following output:

```
abc
abcdefg
```

Notice from the second PRINT statement that if you try to return
more characters from the left of the string than exist, LEFT$( )
returns the entire string and not an error message.

RIGHT$( ) works in the same manner, except that it returns the
rightmost characters from a string, as shown in Listing 9.6.

Listing 9.6. An illustration of the *RIGHT$()* function.

```
a$ = "abcdefg"
PRINT RIGHT$(a$, 1)
PRINT RIGHT$(a$, 20)
```

Listing 9.6 produces the following output:

```
g
abcefg
```

The MID$( ) function accomplishes what LEFT$( ) and RIGHT$( ) cannot: MID$( ) returns characters from the *middle* of a string. MID$( ) uses three arguments: a string followed by two integers. The first integer determines where MID$( ) begins stripping characters from the string (the position, starting at 1). The second integer determines how many characters from the starting position to return. If you do not specify two integers, MID$( ) returns all characters to the right of the start position.

MID$( ) can pull any number of characters from anywhere in the string. Listing 9.7 shows how the MID$( ) function works.

Listing 9.7. An illustration of *MID$()*.

```
a$ = "QBasic FORTRAN COBOL C Pascal"
PRINT MID$(a$, 1, 6)
PRINT MID$(a$, 8, 7)
PRINT MID$(a$, 16, 5)
PRINT MID$(a$, 22, 1)
PRINT MID$(a$, 24, 6)
```

Listing 9.7 produces a listing of these five programming languages, one per line, as shown in the following output:

```
QBasic
FORTRAN
COBOL
C
Pascal
```

The LTRIM$( ) and RTRIM$( ) functions trim spaces from the beginning or end of a string. LTRIM$( ) returns the argument's string without any leading spaces. RTRIM$( ) returns the argument's string without any trailing spaces.

INSTR( ) is a string search function. You use it to find the starting location of a string inside another string. INSTR( ) returns the character position (an integer) at which one string starts within another string.

INSTR( ) looks to see whether the second string expression (INSTR( )'s last argument) exists within the first string expression (INSTR( )'s next-to-last argument). If it does, INSTR( ) returns the starting position of the string within the first string. INSTR( ) assumes a beginning position of 1, unless you override it by including the optional integer as INSTR( )'s first argument. For example, if you give INSTR() a starting value of 5, INSTR() ignores the first four characters of the search string. If INSTR() fails to find the first string within the search string, it returns a 0. Listing 9.8 makes INSTR()'s operation clear.

Listing 9.8. An illustration of *INSTR()*.

```
a$ = "QBasic FORTRAN COBOL C Pascal"
PRINT INSTR(a$, "FORTRAN")        ' Exists at position 8
PRINT INSTR(a$, "COBOL")          ' Exists at position 16
PRINT INSTR(a$, "C")              ' Exists at position 16 too!
PRINT INSTR(a$, "PL/I")           ' PL/I not found
PRINT INSTR(16, A$, "FORTRAN")    ' FORTRAN exists, but not past 16
PRINT INSTR(5, a$, "PL/I")        ' Does not exist
PRINT INSTR(a$, "")               ' NULL always returns 1
PRINT INSTR(5, a$, "")            ' or start value
```

Study Listing 9.8 to see how it produces the following output:

```
8
16
16
0
0
0
1
5
```

> **NOTE**   The reason the third PRINT does not return 22 (the position of the *C* that denotes the C language) is that the *C* is also in COBOL. INSTR() returns only the first occurrence of the string.

Justifying String Statements

The LSET and RSET statements left- or right-justify string data. Although LSET and RSET are statements rather than functions, they operate very much like LTRIM$() and RTRIM$() except that instead of trimming spaces from a string, these statements insert spaces at the beginning or end of a string. They can be used to build output strings and are especially useful for working with disk files (which you learn how to do in Chapter 11).

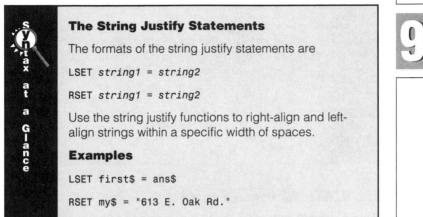

The String Justify Statements

The formats of the string justify statements are

LSET *string1* = *string2*

RSET *string1* = *string2*

Use the string justify functions to right-align and left-align strings within a specific width of spaces.

Examples

LSET first$ = ans$

RSET my$ = "613 E. Oak Rd."

The *string1* in each statement is assumed to already have a value. The length of that string value determines how many spaces have to be used to pad *string2*. Listing 9.9 is an example of the use of LSET and RSET.

Listing 9.9. An illustration of the *LSET* and *RSET* functions.

```
string1$ = "1234567890"    ' 10 characters
LSET string$1 = "left"     ' LSET "left" in those 10 characters
PRINT "¦"; string1$; "¦"   ' Print lines between to see result
string2$ = "1234567890"    ' 10 characters
RSET string2$ = "right"    ' RSET "right" in those 10 characters
PRINT "¦"; string2$; "¦"   ' Print between lines to see result
```

Listing 9.9 produces the following output:

```
¦left      ¦
¦     right¦
```

You must make sure that string1$ and string2$ both have an initial string value before using LSET or RSET. If they do not, QBasic assumes they are null strings (because they have nothing in them) and will not left-justify or right-justify the strings "right" and "left".

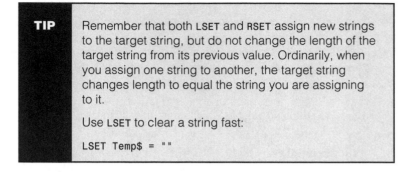

TIP Remember that both LSET and RSET assign new strings to the target string, but do not change the length of the target string from its previous value. Ordinarily, when you assign one string to another, the target string changes length to equal the string you are assigning to it.

Use LSET to clear a string fast:

```
LSET Temp$ = " "
```

The *INKEY$* Input Function

There is a function that seems to be a distant relative of the INPUT statement. It is the INKEY$ function. As with INPUT, INKEY$ gets input from the keyboard. Unlike INPUT, however, INKEY$ can get only one character at a time from the keyboard, not an entire string of characters as INPUT can.

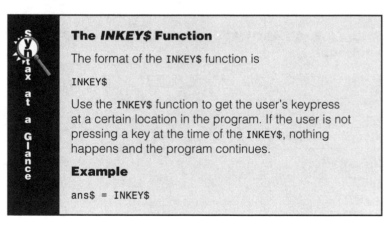

The *INKEY$* Function

The format of the INKEY$ function is

```
INKEY$
```

Use the INKEY$ function to get the user's keypress at a certain location in the program. If the user is not pressing a key at the time of the INKEY$, nothing happens and the program continues.

Example

```
ans$ = INKEY$
```

Because you never pass an argument to INKEY$, it requires no parentheses. The return value of INKEY$ is the character typed at the keyboard. The return value of INKEY$ is typically assigned to a string variable. You might wonder why anyone would want to use INKEY$. After all, it can accept only one character at a time. However, it has one advantage over INPUT: it grabs the key the user presses and stores that character in the string variable without the user having to press Enter. INPUT *requires* the user to press Enter, whereas INKEY$ gets its character input and passes control to the next statement without waiting for an Enter keypress. Unlike INPUT, INKEY$ does not display a question mark.

INKEY$ requires one other consideration. When you want to get a character with INKEY$, you must put the INKEY$ function in a loop. Otherwise, INKEY$ does not wait for the user to type anything. If a key is not being pressed at exactly the same time that the INKEY$ function executes, it returns a null character and moves on.

> **TIP** Programs have a quicker feel to them if the user does not have to press Enter after a menu choice or a yes-or-no question.

Listing 9.10 illustrates INKEY$. The program loops until the user presses a key. If the user presses a *B* on the keyboard, the program beeps. If the user presses *Q*, the program quits.

Listing 9.10. An illustration of *INKEY$*.

```
' Beeps if user presses B; otherwise, quits when user presses
Q
CLS
PRINT "I will beep if you press B"
PRINT "and I will quit if you press Q..."
DO
    ans$ = INKEY$    ' Get a character if one is being pressed
    IF (LCASE$(ans$) = "b") THEN BEEP
LOOP UNTIL (LCASE$(ans$) = "q")
```

Summary

As you have seen in this chapter, QBasic supplies many numeric and string built-in functions. These functions save you work; you do not have to take the time to write the code yourself, but rather, you can call on these functions to do the work for you. You may not use all of these functions, but some will prove useful as you program in QBasic.

Here are some of the things you learned in this chapter:

- Most of the built-in functions require parentheses after their names. The parentheses are where you pass the function data (called *arguments*) to work on.

- Many of the string function names end with the $ suffix to signal that they return a string value. However, some string function names, such as LEN() do not end in the $ suffix.

■ The LEN( ) function serves as a bridge between the numeric and string functions. It is the only function that works with both string and numeric arguments by returning the length (the number of characters of storage) of the argument.

■ Many string functions return portions (such as the leftmost or rightmost characters) of strings.

■ RSET and LSET are not functions, but they act much like QBasic's TRIM$( ) functions by justifying strings within a certain length.

■ INKEY$ is very useful for getting input one character at a time. Unlike INPUT, INKEY$ requires no Enter keypress from the user.

Modular Programming: Subroutines

The preceding chapter taught you about QBasic's built-in functions. Now it's time to learn how to write your own routines that you can execute repeatedly. There is not a built-in function for every task you want to complete. If you write some code to perform a specific task, and you find yourself using that code repeatedly in a program, you can put the code in a *subroutine* and execute it as many times as you want. A subroutine is nothing more than a detour your program takes: your program executes a set of statements in the subroutine, returns to the code that called the subroutine, and continues from there.

This chapter explains two kinds of subroutines: the regular subroutine and the more advanced *subroutine procedure* that acts like a small program within the program. This chapter's approach is a little different from the others. You cannot truly understand subroutine procedures unless you have a brief background in *modular programming* (the process of breaking a program into separate modules).

Subroutines

Any time that you have the same two or more statements being executed in different parts of the same program, consider using subroutines. Subroutines are nothing more than lines of QBasic code that you enter only once in a program but can execute from various locations in the program. Listing 10.1 contains repetitive code and could be improved with subroutines.

Listing 10.1. A program that could be improved with subroutines.

```
' Program without subroutines
PRINT "Welcome to the label printing program!"
PRINT
PRINT "This program prints mailing labels"
PRINT "on your printer, three at a time."

LINE INPUT "What is your name? "; nm$
LINE INPUT "What is your address? "; ad$
LINE INPUT "What is your city? "; ct$
LINE INPUT "What is your state? "; st$
LINE INPUT "What is your zip code? "; zp$

PRINT "Get the printer ready, and press Enter when "
INPUT "you want me to begin printing..."; en$

LPRINT nm$     ' Print first label
LPRINT ad$
LPRINT ct$; ", "; st$; SPC(5); zp$
LPRINT
LPRINT     ' Skip two spaces to the next label

LPRINT nm$     ' Print second label
LPRINT ad$
LPRINT ct$; ", "; st$; SPC(5); zp$
LPRINT
LPRINT     ' Skip two spaces to the next label

LPRINT nm$     ' Print third label
LPRINT ad$
LPRINT ct$; ", "; st$; SPC(5); zp$
LPRINT
LPRINT     ' Skip two spaces to the next label
END
```

Listing 10.1 has much redundant code. The lines that print the name and address are repeated three times. This code begs to be put into a subroutine!

A subroutine *call* is made with a GOSUB. Although their names are similar, GOSUB and GOTO are two very different commands, and GOSUB does not have the drawbacks that GOTO has. The GOTO (as you might recall from Chapter 6, "Making Decisions with Data") is prone to overuse. Too often, programmers stick GOTOs in code instead of planning the code so that it logically flows from top to bottom.

The GOSUB does cause a GOTO-like branch in a program. Unlike the GOTO, however, GOSUB always ensures that the program control eventually returns to the location of the GOSUB. Therefore, if you put a GOSUB in a program, the program branches off and performs the subroutine. When the subroutine finishes, however, program control returns at the GOSUB statement so that the next statement in line (after the GOSUB) can continue.

The program returns from a subroutine when it runs into the RETURN statement. The RETURN statement simply tells the subroutine to give control back to the GOSUB that called it.

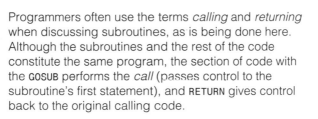

NOTE Programmers often use the terms *calling* and *returning* when discussing subroutines, as is being done here. Although the subroutines and the rest of the code constitute the same program, the section of code with the GOSUB performs the *call* (passes control to the subroutine's first statement), and RETURN gives control back to the original calling code.

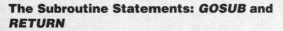

Syntax at a Glance

The Subroutine Statements: *GOSUB* and *RETURN*

The format of the GOSUB and RETURN pair is

GOSUB *line label*

RETURN

Use the GOSUB and RETURN pair of statements to call a subroutine and return from one.

Example

```
GOSUB CompPay    ' Call the compute pay subroutine
   REM ... Rest of subroutine goes here
END
COMPPAY:
   REM ... Rest of subroutine goes here
RETURN    ' This sends control back to the calling
          ' routine
```

A rewritten version of Listing 10.1 might look something like Listing 10.2.

Listing 10.2. Listing 10.1 rewritten with subroutines.

```
' Program with subroutines
PRINT "Welcome to the label printing program!"
PRINT
PRINT "This program prints mailing labels"
PRINT "on your printer, three at a time."

LINE INPUT "What is your name? "; nm$
LINE INPUT "What is your address? "; ad$
LINE INPUT "What is your city? "; ct$
LINE INPUT "What is your state? "; st$
LINE INPUT "What is your ZIP code? "; zp$

PRINT "Get the printer ready, and press Enter when "
INPUT "you want me to begin printing..."; en$

GOSUB PrLabel
GOSUB PrLabel
GOSUB PrLabel

END      ' Execution stops here

PrLabel:
  LPRINT nm$    ' Print first label
  LPRINT ad$
  LPRINT ct$; ", "; st$; SPC(5); zp$
  LPRINT
  LPRINT    ' Skip two spaces to the next label
  RETURN

END
```

Listing 10.2 does exactly the same thing as Listing 10.1 but is much cleaner and does not contain repeated code. Notice the added PrLabel: statement label at the beginning of the label printing routine and the RETURN statement at the end. These additions turned the printing lines into a subroutine that is executed every time the first part of the program calls it with GOSUB PrLabel. Although the GOSUBs are repeated, they take much less space than three sets of the subroutines. Additionally, even if the subroutines are much longer, as they sometimes are, the primary calling code (the part of the program that performs the GOSUBs) does not change.

You can use the concept of subroutines to improve your own code. Many QBasic programmers write several subroutines and save them in separate disk files, loading them into programs that need them and calling them with GOSUB. For another glimpse of what you can do with a subroutine, consider the following code:

```
StrRev:
   print "Before the reverse: s$ is "; s$   ' String to
                                            ' reverse
   new$ = ""            ' Initialize a null string
   FOR i = LEN(s$) TO 1 STEP -1
      new$ = new$ + MID$(s$, i, 1)   ' Build a new string
   NEXT i
   s$ = new$
RETURN
```

This code takes a string stored in s$ and reverses the characters in the string using the MID$() function. There is no built-in string function that reverses strings. Using subroutines, you can use this function and insert it in any program that needs to reverse a string. This subroutine assumes that the string you want to reverse is stored in s$, so if you want to reverse a string named Myself$, you can do so with the following statements:

```
s$ = Myself$
GOSUB StrRev      ' Reverses s$
Myself$ = s$
```

Subroutine Procedures

Computers never get bored. They loop and perform the same input, output, and computations your programs require as long as you want them to. You can take advantage of their repetitive nature by extending the concept of subroutines into subroutine procedures. QBasic distinguishes regular subroutines (the ones you learned about in the previous section) from subroutine procedures by making them almost as separate from the calling part of the program as if they were separate programs altogether.

Breaking your programs into separate subroutine procedures makes a lot of sense. Instead of your program being one huge program file, it becomes a collection of small routines that you then put together. Breaking your code into subroutine procedures, sometimes called *modules*, makes your program much easier to manage. Programs with several hundred lines of code are not uncommon. If the program had no order and was not broken into smaller routines, it would be difficult to figure out later.

Program maintenance, the process of changing and updating programs so that they keep current with the business environment, is a constant challenge for today's businesses. A program you write for a company today, probably will have to be changed within a few years to reflect changes in the business. If you use subroutines when you write the program, whoever revises the program can quickly find the pieces that must change without drastically affecting the rest of the program.

> **NOTE** Today's television sets are extremely modular. If your TV breaks, chances are good that the service person will not "fix" the broken part, but instead will replace an entire module of parts. The electronics industry has learned that a modular television system is much easier to keep working because the modules are made to work independently and can be changed without having to change other parts of the television. A modular program offers the same opportunity for quick maintenance that a modular television system does.

Outlining the Problem

Look at the following program outline to get a feel for the way subroutines work. The outline illustrates a problem that needs to be programmed. The program is supposed to retrieve a list of numbers from the keyboard, sort them, and print them on-screen. You have seen examples of similar programs in previous chapters of this book.

```
' Program to get a list of numbers, sort them, and print them
'
.
.
.
    QBasic statements to get a list of numbers into an array
.
.
.
    QBasic statements to sort those numbers
.
.
.
    QBasic statements to display those numbers to the screen
.
.
.
```

The approach offered in the preceding outline is not the best way to write this program. Even though there are three very distinct sections (or *sub*sections) in the program, it has been written as one long program with one QBasic statement after another.

Because the overall program is obviously a collection of smaller routines, you can group these routines by making them QBasic subroutines. Listing 10.3 shows another approach to the outline just shown, but the routines are broken into distinct subroutines. Additionally, the program contains a new routine at the beginning to control the other subroutines.

Listing 10.3. An outline of a better approach to the same problem.

```
' Program with four routines
' The main (first) one controls the execution of the others
' The next routine is a stand-alone routine that gets numbers
' The next one sorts those numbers
' The last one prints them to the screen
    GOSUB GetNumbers
    GOSUB SortNumbers
    GOSUB DisplayNumbers
    END

' First routine:
GetNumbers:
    QBasic statements to get a list of numbers into an array
.
.
.
    RETURN to Main

' Second routine:
SortNumbers:
    QBasic statements to sort the numbers
.
.
.
    RETURN to Main

' Third routine:
DisplayNumbers:
    QBasic statements to display the numbers on the screen
.
.
.
    RETURN to Main
```

The outline in Listing 10.3 is a much better way to write this program. It is longer to type, but it is much better organized. The first routine simply controls, or *calls*, the other subroutines to do their work in the proper order. After all, it would be silly to sort the numbers before the user types them. The first routine, therefore, ensures that the other routines execute in the proper sequence.

The first routine is not really a QBasic subroutine. It is the main part of the program (QBasic calls this the *main module*). This portion of the program is where you previously would have typed the full program. Now, however, the program consists only of a group of subroutine calls. The primary program in all but the shortest of programs should be simply a series of subroutine-controlling statements.

Again, these listings are obviously not intended to be examples of code, but they are outlines of programs. From these types of outlines, it is easier to write the full program. Before going to the keyboard, you know there are four distinct sections of this program: a primary subroutine-calling routine, a keyboard data-entry subroutine, a sorting subroutine, and a printing subroutine.

The length of each subroutine varies depending on what the subroutine is to do. A good rule of thumb is that a subroutine's listing should not be more than one screen long. If it is, it will be more difficult to edit and maintain with the QBasic editor. Not only that, but if a subroutine is more than one screen long, it probably does too much and should be broken into two or more subroutines. This is not a requirement; you must make the final judgment on whether a subroutine is too long.

If Listing 10.3 were a complete QBasic program, where would the last executed statement be? The last statement executed is in the primary calling routine; it is an END statement. (Without END, execution would *fall through* to the first subroutine, execute it again, and get confused when it reached RETURN.) By returning control to the main module after the last subroutine finishes, it is easier to see the logic from beginning to end.

Summary

In this chapter, you have been exposed to true structured programs. Instead of typing long programs, you should now be able to break them into separate routines. This isolates your routines from one other so that the surrounding code does not confuse things when you are concentrating on a section of your program.

Here are some of the things you learned in this chapter:

■ A subroutine is like a program detour. Control passes to the subroutine and returns back from where the subroutine was called.

■ The GOSUB and RETURN statements control the flow of simple subroutines.

Disk Files

Every example in this book has processed data that resides
inside the program listing or comes from the keyboard. You
learned about the DATA statement that holds numeric and
string data. You assigned constants and variables to other variables and created new data values from existing ones. The
programs also received input with INPUT and INKEY$ and pro-
cessed the user's keystrokes.

The data created by the user with the DATA statement is sufficient for some applications. With the large volumes of data
that most real-world applications have to process, however,
you need a better way of storing that data. For all but the
smallest computer programs, the hard disk offers the solution.
By storing data on-disk, the computer helps you to enter the
data, find it, change it, and delete it. The computer and
QBasic are simply tools to help you manage and process data.

Why Use a Disk?

The typical computer system has at least 640K of RAM and 30
or more megabytes of disk storage. Your disk drive holds
much more data than can fit in your computer's RAM. This is
one of the primary reasons for using the disk for your data.
The disk memory, because it is nonvolatile, also lasts longer.
Nonvolatile memory refers to memory that is not erased when
you turn your computer off. RAM is volatile memory; it is
erased.When you turn your computer off, the disk memory is
not erased, whereas RAM is erased. Also, when your data
changes, you (or more important, your *users*) do not have to
edit the program and look for a set of DATA statements. Instead, the users can run previously written programs that
make changes to the disk data.

By storing data on your disk, you have more storage space. Your disk can hold as much data as you have disk capacity. Also, if your disk requirements grow, you can usually increase your disk space, whereas you cannot always add more RAM to your computer. QBasic cannot access the special *extended* or *expanded* memory that some computers have.

QBasic does not have to access much RAM at once, however, because it can read data from your disk drive and process it. Not all your disk data has to reside in RAM for QBasic to process it. QBasic reads some data, processes it, and then reads some more. If QBasic requires disk data a second time, it rereads that place on the disk.

Data Files and Filenames

You can store two types of files on your computer's disk drive. They are *program files* and *data files*. Program files are the files you write and store on-disk with the File, Save command. Data files don't contain programs; they contain the data that the programs process. For the remainder of this book, *file* refers to a data file unless a program file is specifically mentioned.

A *data file* is a collection of related information stored on your disk. To understand the computer's data files, think of files in a filing cabinet. Files on your computer are treated just as files are in a filing cabinet. You probably have a cabinet or box at home that contains several file folders. You might have a file of your insurance papers, a file of your automobile papers, a file of your home and mortgage information, and several other files. Do you see that these files fit the definition of computer data files? These files are sets of *related information.*

Computer File Example

It helps to take the analogy of computer files and regular paper files one step further. Think about colleges 25 years ago, before they used computers. How did they store their information about students, professors, and classes? They probably had three file cabinets. One of the cabinets probably held the student files.

As each student enrolled, the enrollment clerk completed an enrollment form that included the student's social security number, name, address, city, state, ZIP code, age, and so forth. The clerk would then file that piece of paper in the cabinet. Later, if that student moved and needed his or her address changed, the student would tell the clerk. The clerk would have to go to the filing cabinet, find the student's form, change the address, and then put the form back in the student filing cabinet. The professor file and the class file would be handled similarly.

Now, come back to the present and consider how that same college handles students, professors, and classes with the help of computerized data files. Rather than three file cabinets, that college would have a disk drive with three files on it: the student file, the professor file, and the class file.

As students enroll, the clerk does not fill out a form. Instead, the clerk sits in front of a computer and answers questions on-screen. When the information is complete, the clerk presses a key and the computer stores the information in the student file on-disk. If that student's information changes, the clerk simply calls up the student's information on-screen, changes it, and saves it to the disk file.

The operations are the same in both the manual and the computerized filing systems, except the computer has adopted much of the "physical" labor. The sooner you realize that computer files and files in cabinets are handled the same way, the easier it will be to learn how to use QBasic to create, modify, and delete disk information.

Records and Fields

Before writing a program that creates a data file on-disk, you determine what type of data will be stored in the file. The programmer decides exactly what information is stored and how it is stored. To make proper file decisions, you should understand exactly how data is stored on-disk.

The student data file described in the preceding section might look like the file in Table 11.1. The table shows data for four students. There is no specified order of the file (in this case, it is the order that the students enrolled in the school). This does not mean that file access can be made only in that order. QBasic programs can read this file and print a file listing in any order, including numerical order by social security number and alphabetical order.

Table 11.1. Sample student data.

Social Security	Name	Age	Address	City	State	ZIP
434-54-3223	Jones, Michael	21	9 W. Elm	Miami	FL	22332
231-34-5767	Brown, Larry	19	505 Baker	Tampa	FL	23227
945-65-2344	Smith, Kim	20	14 Oak Rd.	Miami	FL	22331
294-78-9434	Lawton, Jerry	21	6 Main St.	Miami	FL	22356

Your computer files are broken into *records* and *fields*. A record is an individual occurrence in the file. In this case, the file is a collection of students, so each student's information is called a complete student record. If there were 12,000 students in the file, there would be 12,000 records in the file.

The fields are the columns in the file. The student data file has seven columns: Social Security number, Name, Age, Address, City, State, and ZIP. Even if 5,000 student records are added to the file, there still will be only seven fields because there will still be seven columns of data.

You can create files with *fixed-length records* or *variable-length records*. If the records are fixed-length, each field takes the same amount of disk space, even if that field's data value does not fill the field. Fixed strings are typically used for fixed-length records. For instance, most programmers create a data file table for their files. The table shown in Table 11.2 is such a data file; it lists each field name, the type of data in each field, and the length of each field.

Table 11.2. Student description table for a fixed-length data file.

Field Name	Length	Data Type
st.socsec	9	character
st.name$	25	character
st.age	2	integer
st.addr$	30	character
st.city$	10	character
st.state$	2	character
st.zip$	5	character
—		
	83 total characters per record	

The total record length is 83 characters. Every record in this file takes exactly 83 characters of disk space. Just because a city takes only five characters of the 10-character field does not mean that only five characters are stored. Extra spaces are added on the right side of each field that is less than 10 characters. Fixed-length records have a major drawback: They waste disk space. But each field is large enough to hold the largest possible data value.

The fields are the columns in the file (and the table). The student data file has seven columns: social security number, name, age, address, city, state, and ZIP code. Even if you added 5,000 student records to the file, the largest possible data value.

A variable-length file, on the other hand, does not waste disk space. As soon as a field's data value is saved to a variable-length file, the next file's data value is stored immediately after it. There is usually a special separating character between the files so your programs can determine where the files begin and end.

Variable-length files save disk space, but it is not always as easy to write variable-length, file-handling programs as it is to write fixed-length programs. If limited disk space is a consideration, you should definitely use variable-length records. The next two sections discuss each of these types of files.

Filenames

Each file on your hard disk has a unique filename. You cannot have two files in the same directory on your hard drive that have the same name. If that were possible, your computer would have to have another way to differentiate between the two files.

Filenames have naming rules that are much the same way as QBasic variables. A filename can be from one to eight characters long with an optional one-to-three-character *extension*. The filename and extension must be separated with a period. For example, here are some valid filenames:

```
sales89.dat     a.3        testdata     emp_name.ap
```

A filename can consist of letters, numbers, and the underscore (_) character. The underscore character is helpful when you want to separate parts of a name, as in EMP_NAME.AP in the preceding list. Because spaces are not valid in filenames, the underscore helps to group parts of the name, thus making the name more legible.

> **NOTE** A few other special characters are allowed in filenames, including the pound sign and the exclamation point. Many others are not allowed, however, such as the asterisk and the question mark. To be safe, use only letters, numbers, and the underscore.

Types of Disk File Access

Your programs can access files in two ways: through *sequential access* or through *random access.* Your application determines the method you should use. The access mode of a file determines how you read, write, change, and delete data from the file. Some of your files can be accessed in both ways, sequentially and randomly.

A sequential file has to be accessed one record at a time in the same order that the records were written. A sequential file is analogous to a cassette tape. On a cassette, you must play music in the same order it was recorded. (You can quickly fast-forward or rewind over songs that you do not want to listen to, but the order of the songs is still the same.) It is difficult, and sometimes impossible, to insert records in the middle of a sequential file. How easy is it to insert a new song in the middle of two other songs on a tape? The only way to truly add or delete records from the middle of a sequential file is to create a completely new file that combines both old and new songs. Although sequential files might seem limiting, many applications lend themselves to sequential-file processing.

You can access a random-access file in any order you want. Think of records in a random-access file as songs on a compact disc or a record; you can go directly to any song you want without having to play or fast-forward over the other songs. If you want to play the first song, the sixth song, and then the fourth song, you can do so. The order of play has nothing to do with the order in which the songs were originally recorded.

Sequential-Disk Processing

This section introduces QBasic sequential file processing commands. You learn how to create, modify, and manage sequential files on-disk. Using your hard disk for your data storage dramatically increases the power of QBasic. You can process large amounts of data and store it for later use.

The concepts and commands you learn here will be helpful in almost every QBasic application you write. Separating the data and their programs makes your programs much more useful for longterm use and for real-world data processing.

The *OPEN* Statement

The designers of QBasic realized the analogy of disk and filing cabinet files when they wrote the OPEN statement. Before you use a file from your filing cabinet, you must open the filing cabinet. Before creating, modifying, or updating a disk data file in QBasic, you must open the file with the OPEN statement. The format of the OPEN statement is explained in the following syntax-at-a-glance box.

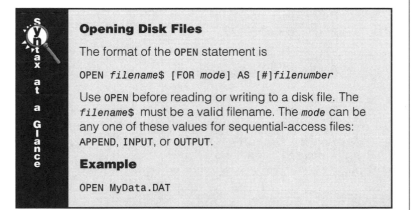

Opening Disk Files

The format of the OPEN statement is

OPEN filename$ [FOR mode] AS [#]filenumber

Use OPEN before reading or writing to a disk file. The filename$ must be a valid filename. The mode can be any one of these values for sequential-access files: APPEND, INPUT, or OUTPUT.

Example

OPEN MyData.DAT

The filenumber must be an integer that links the file to a number used throughout the program. The filenumber can be in the range from 1 to 255. You can open more than one file in one program (up to 255 of them). Instead of typing the complete filename every time you access a file, you refer to the filenumber you associated with that file when you opened it. The pound sign (#) does not have to appear before the filenumber.

The mode refers to the way your program uses the file. If you want to create the file (or overwrite one that already exists), open the file in OUTPUT mode. If you want to read data from a file, open the file in INPUT mode. APPEND mode enables you to add to the end of a file (or create the file if it does not exist).

Suppose you have to create a sequential file containing an inventory of your household items. The following OPEN statement does that:

```
OPEN "house.inv" FOR OUTPUT AS #1
```

The file is ready to accept data from the program.

If you previously created the household inventory file and have to read values from it, you have to write a program that contains the following OPEN statement:

```
OPEN "house.inv" FOR INPUT AS #1
```

After buying several items, you want to add to the household inventory file. To add to the end of the file, you open it in the following way:

```
OPEN "house.inv" FOR APPEND AS #1
```

The *CLOSE* Statement

After using a file, just as you do with a filing cabinet, you must close the file with the CLOSE statement. You should close all files that are open in your program when you are through with them. By closing the files, QBasic frees the file number. That way, the number can be used by other files that are opened later. DOS also updates the disk directory some when you close the file.

TIP Always close all files immediately after you are done using the files, rather than waiting until the end of the program as some programmers do. In the event of a power failure, some of the data in open files might be lost.

You can close all files in a program by placing CLOSE on a line by itself. If you follow CLOSE with one or more integer file numbers separated by commas, QBasic closes the files associated with those numbers.

To close all files in the program, you simply type

```
CLOSE
```

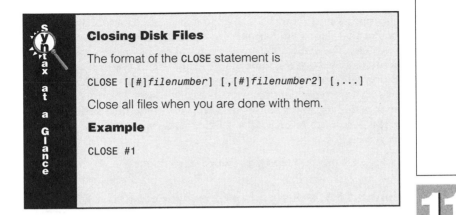

Closing Disk Files

The format of the CLOSE statement is

```
CLOSE [[#]filenumber] [,[#]filenumber2] [,...]
```

Close all files when you are done with them.

Example

```
CLOSE #1
```

Creating Sequential Files

To create a file, open it for OUTPUT. (The APPEND mode also creates a new file, but you should reserve it for adding data to the end of an existing file.) After you have opened the file, you need a way to write data to it. Most data going to a file comes from user input, calculations, DATA statements, or a combination of these. If you save your data in a disk file, it will be there the next time you need it, and you will not have to re-create it each time you run your program.

The PRINT # statement sends output data to a sequential file.

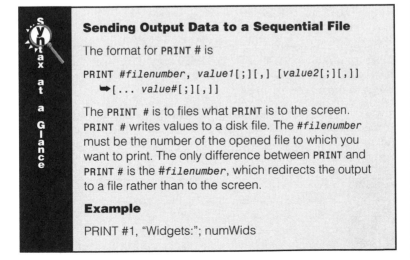

Sending Output Data to a Sequential File

The format for PRINT # is

```
PRINT #filenumber, value1[;][,] [value2[;][,]]
  ➡[... value#[;][,]]
```

The PRINT # is to files what PRINT is to the screen. PRINT # writes values to a disk file. The #filenumber must be the number of the opened file to which you want to print. The only difference between PRINT and PRINT # is the #filenumber, which redirects the output to a file rather than to the screen.

Example

```
PRINT #1, "Widgets:"; numWids
```

It is important to remember that PRINT # prints data to a file *exactly* as that data would appear on-screen with the regular PRINT statement. This means that positive numbers have a space before the number (where the invisible plus sign is). Therefore, the punctuation following the PRINT # statement determines how the data appears on-screen. Semicolons cause data to print next to each other, and the comma causes data to print in the next print zone on the disk (each print zone is 14 characters wide, just as it is on the screen).

Listing 11.1 prints three customer records to a file.

Listing 11.1. Printing customer records to a file.

```
' Write three customer records to a file.
CLS
OPEN "cust.dat" FOR OUTPUT AS #1   ' Open the file on the
                                   ' default drive
PRINT #1, "Johnson, Mike"; 34; "5th and Denver";
                "Houston"; "TX"; "74334"
PRINT #1, "Abel, Lea"; 28; "85 W. 123rd";
                "Miami"; "FL"; "39443"
PRINT #1, "Madison, Larry"; 32; "4 North Elm";
                "Lakewood"; "IL"; "93844"
CLOSE #1   ' Always close open files when you
                ' are through with them.
```

This program produces a file called CUST.DAT that looks like this:

```
Johnson, Mike 34 5th and DenverHoustonTX74334
Abel, Lea 28 85 W. 123rd MiamiFL39443
Madison, Larry 32 4 North ElmLakewoodIL93844
```

This output is an example of a variable-length file. Most sequential files contain variable-length records unless you write fixed-length strings to them.

As with the PRINT statement, you can add a USING option to print formatted data to a disk file. This enables you to format numbers and strings when you send them to disk files, just as when you send them to the screen and the printer.

NOTE There is a major drawback to creating files with PRINT #. There is no easy method of reading the data back to memory. Notice in the preceding file that the data runs together in some places and is separated in other places.

Therefore, QBasic offers the WRITE # statement rather than PRINT # to create sequential files to make things easier for you. The format of WRITE # is similar to that of the PRINT # statement.

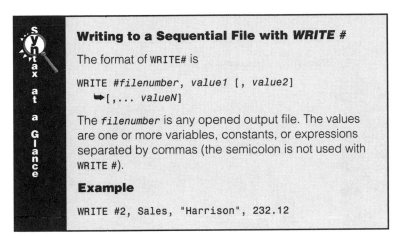

Writing to a Sequential File with *WRITE*

The format of WRITE# is

```
WRITE #filenumber, value1 [, value2]
    ➡[,... valueN]
```

The *filenumber* is any opened output file. The values are one or more variables, constants, or expressions separated by commas (the semicolon is not used with WRITE #).

Example

```
WRITE #2, Sales, "Harrison", 232.12
```

WRITE # makes the variable-length data file much easier to process. WRITE # places quotation marks around strings and separates each field with a comma. Listing 11.2 displays an improved version of the PRINT # program in Listing 11.1.

Listing 11.2. Using the *WRITE* # statement to improve Listing 11.1.

```
' Write three customer records to a file.
CLS
OPEN "cust.dat" FOR OUTPUT AS #1    ' Open the file on the
                                    ' default drive
WRITE #1, "Johnson, Mike"; 34; "5th and Denver"; "Houston";
    ➡"TX"; "74334"
WRITE #1, "Abel, Lea"; 28; "85 W. 123rd"; "Miami"; "FL";
    ➡"39443"
WRITE #1, "Madison, Larry"; 32; "4 North Elm"; "Lakewood";
    ➡"IL"; "93844"
CLOSE #1    ' Always close open files when
            ' you are through with them.
```

Because the program uses WRITE # rather than PRINT #, the output file's fields are much more legible. Here is the output file called CUST.DAT created from this program:

```
"Johnson, Mike",34,"5th and Denver","Houston","TX","74334"
"Abel, Lea",28,"85 W. 123rd","Miami","FL","39443"
"Madison, Larry",32,"4 North Elm","Lakewood","IL","93844"
```

When you use WRITE #, numbers are not enclosed in quotation marks, but each field containing strings is. This file can later be read by sequential input programs like those described in the next section. Although this is a variable-length file, the separating commas and quotation marks make it easy to input the fields later.

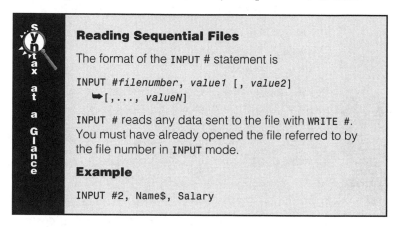

Reading Sequential Files

The format of the INPUT # statement is

```
INPUT #filenumber, value1 [, value2]
  ⮞[,..., valueN]
```

INPUT # reads any data sent to the file with WRITE #. You must have already opened the file referred to by the file number in INPUT mode.

Example

```
INPUT #2, Name$, Salary
```

As with the INPUT statement, you must follow the INPUT # statement with one or more variables separated by commas. Each value in the comma-separated file is input to the INPUT # variable list.

When you read data from an input file, your program takes one of two actions:

- It reads the input values
- It reaches the end of the input file

Most the time, INPUT # returns whatever values were input from the file. When all the values are input, however, there will be no more data. If you try to INPUT # past the end of the file, you get the following error message:

```
Input past end of file.
```

You saw a similar problem when you read data with READ-DATA statements. You needed to test for a trailer DATA record to find out whether the last record was read (otherwise, you had to know in advance exactly how many DATA values there were to read).

With file input, QBasic supplies a built-in function called EOF() that tells you whether you have just read the last record from the file.

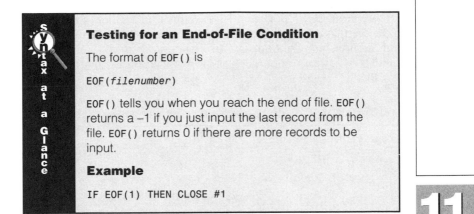

This tells you whether you should continue looping to input more values. Call the EOF() function after each INPUT # to see whether there are more values to input or whether you have input the last one.

Listing 11.3, which follows, reads the first three records from an inventory file. The program that created the file used a WRITE # statement that looked similar (in the number of variables and data types) to the INPUT # used here. Notice that the file must be opened in INPUT mode.

Listing 11.3. Printing from an input file.

```
' Reads and prints the first three records from an input file.
CLS
OPEN "inv.dat" FOR INPUT AS #1

PRINT "Here are the first three records from the file:"
PRINT
PRINT "Part #", "Description", "Quantity", "Price"
' Get the first record
INPUT #1, part.no$, description$, quantity%, price!
PRINT part.no$, description$, quantity%, price!
' Get the second record
INPUT #1, part.no$, description$, quantity%, price!
PRINT part.no$, description$, quantity%, price!
' Get the third record
INPUT #1, part.no$, description$, quantity%, price!
PRINT part.no$, description$, quantity%, price!
CLOSE #1
```

The program shown in Listing 11.4 counts the number of records in the file that the user enters. This program enables the user to find out how many students are in a student file, how many customers are in a customer file, or how many books are in a book data file.

Listing 11.4. Count the number of records in a file.

```
' Counts the number of records in a file.
CLS

PRINT "A Record Counting Program"
PRINT
INPUT "What is the name of the data file ";
INPUT "you want to use for the count"; df$

count = 0     ' Initialize count
OPEN df$ FOR INPUT AS #1
DO UNTIL EOF(1)
    LINE INPUT #1, rec$
    count = count + 1
LOOP

PRINT
PRINT "The number of records in the file is:"; count
CLOSE #1
```

The LINE INPUT # ignores the commas and quotation marks by reading the entire record into rec$. The user must know the name of the data file and type the complete filename and extension.

Appending to Sequential Files

After creating and reading files, you might want to add data to the end of a sequential file. This is easy when you open the file in APPEND mode. All subsequent writes to that file are added to the end of it. This enables users to add data to a file over time.

The only difference between programs that create data files and those that append data to them is the OPEN statement's mode.

Listing 11.5 appends two data files. It asks users for the names of two files. It then adds the second file to the end of the first one. LINE INPUT # is used to read the entire records. Users must ensure that the two data files have the same type and number of fields if they later want to sequentially read the newly appended file.

Listing 11.5. Appending two data files.

```
' Appends one file to the end of the other.
CLS
INPUT "What is the name of the first file"; f1$
PRINT "What file do you want to append to the end of "; f1$;
INPUT f2$

OPEN f1$ FOR APPEND AS #1
OPEN f2$ FOR INPUT AS #2
DO UNTIL ( EOF(2) )
    LINE INPUT #2, rec$
    PRINT #1, rec$
LOOP
CLOSE      ' Close both files
```

Notice that a PRINT # statement is used because WRITE # could add more quotation marks to the file when it writes the records.

Random-Access Disk Processing

This section introduces random-access files. Random-access files enable you to read or write any record in your data file without having to read or write every record before it. You can quickly search for, add, retrieve, change, and delete information in a random-access file. Although you need a few new commands to access files randomly, you will find that the extra effort pays off in flexibility, power, and speed of disk access.

Random File Records

Random files exemplify the power of data processing with QBasic. Sequential-file processing is slow unless you read the entire file into arrays and process the arrays in memory. As explained earlier in this chapter, you have much more disk space than RAM space, and most disk data files do not even fit in your RAM at one time. Therefore, you need a way to quickly read individual records from a file in any order needed and process them one at a time.

Think about the data files of a large credit card organization. When you make a purchase, the store calls the credit card company to receive authorization. There are millions of people in the company's files. Without fast computers, there would be no way that the company could read every record from the disk that comes before yours in a timely manner. Sequential files do not lend themselves to quick access. It is not feasible in many situations to look up individual records in a data file with sequential access.

The credit card companies must use random-access files so that their computers can go directly to your record, just as you go directly to a song on a compact disk or record album. Random-access files are more difficult to set up, but the power you receive is worth the effort.

All random file records must be fixed-length records. The sequential files you read and wrote in the previous sections were variable-length records. When you are reading or writing sequentially, you don't need fixed-length records because you input each field one record at a time, searching for the data you want. With fixed-length records, your computer can calculate exactly where, on the disk, the search record is located.

Although you waste some disk space with fixed-length records (because of the spaces that pad some of the fields), the advantages of random-file access make up for the "wasted" disk space.

> **TIP** With random-access files, you can read or write records in any order. Therefore, even if you want to perform sequential reading or writing of the file, you can use random-access processing and "randomly" read or write the file in sequential record number order.

The Random-Access *OPEN* Statement

Just as with sequential files, you must open random-access files before reading or writing to them. The random-access OPEN statement is similar to the sequential file OPEN statement, except you do not have to include the mode. Random-access files can be read to *and* written to without your having to close and reopen the file—the way you have to with sequential-access files. The OPEN statement must also include the record length of the fixed-length file that you want to access.

Opening Random-Access Files

The format of the random-access file OPEN statement is

OPEN *filename$* AS [#]*filenumber* LEN=*recordlength*

The OPEN statement opens a random-access file and describes its record length. The *filenumber* (with the optional pound sign preceding it) is the file number used in the remainder of the program to refer to this open file. The *recordlength* is the integer length of each record in the file.

Example

OPEN "MyData" AS #2 LEN=62

If you are creating a random-access file, you must know *recordlength* before writing the program. You can determine the record length by deciding exactly which fields you will write to the file and adding the files' lengths together. If you do not specify a record length, QBasic assumes a 128-byte record length, although this length rarely is correct for your data files.

The following code line opens a file called ADDRESS.89, which has a record length of 62 on disk drive D:. The statement then connects the file to file number one (#1).

```
OPEN "D:ADDRESS.89" AS #1 LEN=62
```

The *TYPE* Statement

The TYPE statement describes a fixed-length record. With TYPE, you can define your records, no matter what mixture of fields and data types they might have.

Defining Random-Access Records

The format of TYPE is

```
TYPE recordname
    fieldname AS datatype
    [fieldname2 AS datatype2]
        .
        .
        .
    [fieldnameN AS datatypeN]
END TYPE
```

With TYPE, you can define your own data types to QBasic. Instead of being limited to integers, single- and double-precisions, and strings, you can create new data types that are combinations of all these types.

Example

```
TYPE musicrec
    title     AS STRING * 20    ' Title of the
                                 ' album.
    quantity  AS INTEGER        ' Number of them you
                                 ' have.
    condition AS STRING * 5      ' GOOD, POOR, and so
                                 ' on.
    numsongs  AS INTEGER        ' Number of songs on
                                 ' album.
    pricepd   AS SINGLE         ' Price you paid.
END TYPE
```

recordname is a label for the TYPE you are defining. Its name can consist of one to 40 letters and numbers. Do not use any special characters such as a period or an underscore. The *recordname* has no data type suffix character. It only names a new data type that you are creating. It is the name you refer to when you want to create variables that look like this record. The rest of the TYPE statement describes each field in the record. The *fieldname* can be any name you specify (also consisting of one to 40 letters and numbers), and the *datatype* is any QBasic defined data type from Table 11.3.

Table 11.3. The *TYPE* statement's possible field data types and their lengths.

Datatype	Description	Length
INTEGER	Integer	2
LONG	Long integer	4
SINGLE	Single-precision	4
DOUBLE	Double-precision	8
STRING * N	Fixed-length string	N

Each field you define that contains a string must also include the string length. Because random-access records must be fixed-length records, you must declare each string length in advance. It helps to comment on your record descriptions with remarks after each field description.

The length of musicrec (in the preceding Syntax at a Glance box) is 33. The first field (title) takes 20 characters. The second field (quantity) is an integer that takes two characters. The third (condition) takes five characters, the fourth (numsongs) takes two characters, and the last (pricepd) takes four.

The OPEN statement used for this file might be

```
OPEN "CDCOLLEC.DAT" AS #1 LEN=33
```

> **TIP** Instead of computing the total record length yourself, use the LEN( ) function. The previous OPEN statement could have been
>
> ```
> OPEN "CDCOLLEC.DAT" AS #1 LEN=LEN(musicrec)
> ```

Declaring Record Variables from Your *TYPE*

The TYPE statement only describes your file records. It does not reserve any storage. Notice that no variables are listed in the TYPE statement's format; only field names are described. The TYPE statement only describes the record; you must then define one or more record variables for it. Your programs store data in variables. Therefore, you must create record variables just as you created integer, long integer, string, single-precision, and double-precision variables.

Use a new version of DIM to create record variables.

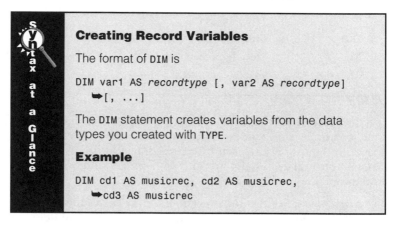

Creating Record Variables

The format of DIM is

DIM var1 AS *recordtype* [, var2 AS *recordtype*]
➥[, ...]

The DIM statement creates variables from the data types you created with TYPE.

Example

DIM cd1 AS musicrec, cd2 AS musicrec,
➥cd3 AS musicrec

The statement in the preceding Syntax at a Glance box creates three variables: cd1, cd2, and cd3. Each of these variables has the type defined in the TYPE statement; in other words, cd1 consists of a 20-character string, followed by an integer, followed by a five-character string, followed by an integer, followed by a single-precision value. If you want an array of music variables, you can do so like this:

DIM cds(500) AS musicrec

The type of the array is not string or integer as you have seen in previous chapters that used arrays; the array type is musicrec. Each element in the array looks like the record you defined with the TYPE statement.

Accessing Fields in a Record

Before saving record variables to a file, you have to assign values to them. In the preceding two Syntax at a Glance boxes, the names title, quantity, condition, numsongs, and pricepd are not variables; they are field names for the record musicrec. The variable

cd refers to a single variable in memory. To fill this variable, use
the dot (.) operator. An example is worth a thousand words:

```
cd.title = "Bruno's Here Again!"
cd.quantity = 1
cd.condition = "GOOD"
cd.numsongs = 12
cd.pricepd = 9.75
```

Notice that to assign values to fields in a record variable, you only
have to precede the field name with the record name and a period.
(This is why record and field names cannot contain a period.) The
dot operator assigns values to the record. The record is now ready
to be written to disk. Notice that some of the fields have been pad-
ded with spaces; this is how QBasic retains the fixed-length
records it needs for random-access files.

These `recordname.fieldname` pairs combine to form individual values that you can print, assign, or pass to subroutines and functions. The first part of the name before the period specifies the
record, and the last part specifies the field in that record.

Reading and Writing to Random-Access Files

After setting up your random-access record with TYPE, it is easy to
read or write that data to a file. The location of the record in the
file becomes important when working with random-access files.
The record number is the key to finding whatever record you want
to write or read. To create or read files, you cannot use the sequential file INPUT # and PRINT # statements because they do not
enable you to change the location of the next read or write.

Using the random-access reading and writing commands enables
you to specify which record in the file to read or write next.

Creating Random-Access File Data

You must use the PUT # statement to create a random-access file.
After you define the record to write and initialize the fields in that
record with data, PUT # writes that record to the disk.

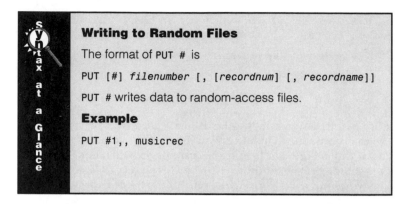

Writing to Random Files

The format of PUT # is

PUT [#] *filenumber* [, [*recordnum*] [, *recordname*]]

PUT # writes data to random-access files.

Example

PUT #1,, musicrec

The *filenumber* is the open random-access file to write to. The pound sign is optional, although most programmers include it. The *recordnum* is an integer or a long integer that specifies the record number to write to. If you do not specify a *recordnum*, QBasic uses, as the default, the record following the last one written. The comma is mandatory regardless of whether you specify a record name. If the comma is not present, QBasic will interpret the item as a record and not a record number. The *recordname* is the record's name created with a TYPE statement.

Listing 11.6. creates a random inventory file.

Listing 11.6. Creating a random-access inventory file.

```
' Creates a random-access inventory file.
CLS
TYPE invrec
    partno   AS STRING * 5
    descrip  AS STRING * 10
    quantity AS INTEGER
    price    AS SINGLE
END TYPE
DIM item AS invrec      ' A nonarray variable of the record.
OPEN "C:INVEN.DAT" AS #1 LEN=21
' Get the data from the user
DO
    PRINT
    INPUT "What is the part number"; item.partno
    INPUT "What is the description"; item.descrip
    INPUT "What is the quantity"; item.quantity
    INPUT "What is the price"; item.price
    INPUT "Is there another part (Y/N)"; ans$
    PUT #1,, item
```

```
' No record number is needed.
' The record number defaults to the next one.
LOOP WHILE ( LEFT$(UCASE$(ans$),1) = "Y" )
CLOSE
```

This code also shows that the record number is optional. If you do not specify a record number in the PUT # statement, QBasic inserts the next record after the last one written in the file. Whether or not you specify a record number, you must still include the comma.

> **NOTE** Keep in mind that this is a random-access file, although you are creating it in a sequential manner: The first record is followed by the second, and so on. Later, you can read this file randomly or sequentially using random-access commands.

Reading Random-Access Files

You must use the GET # statement to read from random-access files. GET # is the mirror image of PUT #. GET # reads records from the disk file to the record you define with TYPE or FIELD.

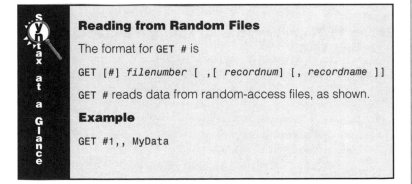

Reading from Random Files

The format for GET # is

GET [#] *filenumber* [,[*recordnum*] [, *recordname*]]

GET # reads data from random-access files, as shown.

Example

GET #1,, MyData

The *filenumber* is the open random-access file from which GET # reads. Notice that the pound sign is optional, although most programmers include it. The *recordnum* is an integer or a long integer that specifies the record number to read. If you do not specify a *recordnum*, QBasic reads the default record—the one following the last one read. The comma here is mandatory. The *recordname* is the record's name created with a TYPE statement.

It might be helpful to use the LOF() function to determine how many bytes are in the file.

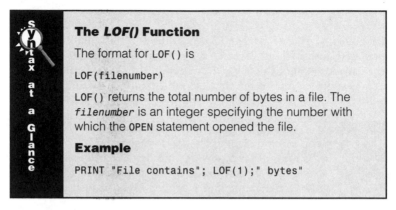

The *LOF()* Function

The format for LOF() is

LOF(filenumber)

LOF() returns the total number of bytes in a file. The *filenumber* is an integer specifying the number with which the OPEN statement opened the file.

Example

PRINT "File contains"; LOF(1);" bytes"

LOF() always returns the total number of bytes written to the file. By dividing the LOF() value by the record length, you can determine exactly how many records there are in the file. You can then avoid reading past the end of the file. You can also append to the end of a random-access file by knowing the last record number.

Listing 11.7 reads the inventory file created in Listing 11.6. It reads the file with GET #, but it reads from the first record to the last as if it were a sequential file.

Listing 11.7. Reading the inventory file created in Listing 11.6.

```
' Reads a random-access inventory file created earlier.

CLS

TYPE invrec
   partno   AS STRING * 5
   descrip  AS STRING * 10
   quantity AS INTEGER
   price    AS SINGLE
END TYPE

DIM item AS invrec    ' A nonarray variable of the record.

OPEN "C:INVEN.DAT" AS #1 LEN=21

num.recs = LOF(1) / 21      ' The total number of records.
```

```
FOR recnum = 1 TO num.recs  ' Loop through the file.
   GET #1, recnum, item     ' Get the next record.
   PRINT
   PRINT "The part number: "; item.partno
   PRINT "The description: "; item.descrip
   PRINT "The quantity:"; item.quantity
   PRINT "The price:"; item.price
NEXT recnum
CLOSE
```

Changing a Random-Access File

When you find a random-access record, you can change it and
write it back to the file. The advantage of random-access files over
sequential files is that the entire file does not have to be rewritten;
only the record you want to change has to be rewritten. When you
find the record to change, you only have to perform a PUT #.
QBasic remembers exactly where the record just read (with GET #)
came from. After changing the record's field data (you can change
any of the field data by assigning them other values), issue a PUT #
to put the record back in its place.

Suppose a company decides to add a letter *C* to each customer
number stored in a customer file, and a *V* to each vendor number
in a vendor file. (The company left enough room in these fields to
add the prefix letter.) Listing 11.8 opens the customer file and
reads each customer record. It inserts a *C* before the customer
number and writes each record back to the file. No other customer
data is changed. Then the program does the same for the vendors.

Listing 11.8. Manipulating records in a customer file.

```
' This program reads each record in a customer and vendor
' file and inserts a C or V in each file's customer
' number and vendor number.
' No other fields in the files are changed.
'
TYPE custrec
   custnum  AS STRING * 8
   custname AS STRING * 15
   custaddr AS STRING * 20
   custcity AS STRING * 10
   custst   AS STRING * 2
```

continues

Listing 11.8. Continued

```
    custzip  AS STRING * 5
    custbal  AS DOUBLE
END TYPE

TYPE vendrec
    vendnum  AS STRING * 10
    vendname AS STRING * 20
    vendaddr AS STRING * 20
    vendcity AS STRING * 10
    vendst   AS STRING * 2
    vendzip  AS STRING * 5
END TYPE

DIM customer AS custrec
DIM vendor   AS vendrec

OPEN "c:CUSTDATA.DAT" FOR RANDOM AS #1 LEN = LEN(customer)

cus.num.recs = LOF(1) / LEN(customer)
    ' Total records in customer file

    ' Add the C to the customer number field.
FOR rec = 1 TO cus.num.recs
    GET #1, rec, customer
    customer.custnum = LEFT$(("C" + customer.custnum), 8)
    ' Insert the C
    PUT #1, rec, customer
    ' No other data have to be changed.
NEXT rec
CLOSE #1

    ' Add the V to the vendor number field.
OPEN "c:VENDDATA.DAT" FOR RANDOM AS #2 LEN = LEN(vendor)
ven.num.recs = LOF(2) / LEN(vendor)
    ' Total records in vendor file
FOR rec = 1 TO ven.num.recs
    GET #2, rec, vendor
    vendor.vendnum = LEFT$(("V" + vendor.vendnum), 10)
    ' Insert the V.
    PUT #2, rec, vendor
    ' No other data have to be changed.
NEXT rec
CLOSE #2
```

Summary

You can now work with sequential and random-access files in QBasic. You saw that random-access files can still be read sequentially, but you can also read and write them in any order. You can also change a record in the middle of the file without affecting any surrounding records in the file. You now have the capability to store a large amount of data without relying on DATA statements to hold data. By using random-access files for your changing data, you ensure that you can easily update that data later.

Here are some of the things you learned in this chapter:

■ Files hold much more data than memory.

■ The two types of file access are sequential and random.

■ Open all files before you access them, and close them when you are finished.

■ You can only read and write (and append to) sequential-access files in the order that the data was initially stored.

■ You can read and write to random-access files in any order.

■ To help you store data in a random-access file, you should use the TYPE statement to consolidate your file data.

Sound and Graphics

It's time to have some fun! QBasic provides lots of sound and graphics capabilities that you can use to write game programs and to make business programs more interesting. One of the most fun aspects of programming with QBasic is its graphics capabilities. Drawing is not only for playing; it is useful also for business graphics. It is said that a picture is worth a thousand words. Executives don't want to see a long list of numbers when a graph can show at a glance where the numbers are headed.

You must have a graphics adapter inside your computer and a graphics monitor attached to it before the drawing routines in this section will work. Available graphics adapters include the HGA (Hercules Graphics Adapter), CGA (Color Graphics Adapter), EGA (Enhanced Graphics Adapter), VGA (Video Graphics Array), and the MCGA (MultiColor Graphics Array) video cards.

There are many video graphics adapters on the market, and QBasic supports most of them. Sometimes the number of graphics adapters and possible colors confuses beginning programmers. You should concentrate on the modes that match your graphics adapter.

Your Screen

The difference in graphics adapters is measured by the number of colors each supports and the highest *resolution* possible. Resolution refers to the number of lines and columns on your screen. You already know that your PC screen can support 80 rows of 25 lines of text. In a graphics mode, the screen has more rows and columns. The intersection of a row and a column represents a *picture element*, or a *pixel*, which is a dot on the screen. The more rows and columns (or the higher the resolution), the smaller each pixel is and the better picture you can draw—the lines are smoother and the image is more crisp.

The higher your screen's resolution, the sharper its picture is. Several graphics modes are possible with most graphics adapters. When your program switches among modes, it selects a resolution and color combination. For instance, when you display graphics, your screen must be in a graphics mode. If text was on the screen before the mode change, it is erased.

> **NOTE** The LOCATE command locates the next printed text at a row and column position but has no effect on locating pixels for graphics. You must use the graphics commands that are described later to locate and display pixels of graphics. If you are in a graphics mode, you can use LOCATE to print text.

The upper-left screen pixel is called the *home* location. It is located at column 0, row 0. This pixel is designated also with (0, 0). This designation, in which the column number always comes first, is common. In other words, a pixel located at (34, 50) would be at graphics column *34* and graphics row *50*.

When you designate a pixel's location with its row and column intersection, it is known as a pixel *coordinate*. Obviously, the higher the resolution, the more coordinates are possible, and the higher the row and column numbers can be. QBasic borrows from mathematics when it refers to its screen coordinates. The columns across the screen are known as the *x* coordinates, whereas the rows down the screen are known as the *y* coordinates. Therefore, the coordinate *(9, 56)* would refer to x-position *9* and y-position *56*.

The SCREEN statement sets your computer's graphics card to a certain resolution and color combination.

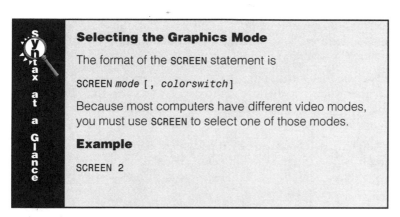

Selecting the Graphics Mode

The format of the SCREEN statement is

SCREEN *mode* [, *colorswitch*]

Because most computers have different video modes, you must use SCREEN to select one of those modes.

Example

SCREEN 2

The *mode* can be one of the values in Table 12.1 (check your QBasic Reference Manual for a full list). Notice that in some modes, SCREEN supports several different resolutions of several different graphics adapters and monitors.

Table 12.1. Some common graphics modes for *SCREEN*.

Mode	Description
1	320 x 200 graphics resolution. Also supports 40 x 25 text mode (all LOCATEs must be in this range). Supports 4 of 16 colors and one video page (0). For use with CGA, EGA, VGA, or MCGA.
2	640 x 200 graphics resolution. Also supports 80 x 25 text mode. Supports 2 of 16 colors with EGA, VGA, or MCGA; black and white only with CGA and one video page (0). For use with CGA, EGA, VGA, or MCGA.
12	640 x 480 graphics resolution. Also supports 80 x 30 text modes. Supports 16 of 256K colors and one video page (0). For use only with VGA.

When you use a SCREEN statement to set a graphics mode, the rest of your graphics commands must be aware of the resolution you set with the SCREEN statement. In other words, if you type SCREEN 1 to initialize the screen to 320 x 200 resolution, no graphics commands can display a pixel past row 200. Many examples in this book use the graphics modes 1 and 2 because these are so common and are available on almost every computer (from CGA adapters to VGA adapters).

It is a good idea to add the SCREEN 0 statement to the end of every program you write that uses graphics. This returns the video adapter to an 80-column text screen if you were in a graphics mode before.

If you have a CGA adapter card and need to initialize a program for graphics, you can put the following statement at the top of your program:

SCREEN 1

This initializes your screen to 320 x 200 resolution.

If you want to display graphics in the highest possible resolution, type the following statement at the top of your program:

SCREEN 12

TIP	You do not have to clear the screen (with CLS) before changing graphics modes. The SCREEN statement automatically clears the screen for you.

Drawing Pixels on the Screen

The most fundamental of all graphics statements turns pixels on and off. Later, you will learn how to add color to your programs. For now, it is easiest to ignore colors and work with the default colors (white pixels on a black background) that QBasic assumes. After you master the drawing commands, you can easily add colors.

The two commands that turn pixels on and off are PSET and PRESET.

The x and y values are integer numbers or variables representing the column and row intersections you want to turn on or off. The x and y values are absolute if you do not specify the STEP keyword. (You will read about the *color* value later in this chapter.) In other words, the statement

PSET (30, 67)

turns on the pixel at graphics x-position (column) 30 and y- position (row) 67. However, if you include the optional STEP keyword, as in

PSET STEP (30, 67)

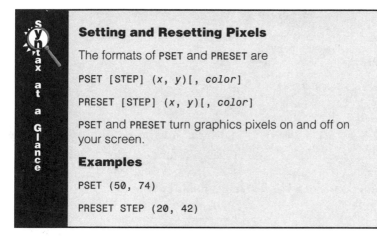

Setting and Resetting Pixels

The formats of PSET and PRESET are

PSET [STEP] (*x, y*)[, *color*]

PRESET [STEP] (*x, y*)[, *color*]

PSET and PRESET turn graphics pixels on and off on your screen.

Examples

PSET (50, 74)

PRESET STEP (20, 42)

QBasic turns on the pixel located at 30 and 67 positions away from the last PSET or PRESET statement. If there was not another graphics PSET or PRESET performed before the PSET STEP, QBasic turns on the pixel that is 30 and 67 positions away from the middle of the screen.

PRESET turns off any pixel located at its row and column (or relative to its row and column if you include STEP). If there is no pixel turned on at that location, PRESET does nothing.

PSET and PRESET are useful only when you need to do complex drawings. You can take advantage of the faster LINE and CIRCLE statements (described in the next section) for drawing lines and circles.

Listing 12.1 is fancy; it draws pixels randomly on the screen until the user presses any key. The RND function determines the next screen coordinate to turn on or off. (RND produces a random number from 0 to 1.) Each time through the loop, the program calculates a random value of x and y coordinate pairs to turn on and another to turn off. Eventually, the screen fills up with blinking lights.

Listing 12.1. Drawing with pixels.

```
' Randomly draws and turns off pixels until the user
' presses a key.
SCREEN 2    ' 640 x 200 resolution
LOCATE 12, 30
PRINT "Press any key to quit..."
DO
    x = INT(RND * 640)    ' Select a random coordinate
    y = INT(RND * 200)
    PSET (x, y)    ' Turn it on

    x = INT(RND * 640)
    y = INT(RND * 200)
    PRESET (x, y)    ' Turn another one off

    key.press$ = INKEY$    ' Look for a keypress
LOOP UNTIL (key.press$ <> "")
```

Figure 12.1 shows the output from this program.

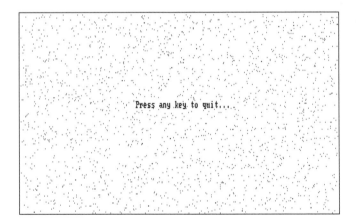

Figure 12.1. *A screenful of on and off pixels appears.*

Drawing Lines and Boxes

Although the PSET is good for individual pixels, it is slow for drawing lines and boxes. Because your program first has to calculate each pixel in the line or box, the results are fairly slow. QBasic offers the LINE statement to help make your line drawing easier and faster. Instead of collecting a group of PSET statements to draw a line or box, the LINE statement does all the work at once. The LINE statement draws both lines and boxes, depending on the format you use. The simplest format of LINE draws a line from one coordinate to another.

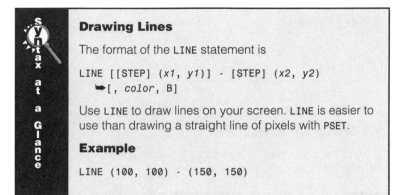

Drawing Lines

The format of the LINE statement is

LINE [[STEP] (x1, y1)] - [STEP] (x2, y2)
↪[, color, B]

Use LINE to draw lines on your screen. LINE is easier to use than drawing a straight line of pixels with PSET.

Example

LINE (100, 100) - (150, 150)

The x1 and y1 values define the beginning point (coordinate) of the line, and the x2 and y2 coordinates define where the line ends. Of course, the coordinates cannot exceed the boundries of the screen mode set with the SCREEN statement. The B indicates that you want to draw a box, as described later. The LINE statement in the preceding example draws a line from pixel (100, 100) to pixel (150, 150).

As with PSET and PRESET, the STEP option draws the line relative to the starting location (the last pixel drawn or turned off). You do not have to include the starting coordinate pair because STEP knows where to begin. Therefore, by using STEP, some of the coordinates may be negative, such as

LINE STEP(-15, 0) - (10, 1)

(which means draw a line from the last pixel drawn to a point 15 pixels to the left of the last pixel drawn). If you have not drawn anything, STEP draws 15 pixels to the left of your screen's center pixel. There is no mandatory order of LINE's parameters. You can draw up, down, to the left, or to the right.

You can add an option to LINE to draw a box or rectangle with a single LINE statement. The B option of LINE is required to draw boxes. You can put an optional color attribute before the B. If you do not specify a color (which you will learn to do later), you still need to include the empty comma before the B. The two coordinates specify the upper-left and the lower-right corners of the rectangle.

Listing 12.2 draws a single box on-screen in the screen's default colors of white on black.

Listing 12.2. A program that draws a box in the default colors.

```
' Draws a box on the screen
SCREEN 2     ' 640 x 200
LINE (20, 20) - (100, 100),,B
```

Drawing Circles

The CIRCLE statement enables you to draw circles and ellipses (stretched circles).

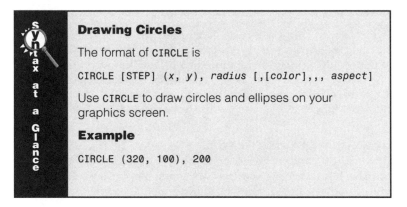

Drawing Circles

The format of CIRCLE is

CIRCLE [STEP] (x, y), radius [,[color],,, aspect]

Use CIRCLE to draw circles and ellipses on your graphics screen.

Example

CIRCLE (320, 100), 200

The x and y values determine the center point of the circle, and the radius is the distance in pixels between the center point of the circle and its outer edge. If you include the STEP keyword, the x and y coordinates are relative (negative values are allowed) from the current (last-drawn) pixel. To draw a stretched circle (an ellipse), you must also add an *aspect ratio* to the CIRCLE statement (after some commas that are placeholders for color commands you learn later).

aspect means two different things, depending on its value. If the value is less than 1, it refers to the x-radius (the circle is stretched *widely* across the x coordinate). If the aspect is greater than or equal to 1, it refers to the y-radius (the circle is stretched *lengthwise* up and down the y coordinate).

The *aspect* ratio acts as a multiplier of each radius. For example, an aspect of *4* means that the circle is vertically stretched four times the regular circle's height. An aspect ratio of *(4/10/2)* (or *.2*) means the circle is horizontally stretched five times its regular radius (one-half of 40 percent).

Adding Color

This section expands on some of the graphics statements you learned in the previous section. Depending on your graphics adapter, you can add different colors to your drawings. Colors make your programs more interesting and enjoyable.

There are so many color options available in QBasic that it would be difficult to cover them all here, especially in light of the fact that each graphics adapter handles colors in a different way. Instead of being an exhaustive walk-through of every possible color option for every possible graphics adapter and monitor, this section attempts to explore some of the common routines available for the graphics adapters that most readers own. When you master the basic color concepts, you will find it easy to program the specific options available for your adapter.

QBasic and Color

The authors of QBasic chose to give you a wide variety of color programming tools, many of which you might never use. Color graphics add flair to almost any application. Suppose you decide to write a payroll program that you want to sell. A colorful opening graphics screen gets your customers' attention and makes your program look as though you put much work into it (although graphics do not necessarily require much work).

To give you an idea of the range of possible colors, look at Table 12.2, which is the QBasic color attribute chart that shows possible colors for both color and monochrome video adapters in each of the SCREEN modes. Of course, no color is possible with monochrome adapters except the adapter's native two-color mode, but you can set attributes, such as underlining and high intensity, with a monochrome adapter. Table 12.2 explains those attributes. Most of the examples in this book stay with common color combinations that are possible for users with CGA, EGA, and VGA adapters. If your video adapter is VGA or MCGA, you might want to experiment with other color settings.

Table 12.2. The range of possible color attributes for color and monochrome adapters.

Color Monitors		Monochrome Monitors	
Color Attribute	Displayed Color	Default Color Value	Displayed Color
0	Black	0[a]	Off
1	Blue		Underlined[b]
2	Green	1[a]	On[b]
3	Cyan	1[a]	On[b]
4	Red	1[a]	On[b]
5	Magenta	1[a]	On[b]
6	Brown	1[a]	On[b]
7	White	1[a]	On[b]
8	Gray	0[a]	Off
9	Light blue		High-intensity Underlined
10	Light green	2[a]	High-intensity
11	Light cyan	2[a]	High-intensity
12	Light red	2[a]	High-intensity
13	Light magenta	2[a]	High-intensity
14	Yellow	2[a]	High-intensity
15	High-intensity white	2[a]	High-intensity

SCREEN Mode 1 only

0	Black	0	Off
1	Light cyan	2	High-intensity
2	Light magenta	2	High-intensity
3	High-intensity white	0	Off-white

Notes:
(a) Only for mode 0.
(b) Off when used for background.

Not all the color resolutions are covered here (for instance, SCREEN modes 10 and 11 are omitted), because not all of them support colors.

The color value in the graphics statements you learned earlier is a number from Table 12.2 that is consistent with the SCREEN mode you are in. For example, if you have an EGA graphics adapter that has less than 64K of RAM and you set the SCREEN mode to 9, the color values can range from 0 to 3 to get the colors black, light cyan, light magenta, and high-intensity white, respectively.

Listing 12.3 is a box drawing program similar to the one in Listing 12.2. It draws three rectangles, each with a different color. It uses SCREEN mode 1, which limits the number of colors to three. There are four possible colors in SCREEN mode 1; however, the background is black, so you couldn't see a black rectangle if it was drawn.

Listing 12.3. Box drawing program.

```
' Draws three rectangles on the screen in three different
' colors.
SCREEN 1    ' 320 x 200
' Draw the boxes of different colors
LINE (80, 50)-(120, 100), 1, B    ' Box of light cyan color
LINE (130, 50)-(170, 100), 2, B   ' Box of light magenta color
LINE (180, 50)-(220, 100), 3, B   ' Box of high-intensity
                                  ' white color
```

Making Music and Special Sounds

Now that you can display graphics, you might want to stimulate your aural senses as well by producing music and sound effects. This section explains the basics of generating sound through various sound-producing commands.

The BEEP statement was your first introduction to the PC speaker. Rather than a single tone (as produced by BEEP), you can create your own Top 40 hits.

The *SOUND* Statement

The SOUND statement is the foundation of music on your PC. Each sound statement produces a sound similar to that of a single piano key. You can produce any note for any duration.

Although you do not need a degree in music theory to produce music with SOUND, understanding musical notation helps you understand the SOUND statement.

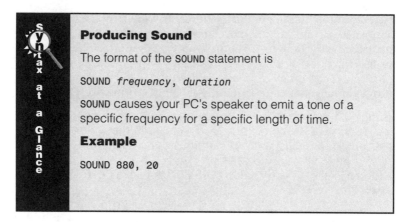

Producing Sound

The format of the SOUND statement is

SOUND *frequency, duration*

SOUND causes your PC's speaker to emit a tone of a specific frequency for a specific length of time.

Example

SOUND 880, 20

The frequency value (in hertz) must be a number from 37 to 32,767 (therefore, it can be an integer constant, integer expression, or integer variable). *Hertz* is the number of cycles per second the note "sings." On a piano, the A below middle C (the middle note of the 88 keys) has the frequency of 440 hertz. Therefore, a frequency of 440 produces the same note and key as pressing the A below middle C.

The duration must be a number from 0 through 65,536. It must be a constant, an expression, or a variable (any data type except an integer, because 65,536 is too large to fit in an integer variable). The duration measures the length of the note (how long it sounds) in *clock ticks*. A clock tick is based on the CPU's built-in timing clock. There are 18.2 ticks in one second. Therefore, if you want to produce the A below middle C for one second, you would write the following statement:

SOUND 440, 18.2

The value of 440 hertz is important. It defines each octave available with sound. Each multiple of 440 (880, 1,320, 1,760, and so on) is the next octave A. Sound becomes inaudible at 28,160 hertz. SOUND is good for producing gliding crescendos and sirens when matching a tone to a specific note is not as important as the actual sound.

Listing 12.4 simply uses SOUND to produce every possible A from its lowest frequency of 110 to its highest (and inaudible) frequency of 28,160.

Listing 12.4. Program producing all possible A octaves.

```
' Program that produces each octave of A's.
SOUND 110, 20      ' Three A's below middle C
SOUND 220, 20      ' Two A's below middle C
SOUND 440, 20      ' A below middle C
SOUND 880, 20      ' One A above middle C
SOUND 1760, 20     ' Two A's above middle C
SOUND 3520, 20     ' Three A's above middle C
SOUND 7040, 20     ' Four A's above middle C
SOUND 14080, 20    ' Five A's above middle C
SOUND 28160, 20    ' Six A's above middle C, inaudible
```

Listing 12.5 uses a FOR-NEXT loop to cycle through every note that is possible with SOUND.

Listing 12.5. Cycling through all possible notes with a *FOR-NEXT* loop.

```
' Program that cycles through every note of SOUND.
FOR n = 37 TO 32767
    SOUND n, 1    ' Sound each note for a very short duration
NEXT
```

Summary

Although this chapter made a whirlwind tour through graphics and sound, it gave you the fundamentals for producing eye-catching displays and ear-ringing sounds.

Here are some of the things you learned in this chapter:

- You must have a graphics adapter and matching monitor before you can display graphics.

- The SCREEN statement ensures that your graphics adapter is ready to display graphics.

- To turn individual pixels (*picture elements*) on and off, use the PSET and PRESET commands.

- QBasic supplies statements that let you draw lines, circles, and boxes.

- The SOUND command sends whatever note and duration you need to the PC's speaker.

INDEX

Symbols

! PRINT USING string control
code, 83
PRINT USING numeric control
code, 86, 89
$$ PRINT USING numeric
control code, 87
% in format strings, 88-89
& PRINT USING control code,
83-84
% integer variable suffix, 33
, (comma)
in input strings, 77-79
in PRINT statements, 41-43
PRINT USING numeric control
code, 87-89
printing effects, 204
' in REM statements, 49
" (quotation marks) as string
constants, 39, 62
( ) parentheses
hierarchy
of operators, 106
of variables, overriding, 57
tab commands, 43
− (minus sign)
PRINT USING numeric control
code, 83, 87
subtraction operator, 52

... (ellipses) in commands, 17
^ (exponentiation operator),
52
* (asterisk) multiplication
operator, 52
** (asterisks) PRINT USING
numeric control code, 87
**$ PRINT USING numeric
control code, 87
+ (plus sign)
addition operator, 52
PRINT USING numeric
control code, 87
string concatenation
operator, 67-68
/ (division operator), 52
// PRINT USING control code,
83-84
/? command-line option, 13
: (colon), statement separator,
112-113
; (semicolons)
in INPUT commands, 80-81
in PRINT statements, 41-49
in tab commands, 44
printing effects, 204
< (less than) relational
operator, 101
<= (less than or equal to)
relational operator, 101

< > (not equal to) relational
operator, 101
= (equal sign) relational
operator, 101
> (greater than) relational
operator, 101
? (question marks)
in INPUT statements, 73-75
eliminating, 78-79
in LINE INPUT statements, 79-
80
\ (integer division operator),
52-53
^ ^ ^ ^ PRINT USING numeric
control code, 87

A

ABS( ) function, 173
accessing files, 200-202
active commands, 109
adapters
graphics, 13, 223-226
color handling, 231
monochrome, 231-232
video, 13, 231-232
Alt-H (display help menu)
command, 21
Alt-key combination (display
menus), 15
ampersand (&), in PRINT USING
command, 83-84
AND operator, hierarchical
status, 107
AND truth table, 104
apostrophes ('), in REM
statements, 49

APPEND mode, 202-203, 208
arguments, 168
arrays, 143
character-string, 146
data type, declaring, 146-147
dimensioning, 146-152,
160-166
elements, erasing, 159-161
multidimensional, 160-166
numeric, zeroing out, 159
parallel, 149
single-dimension, 160-161
single-precision, 146
sorting, 155-160
bubble sort, 156-158
descending, 154
quicksort, 156
shell sort, 156
subscripts, 143
designating, 152
numbers, 145
values, searching, 154-155
ASC( ) function, 174
ASCII
QBasic programs, 13
string functions, 174-176
table, 92-94, 103, 174
aspect ratios, 230
assigning values, 35-39
READ/DATA commands,
107-111
to string variables, 62-63
assignment statements, 35-39
matching data types, 68-69
valid/invalid, 69
asterisks, floating, 87
asterisks (**), PRINT USING
numeric control code, 87

B

/B command-line option, 13
background color, 17-29, 94-96
backslashes (\\), PRINT USING
control code, 83-84
Backspace key, 23
.BAS filename extension, 21
BASIC (Beginner's All-purpose
Symbolic Instruction Code)
programming language, 6
versions, 6, 14
BEEP command, 92
blank lines, printing to
screen, 38
block
IF command, 117
IF-THEN-ELSE command,
115-117
bookmark keys, 25
borders, colors, 94-96
boxes, drawing, 176, 228-230
brackets (dialog box), 19
branching statements, 99-101
bubble sort arrays, 156-158
buttons, Help, 19

C

calculations, printing, 58-59
calling
routines, 193
subroutines, 188-189
carriage return-line feeds,
suppressing, 41
CASE ELSE command, 120

CGA (Color Graphics Adapter),
94, 223
screens, snow, eliminating, 13
character
functions, string, 179-182
strings, comparing, 103
character-string arrays, 146
characters
color, changing, 17
empty space (Tab keypress),
setting, 19
filename, 27
high-intensity, 13
in string variables, storing, 93
in strings, reversing, 191
line-drawing, 94
nonprinting, 93
permitted in filenames, 200
special, printing, 92-94
checks, printing, 87
CHR$( ) function, 93-94, 167,
174
CINT( ) integer function,
169-170
limitations of return
values, 171
CIRCLE command, 230-231
circles, drawing, 230-231
Clear command (Edit menu), 17
clearing
screens, 46, 226
in desired color, 96
windows, 28
CLNG( ) integer function,
169-171
CLOSE command, 202-203
closing files, 202-203
CLS command, 46, 96

codes, control, 89
PRINT USING command, 83-98
colon (:) statement separator, 112-113
COLOR command, 94-96
Color Graphics Adapter, 223
colors
borders, 94-96
characters, changing, 17
foreground/background, 17-19, 94-96
printing to screen, 94-96
numbers for COLOR statement, 95-98
text, changing, 17-18
command-line options, 12-13
commands, 32
Alt-H (display help menu), 21
BEEP, 92
block
IF, 117
IF-THEN-ELSE, 115-117
CASE ELSE, 120
CIRCLE, 230-231
Clear (Edit menu), 17
CLOSE, 202-203
CLS (Clear Screen), 46, 96
COLOR, 94-96
Contents (Help menu), 21
Continue (Run menu), 16, 22
Copy (Edit menu), 17
Ctrl-Break (Stop), 22
Cut (Edit menu), 17
DATA, 107-111, 195
DIM, 146-152, 214
DO UNTIL-LOOP, 137-139
DO WHILE-LOOP, 134-135
DO-LOOP UNTIL, 139-140

editing, 24
ELSE, 114-115, 155
ELSEIF, 117-119, 155
END, 47, 194
END IF, 116
ERASE, 159-161
executing, 15-16
Exit (File menu), 28
EXIT DO, 140-142
EXIT FOR, 130-132
F1 (Help), 21
F5 (Continue), 22
FOR/NEXT, 123-132, 154
GET #, 217
GOSUB, 188-191
GOTO, 99-103, 188
"grayed out," 16
Help, 16
IF, 102-107, 113
IF-THEN, 154
IF-THEN-ELSE, 114-115
Index (Help menu), 21
INPUT, 71-81, 184
INPUT #, 206-208
Last Find (Repeat menu), 16
LET, 35-36, 72
LINE, 228-230
LINE INPUT, 79-81
LINE INPUT #, 208
listing, 21
LOCATE, 96-98, 224
LPRINT, 45, 58-59, 63-66, 90
LPRINT USING, 82-84
names, 61
New (File menu), 28
OPEN, 15, 201-215
OPEN, random-access, 210-211
OPTION BASE, 152-153, 162-163

Output Screen (View
 menu), 16
passivity/activity, 109
Paste (Edit menu), 17
PRESET, 226-229
PRINT, 38-45, 58-59, 63-66, 90
PRINT #, 203-206, 209
PRINT USING, 82-83
Print... (File menu), 28
Procedure Step (Debug
 menu), 17
PSET, 226-228
PUT #, 215-221
READ, 107-111
READ-DATA, 138, 148, 206
REM, 48-50
RESTORE, 111-112
RETURN, 189-191
Save (File menu), 27
Save As... (File menu), 27
SCREEN, 224-226
Scroll Bars, 18
SELECT CASE, 119-121
selecting, 14-16
Shift-F5 (Start), 22
SOUND, 233-235
Start (Run menu), 17, 22, 39
startup, 12-13
STEP, 229-230
Step (Debug menu), 16
string, justifying, 182-184
SUBs..., 16
SWAP, 155-160
tab, 43-45
Tab Stops, 18
Toggle Breakpoint (Debug
 menu), 16
Topic (Help menu), 21
TYPE, 211-214

USING, 204
Using Help, 17, 20
WHILE-WEND, 133-134
window, 25-29
WRITE #, 205-206, 209
commas
 in input strings, 77-79
 in PRINT statements, 41-43
 PRINT USING numeric control
  code, 87-89
 printing effects, 204
comparing strings, character, 103
comparison operators, *see*
 relational operators
components, data, 31
compound logical operators,
 104-106
 relational tests, 104-106
concatenation, string, 67-68
constants, 31, 36-37
 double-precision, 37
 fixed point, 37
 floating point, 37
 in DATA commands, 108
 integer, 37
 long integer, 37
 numeric
  ranges, 37-39
  types, 37
 single-precision, 37
 string, 59-60, 62-70
  printing, 39-40
  storing in string variable, 64
Contents command (Help
 menu), 21
context-sensitive help, 21
Continue command (Run menu),
 16, 22

control codes, 89
    PRINT USING command,
        83-98
conversion functions, string,
    176-179
conversions, numeric, 13
coordinates, pixel, 224
Copy command (Edit menu), 17
Count from 1 to 5 program,
    125-126
    (without FOR/NEXT), 125-126
counter variables, 129
Ctrl-Break (Stop) command, 22
cursor control, INPUT/LINE
        INPUT commands, 80-81
cursors
    keys, 24
    moving, 23
    positioning, 96-98
Cut command (Edit menu), 17

D

dash (–), PRINT USING control
    code, 83
data
    aligning in columns, 65
    components, 31
    files, 196-200
    numeric, converting to
        string, 178
    processing, 7
    similar, storing in single
        variable, 144-146
    storage
        in string variables, 62-63
        in numeric variables, 61
    string, 60
    trigger, 110

types
    arrays, declaring, 146-147
    matching in assignment
        statements, 68-69
    TYPE command, 213
DATA command, 107-111, 195
data-driven programs, 99
decision statements, 102
declaring arrays, data types,
    146-147
defining records, random-access,
    211-213
deleting text, 23
descending sort, arrays, 154
designating arrays,
        subscripts, 152
designing programs, 8-9
dialog boxes, 17-19
    brackets, 19
    Display.... (Options menu),
        17-19
DIM command, 146-152, 214
    combining, 163
    dimensioning multiple
        arrays, 149
    memory, reserving for
        multidimensional
        arrays, 160
dimensioning
    array elements, 146-152
    arrays, multidimensional,
        160-166
    tables, 162-163
directories, DOS, 11
disk drives, 195-196
disk operating system, *see* DOS
disks
    files, saving programs to, 9
    hard, 195-196
Display.... dialog box (Options
    menu), 17-19

DO loops, 134-142
DO UNTIL-LOOP command,
    137-139
DO WHILE-LOOP command,
    134-135
DO-LOOP loop, 149
DO-LOOP UNTIL command,
    139-140
DO-LOOP WHILE command, 136
dollar signs ($$), PRINT USING
    numeric control code, 87
DOS (disk operating system), 8
    directories, 11
    Version 5.0, 5
double quotation marks ("),
    string constants, 39
double-precision
    constants, 37
    variables, 33
drawing
    boxes, 176, 228-230
    circles, 230-231
    ellipses, 230-231
    lines, 228-230
    pixels, 226-228
duration, 234

E

editing
    commands, 24
    hints, 23
    keys, 24
/EDITOR command-line
    option, 13
EDITOR (MS-DOS), 13
editors, 9
    program, 22-28

EGA (Enhanced Graphics
    Adapter), 223
    monitors, 94
ellipses (figures), drawing,
    230-231
ellipses (...), in commands, 17
ELSE command, 114-115, 155
ELSEIF command, 117-119, 155
empty string, 63
END command, 47, 194
END IF command, 116
Enhanced Graphics Adapter, 223
EOF( ) function, 206-221
equal sign (=) relational
    operator, 101
ERASE command, 159-161
erasing elements, arrays, 159-161
errors
    messages, 27
    syntax, 27
    READ commands, 109
exclamation point (!), PRINT
    USING control code, 83
executing
    commands, 15-16
    programs, 7, 26-27
Exit command (File menu), 28
EXIT DO command, 140-142
EXIT FOR command, 130-132
    conditional, 132
    unconditional, 131
exiting
    programs, 22
    QBasic, 28
expanded
    memory, 196
    scientific notation, 87
exponentiation operator ($\wedge$), 52
expressions, value, printing,
    58-59
extensions, filename, 21, 199

F

F1 (Help) command, 21
F5 (Continue) command, 22
fieldnames, 212
fields, 198-199
  assigning values to, 214-215
File pull-down menu, 15
filenames, 27, 196, 199-200
  characters permitted, 200
  extensions, 21
files
  accessing, 200-202
  closing, 202-203
  data, 196-200
  disk, saving programs to, 9
  fields, 198-199
  input, reading data from, 206
  overwriting, 27
  program, 196
  random-access, 200, 209-217
    changing, 219-220
    creating, 215-217
    opening, 210-211
    reading, 217-219
  records, 198-199
  sequential, 200-203
    appending to, 208-209
    creating, 203-208
    reading, 206-208
    writing to, 203-208
    variable-length, 204
FIX( ) integer function, 169, 170
fixed point constants, 37
fixed-length
  records, 198-199
  string variables, 60
floating
  asterisks, 87
  dollar signs, 87

floating point constants, 37
FOR loops, exiting early, 130-132
FOR-NEXT command, 154,
  123-132
FOR-NEXT loops, 145-146,
  149, 235
  nested, 163-166
foreground colors, 17-19, 94-96
format strings, 82-83, 86-90
  in variables, 84
formats
  DATA command, 108
  DIM command, 146
    for multidimensional
    arrays, 161-166
  ERASE command, 159
  EXIT FOR command, 131
  integer functions, 169
  LINE INPUT command, 79
  OPTION BASE command,
    152-153
  READ command, 108
  scientific notation
    E+xx, 87
    E+xxx, 87
  SELECT CASE command, 119
formulas, assigning to
  variables, 54
FORTRAN programming
  language, 6
free-form programs, 27
frequency values, 234
functions, 32, 167
  arguments, 168
  ASCII string, 174
  CHR$( ), 93-94, 167
  EOF( ), 206-221
  INKEY$, 184-185
  integer, 168-172
  LOF( ), 218

math, 168-185
mirror-image, 178
SPC( ), 90-92, 167
string, 174-185
  character, 179-182
  conversion, 176-179
  search, 181-182
TAB, 90-92
TAB( ), 167
values, returning, 168

Help Survival Guide, 19-20
  bypassing, 19-20
Hercules Graphics Adapter
  (HGA), 223
hertz, 234
hierarchy
  math operators, 54-56
  operators, 106-113
high-intensity characters, 13
hints, editing, 23
home location, pixels, 224

G

/G command-line option, 13
GET # command, 217
GOSUB command, 188-191
GOTO command, 99-101, 188
  with IF command, 102-103
graphics
  adapters, 223-226
  color handling, 231
  modes, 224-225, 231
"grayed out" commands, 16
greater than or equal to sign
  (>=), relational
  operator, 101
greater than sign (>), relational
  operator, 101

H

/H command-line option, 13
help (on-line), 19-21
  context-sensitive, 21
Help button, 19
Help command, 16
Help pull-down menu, 20

I

IEEE (Institute of Electrical and
  Electronics Engineers), 13
IF command, 102-107, 113
IF-THEN command, 154
IF-THEN-ELSE command,
  114-115
  block, 115-117
indentation of loops, 128-129
indeterminate loops, 134
Index command (Help
  menu), 21
INKEY$ function, 184-185
  loop requirements, 185
input
  files, reading data from, 206
  strings, commas in, 77-79
INPUT # command, 206-208
INPUT command, 71-79, 184
  blanks, 75
  cursor control, 80-81
  prompting the user, 74-78
INPUT mode, 202
input-checking routines,
  loops, 136

inputting, strings, 77-78
Insert mode, 23
INSTR( ) function, 181-182
INT( ) integer function, 169-172
integer
  constants, 37
  functions, 168-172
  variables, 33-34

J-K

justifying commands, string,
  182-184

keys
  Backspace, 23
  bookmark, 25
  cursor movement, 24
  editing, 24
  shortcut
    Alt-key combination
    (menus, displaying), 15
    F1 (Help) command, 21
    F5 (Continue)
      command, 22
    text-copying, 25
    text-deleting, 25
    text-inserting, 25
    text-scrolling, 24
    text-selection, 24
  window commands, 25-29

L

labels statement, 100, 111
Last Find command (Repeat
  menu), 16
LCASE$( ) function, 177
leading blanks, 178

left justification, 85
LEFT$( ) function, 180-181
LEN( ) function, 173-174, 180
length-of-file function, *see*
  LOF( ) function
lengths, subroutines, 194
less than or equal to sign (<=),
  relational operator, 101
less than sign (<), relational
  operator, 101
LET assignment statement, 62-63
LET command, 35-36, 72
LINE command, 228-230
LINE INPUT # command, 208
LINE INPUT command, 79-80
  cursor control, 80-81
  format, 79
line-drawing characters, 94
lines, drawing, 228-230
listing commands, 21
loading
  programs, 21-22
  QBasic, 11-12
LOCATE command, 96-98, 224
LOF( ) function, 218
logical operators, compound,
  104-106
long integer
  constants, 37
  variables, 33
loops, 123
  DO, 134-142
  DO-LOOP, 149
  early exiting, 150
  FOR, exiting early, 130-132
  FOR-NEXT, 123-132, 145-146,
    149, 235
    nested, 127-130, 163-166
    printing data values inside,
    125-126
  indentation, 128-129
  indeterminate, 134

input-checking, 136
memory, running out of, 150
requirements, INKEY$
    function, 185
WHILE-WEND, 133-134
lowercase, converting to
    uppercase, 176-179
LPRINT command, 45, 58-59,
    63-66, 90
LPRINT USING command, 82-84
LSET command, 182-184
LTRIM$( ) function, 181

M

maintenance programs, 191
math
    functions, 168-185
    operators, 51-57
        hierarchical status, 54-56,
        106-107
/MBF command-line option, 13
MCGA (MultiColor
        Graphics Array)
    monitors, 94
    video cards, 223
memory
    expanded, 196
    reserving, DIM command, 160
    running out of, loops, 150
    volatile/nonvolatile, 195
menu bars, 14-15
menus
    Options, 17
    program, 120
    pull-down, 14-16
        File, 15
        Help, 20-21
        Run, 26
    shortcut keys, 16-17

messages
    error, 27
    Press any key to continue, 26
    prompt, 76-77
Microsoft Corporation, 6
MID$( ) function, 181, 191
minus sign (–), PRINT USING
        numeric control code, 87
mirror-image functions, 178
MOD (Modulus operator), 52-53
modes, 201-215
    graphics, 224-225, 231
    Insert, 23
    Overtype, 23
modular programming, 187
modules, 191-194
monitors
    color, 94-96
    EGA, 94
    MCGA, 94
    VGA, 94
    monochrome, 13
monochrome adapters, 231
    possible color attributes, 232
mouse, 14
moving cursors, 23
MS-DOS EDITOR, 13
MultiColor Graphics Array, *see*
        MCGA
multidimensional
    arrays
        dimensioning, 160-166
        values, storing, 164
        tables, looping, 163-166
multiple
    arrays, dimensioning, 149
    statements on one line,
        112-119
    values, printing to a single
        line, 40

N

names, command, 61
naming variables, 32-33
  string, 61-62
nested loops, 127-130
  FOR-NEXT, 163-166
New command (File menu), 28
/NOHI *filename* , 13
nonprinting characters, 93
nonvolatile memory, 195
not equal to (< >), relational
  operator, 101
NOT truth table, 105
notation, scientific
  E+xx format, 87
  E+xxx format, 87
null strings, 63, 159, 180
numbers
  ASCII, 93
  changing power of, 53
  color, 95-98
  converting to strings, 176-179
  printing with PRINT USING
    command, 86-90
  subscript, arrays, 145
numeric
  arrays, zeroing out, 159
  constants
    ranges, 37-39
    types, 37
  conversions, 13
  data, converting to string, 178
  variables, 60
    storing data in, 61
    suffixes, 62
    types, 33-34

O

on-line help, 19-21
  context-sensitive, 21
OPEN command, 15, 201-215
  random-access, 210-211
opening random-access files,
  210-211
opening screen, 11
operators
  + (plus sign), string concat-
    enation, 67-68
  hierarchy, 106-113
  logical, compound, 104-106
  math, 51-57
    hierarchical status, 54-56,
      106-113
  relational, 101
    hierarchical status, 106-113
  unary, 52
OPTION BASE command,
  152-153, 162-163
Options menu, 17
OR truth table, 104-105
outlines, nested loops, 127
OUTPUT mode, 202
Output Screen command (View
  menu), 16
overriding subscripts, 162
Overtype mode, 23
overwriting
  files, 27
  text, 23

P

paper, printing to, 45
parallel arrays, 149

parentheses
    hierarchy of variables,
        overriding, 57
    in hierarchy of operators, 106
    tab commands, 43
passive commands, 109
Paste command (Edit menu), 17
percent sign (%)
    in format strings, 88-89
    integer variables, 33
picture elements, *see* pixels
pixels, 224-226
    coordinates, 224
    home location, 224
    turning on/off, 226-228
plus sign (+)
    PRINT USING numeric control
        code, 87
    string concatenation operator,
        67-68
positioning cursor, 96-98
pound sign (#), PRINT USING
    numeric control code,
    86, 89
precedence, operator, 54-56
PRESET command, 226-229
Press any key to continue
    message, 26
PRINT # command, 203-206, 209
PRINT command, 38-45, 49,
    58-59, 63-66, 90
PRINT USING command, 82-83
    ampersand (&), 84
    control codes, numeric, 86-98
    numbers, printing, 86-90
    string control codes, 83-86
print zones, 42-43
Print... command (File menu), 28

printing
    characters, special, 92-94
    checks, 87
    colors to screen, 94-96
    constants, string, 39-40
    control codes, in PRINT
        USING statements, 86
    multiple values to a line, 40-49
    numbers, with PRINT USING
        command, 86-90
    programs, 28
    SPC( ), 90-92
    to paper, 45
    to screen, 38-45
        blank lines, 38
    values, expressions, 58-59
    variables, string, 63-66
    with TAB commands, 43-45
Procedure Step command
    (Debug menu), 17
procedures, subroutine, 187,
    191-194
processing data, 7
program
    editing window, 14, 23
    clearing, 28
    editor, 22-28
    files, 196
program listings
    2.1. Your first QBasic
        program, 26
    3.1. Using commands with
        PRINT, 42
    3.2 Using TAB to print a
        report, 44
    3.3. Screen-clearing
        program, 46
    3.4. Program with an END
        statement, 47

3.5. Program using both types of comments, 49

4.1. Payroll computation program, 54

4.2. Payroll computation program (without variables), 58

4.3. Program using QBasic operators, 59

4.4. Program that stores/prints book variables, 64

4.5. Modified program that stores/prints book variables, 65

4.6. Program to compute payroll and print check, 66

5.1. Sales tax program, 72-73

5.2. Averaging program, 73

5.3. Averaging program (with print option), 74

5.4. Addition program for children, 75

5.5. Song title program, 77

5.6. Quotes request/display program, 80

5.7. Program using extra semicolon in INPUT, 81

5.8. Program illustrating types of string format characters, 85

5.9. Payroll program (with dollar signs), 88

5.10. Program illustrating the PRINT USING numeric format strings program, 89-90

5.11. TAB( ) and SPC( ) comparison program, 91-92

5.12. Program illustrating the COLOR statement program, 96

6.1. Program overusing GOTO statement program, 101

6.2. Age verification program, 103

6.3. Password program, 104

6.4. Age verification program (revised), 106

6.5. Inventory program, 110

6.6. Inventory program (revised), 112

6.7. Multiline separator program, 113

6.8. Overtime pay program, 117

6.9. Math tutorial program, 120-121

7.1. Name/Age program, 125-126

7.2. Odd/Even numbers printing program, 126

7.3. Numbers 1 to 4, printing program, 128

7.4. Loop/Counter variable program, 129

7.5. Unconditional EXIT FOR program, 131

7.6. Unconditional EXIT FOR program, (revised), 132

7.7. User Response program (WHILE-WEND), 134

7.8. User Response program (DO WHILE-LOOP), 135

7.9. User Response program (DO-LOOP WHILE), 136

7.10. User Response program (DO UNTIL-LOOP), 137-138

7.11. DO UNTIL-LOOP program, 138

7.12. DO UNTIL-LOOP (city names) program, 139

7.13. Counting program, 140

7.14. DO UNTIL-LOOP (city names) program, (revised), 141-142

8.1. Neighborhood association program (35 families), 149

8.2. Neighborhood association program (500 families), 150

8.3. Monthly salary program, 151

8.4. Temperature averaging program, 152

8.5. Days-of-the-week program, 153

8.6. Days-of-the-week program with OPTION BASE, 153

8.7. Program to compute highest sales, 155

8.8. Sorting numbers program with bubblesort, 156-157

8.9. Sorting numbers program in descending order with bubblesort, 157-158

8.10. Sorting names program with bubblesort, 158

8.11. Softball league statistics program, 165-166

9.1. Integer functions program, 171

9.2. Program to determine memory requirements when dimensioning an array, 173

9.3. LCASE$( ) and UCASE$( ) demonstration program, 177

9.4. VAL( ) function demonstration program, 178

9.5. LEFT$( ) function, demonstration program, 180

9.6. RIGHT$( ) function, demonstration program, 180

9.7. MID$( ) function, demonstration program, 181

9.8. INSTR( ) function, demonstration program, 182

9.9. LSET/RSET functions, demonstration program, 183

9.10. INKEY$ function, demonstration program, 185

10.1 Program without subroutines, 188

10.2 Program with subroutines, 190

10.3. Program with four routines, 193

11.1. Printing records to file program, 204

11.2. Printing records to file program using WRITE#, 205

11.3. Input file printing
program, 207
11.4. Counting records in a
file program, 208
11.5. Appending two data
files program, 209
11.6. Program to create a
random-access inventory
file, 216-217
11.7. Program to read a
random-access inventory
file, 218-219
11.8. Customer file records
program, 219-220
12.1. Drawing with pixels
program, 228
12.2. Drawing box in
default colors program, 230
12.3. Drawing box in three
colors program, 233
12.4. Octaves of A's
program, 235
12.5. All possible notes
program (SOUND), 235
programming, modular, 187
programs, 7-8
Count from 1 to 5 program
(without FOR/NEXT),
125-126
Count from 1 to 5 program,
125-126
data-driven, 99
designing, 8-9
executing, 26-27
exiting, 22
free-form, 27
loading, 21-22
maintenance, 191
menus, 120
printing, 28

restarting, 22
running, 7
saving, 9, 27
stopping, 22
typing, 23-25
writing, 9
prompt messages, 76-77
PSET command, 226-228
pull-down menus, 14-16
File, 15
getting help, 21
Help, 20
Run, 26
PUT # command, 215-221

Q

QBasic
color attribute chart, 231-232
exiting, 28
getting help, 20
loading, 11-12
opening screen, 11
screens, 13-14
question marks (?) in INPUT
statements, 73-75
eliminating, 78-82
in LINE INPUT statements, 79
quicksort arrays, 156
quotation marks ("), 62

R

RAM, 195-196
random-access, 200
files, 209-217
changing, 219-220
creating, 215-217

opening, 210-211
reading, 217-219
records, defining, 211-213
OPEN command, 210-211
ranges
constants, numeric, 37-39
variable values, 34
READ command, 107-111
syntax errors, 109
READ-DATA command, 138, 206
data storage, 148
record variables, creating, 214
recordname, 212
records, 198-199
random-access, defining,
211-213
relational
operators, 101
hierarchical status, 106
tests, 114-117, 133-134
compound, 104-106
DO UNTIL-LOOP
command, 137-139
DO-LOOP UNTIL, 140
DO-LOOP WHILE
command, 136-142
false, 137
REM (remark) statements, 27,
48-50
resolution, screen, 223-226
restarting programs, 22
RESTORE command, 111-112
RETURN command, 189-191
returning
from subroutines, 189
values, functions, 168
RIGHT$( ) function, 180-181
RSET command, 182-184
RTRIM$( ) function, 181
/RUN *filename*, 13
Run pull-down menu, 26

S

Save As... command (File
menu), 27
Save command (File menu), 27
saving programs, 9, 27
scientific notation
E+xx format, 87
expanded, E+xxx format, 87
SCREEN modes, 231-233
SCREEN command, 224-226
screens
CGA, snow, eliminating, 13
clearing, 46, 226
in desired color, 96
cursors, positioning, 96-98
print zones, 42-43
QBasic, 13-14
resolution, 223-226
VGA, 13
scroll bars, 18-19
Scroll Bars command, 18
searching arrays, values, 154-155
SELECT CASE command,
119-121
selecting
colors, 18-19
commands, 14-16
semicolons (;)
in INPUT commands, 80-81
in PRINT statements, 41-49
in tab commands, 44
printing effects, 204
sequential
access, 200
files, 200-203
appending to, 208-209
creating, 203-208
settings
empty spaces (Tab
keypress), 19
values, subscripts, 162-163

SGN( ) function, 173
shell sort arrays, 156
Shift-F5 (Start) command, 22
shortcut keys
  Alt-key combination (display
    menus), 15
  bookmarks, 25
  cursor movement, 24
  F1 (Help) command, 21
  F5 (Continue) command, 22
  menu, 16-17
  text
    copying, 25
    deleting, 25
    inserting, 25
    scrolling, 24
    selection, 24
  window commands, 25-29
sign function, *see* SGN( )
  function
single-dimensional arrays,
  160-161
single-precision
  arrays, 146
  constants, 37
  variables, 33-34
sorting arrays, 155-160
  descending order, 154
SOUND command, 233-235
space value, 90-92
SPACE$( ) function, 176
spaces
  in programs, 27
  in variable names, 32
  inserting at ends of
    strings, 182
  trimming from ends of strings,
    181-182
SPC( ) function, 90-92, 167, 176
SQR( ) function, 172

square root function, *see*
  SQR( ) function
Start command (Run menu), 17,
  22, 39
startup, command-line options,
  12-13
statement separators, colon (:),
  112-113
statements
  assignment, 35-39, 62-63
    matching data types, 68-69
    valid/invalid, 69
  branching, 99-101
  decision, 102
  END, 47
  labels, 100, 111
  multiple, on one line, 112-119
  PRINT, 38-45, 49
  REM (remark), 27, 48-50
  TAB, 63-66
STEP command, 229-230
Step command (Debug
  menu), 16
STEP keyword, 226, 230
STEP values, 124
stopping programs, 22
storing
  characters, in string
    variables, 93
  data
    in numeric variables, 61
    in string variables, 62-63
  similar data in a single
    variable, 144-146
  values, multidimensional
    arrays, 164
STR$( ), 176-178
string constants, 39-40, 59
  printing, 39-40
STRING$( ) function, 175

strings
    breaking into smaller strings, 179-182
    changing sections of, 179
    characters
        comparing, 103
        reversing, 191
    commands, justifying, 182-184
    concatenating, 67-68
    constants, 60-70
        storing in string variable, 64
    control codes, PRINT USING command, 83-86
    converting to numbers, 176-179
    data, 60
    format, 82-83, 86-90
        % (percent sign), 88-89
        in variables, 84
    functions, 174-185
        character, 179-182
        conversion, 176-179
        search, 181-182
    input (,) commas in, 77-79
    inputting, 77-78
    inserting spaces at ends, 182
    null, 63, 180
    in ERASE command, 159
    trimming spaces from ends, 181-182
    variables, 51, 60-66
        assigning values to, 62-63
        data storage in, 62-63
        naming, 61-62
        printing, 63-66
        storing characters in, 93
subroutines, 187-194
    calls, 188-189
    lengths, 194
    procedures, 187, 191-194

SUBs... command, 16
subscripts
    arrays
        designating, 152
        numbers, 145
        variables, 143
    overriding, 162
    values, setting, 162-163
suffixes, variables, 33-36
    numeric, 62
SWAP command, 155-160
symbols, variables, types, 147
syntax errors, 27
    READ commands, 109

T

tab commands, 18, 63-66
    printing with, 43-45
    semicolons (;) in, 44
TAB( ) function, 90-92, 167
tables, dimensioning, 162-163
tests
    relational, 114-117, 133-134
        compound, 104-106
        DO UNTIL-LOOP, 137-142
        DO-LOOP UNTIL, 140
        DO-LOOP WHILE, 136-142
        false, 137
text
    color, changing, 17-18
    deleting, 23
    overwriting, 23
    printing, before string variables, 63
    underlining, 176
text-copying keys, 25
text-deleting keys, 25
text-inserting keys, 25

text-scrolling keys, 24
text-selection keys, 24
Toggle Breakpoint command
    (Debug menu), 16
Topic command (Help
    menu), 21
trailer DATA records, 110
trailing semicolons, 41
trigger data, 110
truncated values, 170
truth tables, 104-106
two-dimensional tables, 160-162
TYPE command, 211-214
types
    constants, numeric, 37
    data
        matching in assignment
        statements, 68-69
        TYPE command, 213
    variables, 33-34
    symbols, 147
typing programs, 23-25

U

UCASE$( ) function, 177
unary operators, 52
underlining text, 176
uppercase, converting to
    lowercase, 176-179
USING command, 204
Using Help command, 17, 20

V

VAL( ) function, 176-178
values
    arrays, searching, 154-155
    assigning, 35-39

to fields, 214-215
to string variables, 62-63
variables, 107-111
expressions, printing, 58-59
frequency, 234
getting from the keyboard, 72
multiple, printing to a single
    line, 40
returning, functions, 168
space, 90-92
STEP, 124
storing, multidimensional
    arrays, 164
subscripts, setting, 162-163
truncated, 170
variables
    assigning at programming
    time, 72
    assigning at run time, 72
    ranges, 34
variable-length
    files, 204
    records, 198-199
    string variables, 60
variables, 31
    array, 143
        subscripts, 143
    assigning formulas to, 54
    counter, 129
    double-precision, 33
    in INPUT statements, 71
    in READ commands, 108
    integer, 33-34
    long integer, 33
    naming, 32-33
    numeric, 60
        storing data in, 61
        suffixes, 62
    records, creating, 214
    single precision, 33-34
    string, 51, 60-66
        assigning values to, 62-63
        data storage in, 62-63

format, 84
naming, 61-62
printing, 63-66
storing characters in, 93
storing string constants
in, 64
types, 60
suffixes, 33-36
tracing through loops, 130
types, 33-34
symbols, 147
values
assigning, 35-39, 72,
107-111
ranges, 34
VGA (Video Graphics Array)
video cards, 223
monitors, 94
screens, 13
video adapters, 13, 231
possible color attributes, 232
Video Graphics Array (VGA)
video cards, 223
volatile memory, 195

W-X-Y-Z

WHILE-WEND command,
133-134
window command keys, 25-29
windows
clearing, 28
commands, 25-29
program editing, 14, 23
WRITE # command,
205-206, 209
writing programs, 9
XOR truth table, 105
zeroing out numeric arrays, 159